From Charlotte Square to Fingal's Cave

Krystyn Lach-Szyrma (1791–1866). The portrait was probably painted during the 1830 Rising when Lach-Szyrma became the leader, with the rank of colonel, of the Academic Youth of Warsaw and Cracow Universities. He is wearing a military jacket but with a civilian shirt and cloak.

From Charlotte Square to Fingal's Cave

Reminiscences of a Journey through Scotland 1820–1824, by Krystyn Lach-Szyrma

Edited and introduced by
MONA KEDSLIE McLEOD
Based on the translation by
Helena Brochowska

TUCKWELL PRESS

First published in Great Britain in 2004 by
Tuckwell Press
The Mill House
Phantassie
East Linton
East Lothian, Scotland

ISBN 1 86232 218 X

The Publishers acknowledge the support of the
Scotland Inheritance Fund in the publication of this volume

The Publisher gratefully acknowledges financial assistance
from the Russell Trust

British Library Cataloguing-in-Publication Data
A catalogue record for this book is available
on request from the British Library

Typeset in Scotch Roman by
Koinonia, Manchester
Printed and bound by
The Cromwell Press, Trowbridge, Wiltshire

Contents

Contents

Contents

List of Illustrations

Foreword

Brilliant and unexpected as a meteor, here comes a new and unknown source for Scotland's history. Krystyn Lach-Szyrma, a clever and inquisitive young Pole, spent four years in Scotland in the 'Silver Age' of the Enlightenment. His job was to escort and tutor the two sons of a Polish prince during their studies at Edinburgh. But he used his time to find out how Scotland worked and what had made it into a centre of European ideas – philosophical, literary, scientific and technical. To achieve this, he travelled on foot through the Highlands, visited the Lowland cities and factories of the early industrial revolution, and inspected (in fascinating detail) the modernising and improved tenant farming of the Lothians.

Luckily for us, Lach-Szyrma took a broad view of research. He made his way into grand company, meeting Scott, Hogg, Wilson, Dugald Stewart and most of the other literary and philosophical talents of Edinburgh. A party-addict of genius, he witnessed a dirk-fight at the Celtic Society dinner and saw Walter Scott rescue James Hogg when he forgot his lines in the midst of a recitation at the Pitt dinner. He was a guest at countless important and sometimes hard-drinking suppers, and recorded with delight the minutiae of Scottish society manners.

He had the gifts of a first-class journalist (and many years later he became one). The detail of his observations – farm machines, the pay structure for professors, advances for authors, the precise structure and administration of prisons and lunatic asylums, the formalities and menus of dinner parties in the New Town – are precious now. But he used his data to generalise about a nation he came to love and admire – and sometimes to laugh at. As a Pole, from a country which had recently been wiped off the map by its neighbours, he had passionate sympathy for a people which compensated for the loss of independence by cherishing its music, songs and traditions.

Krystyn Lach-Szyrma had both intelligence and charm. This book leaves the reader with a new friend, somebody one would long to meet and know. Whether he is scaling Ben Lomond in the rain, well provisioned with whisky, or leaping impulsively into the sea to swim into Fingal's Cave (he nearly drowned and had to be dragged out), or exploding with rage over Lord Elgin's theft of the Parthenon Marbles, or working out how to pass a large sailor on a narrow Edinburgh pavement, his vivid writing is irresistible. And how well he wrote! A Romantic addicted to Ossian, he was also alight with the universal humanism of the Enlightenment: 'Music and song ... influence the heart, and all virtue springs from the heart. And thus the Laplander runs across the snow and the inhabitant of Angola across the burning sands to see the love of his heart; both try to shorten their way with song'.

Why this voice has been unknown to Scots until now is not a mystery – Scotland continues to ignore its ancient and rich connection with Poland. But it is a crime. All honour to Mona McLeod, herself descended from Scottish settlers in Poland, for letting Lach-Szyrma at last thank in person the country he enjoyed so intensely.

Acknowledgements

IN 1820 Prince Adam Jerzy Czartoryski, the head of the most powerful family in Poland, decided to send the young princes, Adam and Konstanty and their cousin Prince Sapieha, to study at Edinburgh University. As their tutor, Krystyn Lach-Szyrma spent four years in Scotland. On his return with a doctorate from Edinburgh, he was offered the Chair of Philosophy at the newly-founded University of Warsaw. His three-volume *Reminiscences of a Journey through England and Scotland, 1820–1824,* was published in 1828. Two years later he led the students of both Warsaw and Cracow Universities in the 1830 Rising against Russian misrule. Its failure led to the closure of Warsaw University and Lach-Szyrma's lifelong exile in Britain.

In 1941, Helena Brochowska, another exile from Poland, found a copy of the *Reminiscences* in the Library of the British Museum. The first two volumes relate to Scotland and from these she translated everything which she thought might interest Sir James Fraser. A distinguished surgeon, he had played a significant role in the creation of the Polish Medical School at Edinburgh University: the translation was an expression of her gratitude.

The Fraser family has very generously allowed me to edit and publish this, the only translation known to me. The late Sir James Fraser showed me the manuscript some years ago and, after his death, his widow Maureen and son Iain hunted bookshelves and attics before discovering its safe hiding place. My granddaughters, Shian and Sarah Holt, transferred a frail typewritten document to disk and guided me through the hazards of computing. Peter Pininski translated the many details omitted from the text by Brochowska. The son of a Polish and a Scottish graduate of St Andrews University, he has a rare understanding of the culture of both countries. His translations are from his own copy of the 1828 edition and his familiarity with the Polish background has made his assistance invaluable. Additional material has been translated by Anna Frackiewicz, the historian of the Polish service men and women

Acknowledgements

who graduated from St Andrews. Professor Bruce Lenman's profound knowledge of Scottish history has eliminated many errors from the footnotes and Iseabail Macleod, with her customary generosity and great professional skills, has eliminated many more. Elizabeth Barry has allowed me to reproduce illustrations from her 1792 edtion of Francis Grose's *Antiquities of Scotland*. These, and many illustrations from my own books, have been photographed by Mary Burkett. To all of them, and to my husband Robert for his patient support, I am deeply grateful.

For permission to reproduce illustrations the publishers would like to thank the following: Francis Lach-Szyrma: Frontispiece. Instytut Sztuki, Warsaw: 1. Foundation of the Princes Czartoryski, National Museum, Cracow: 2. Elizabeth Barry: 3–5, 30, 38–40, 42, 43, 58, 60, 65, 67, 68, 70, 72. The Editor: 1, 6, 7–9, 11–15, 18–22, 29, 35, 37, 41, 45, 53–57, 59, 64, 69, 74. James Holloway: 10. Edinburgh University Library: 6, 33, 50, 51, 61, 63, 66. Edinburgh City Libraries: 17, 26–28, 36, 48, 52, 76. Peter Pininski; 23. Scottish National Portrait Gallery: 24. Lady Evelyn Brander: 25. Jagiellonian Library, Cracow: 31. Trustees of the National Library of Scotland: 32, 46, 47, 73. National Museums of Scotland: 71. Viscount Runciman of Doxford: 44. The late Lady Isabel Linda: 75.

Editor's Introduction

ON his return to England in 1824 Krystyn Lach-Szyrma, in a letter to his friend Alexander Young of Harburn, wrote:

> When I am asked about Scotland how did I like it, my enthusiasm for it makes people repent of their question and I must remember that I am in England which is jealous of the land of the mountain and the flood.

As tutor to the young Czartoryski princes he had spent four years in Scotland. Their Grand Tour had been extended from Germany, Switzerland and France to Britain. A Scottish connection had been established in 1659 when Lady Catherine Gordon, a lady-in-waiting at the court of Queen Marie Louise of Poland, married into the Morsztyn family. Her daughter Izabela married Prince August Czartoryski and, in 1757, their son, Prince Adam Kazimierz, was persuaded to visit Scotland by Lord Mansfield, the Scottish Lord Chief Justice of England. Like Lach-Szyrma, he fell in love with Scotland and returned with his wife, Princess Izabela. She in her turn returned with their son Adam Jerzy. On his first visit to Edinburgh in 1787 his father had written:

> The main purpose of this journey is to gather materials necessary for the moment when you are chosen to serve your country

His second visit with Princess Izabela was in 1793. After studying the British parliamentary system at work at Westminster, he and his mother travelled north, visiting factories and 'Improved' farms on their way. In Scotland Adam Jerzy attended classes at Edinburgh University, then at the height of its fame, before continuing his tour of observation. By this time Izabela was tired of industrial developments and left her son to look at more factories while she toured some of the great landscaped gardens, going as far north as Blair Castle in Perthshire and as far west as Inveraray in Argyll. On her return to Poland the Scottish gardeners whom she had recruited transformed the park round her home at

Puławy, replacing parterres and formal avenues with the grottoes and waterfalls of a romantic 'English' garden. By 1824 there were at least 300 'English' gardens in Poland and the princess's book, *Varied Thoughts on the way of Designing Gardens*, had gone into several editions.

Adam Kazimierz had created a precedent. To extend their Grand Tours to visit Scotland and attend lectures at Edinburgh University became a standard practice for the more enlightened members of the Polish upper classes. Amongst these were Count Jan Potocki whose Tour took him as far as the Orkneys in 1787, General Jan Komarzewski, who searched Edinburgh and Glasgow for an improved telescope, and Count Fryderyk Skarbek who became a disciple of Adam Smith. Two generations of Zamoyski counts studied agriculture and economics, and the agricultural improvers, Generals Pac and Chlapowski, reinforced their study of agricultural theory by prolonged working visits to model farms.

The Czartoryskis were one of the most powerful and intelligent of the powerful and wealthy families in Poland. During the eighteenth century they had built up bases of power throughout the country and there were few families of importance with whom they were not connected by marriage. Collectively they became known as 'The Familia'. Konstancja, one of the Czartoryski princesses, was the mother of Stanisław August Poniatowski, the last King of Poland. Given that he was a former lover of Catherine the Great of Russia, her influence and that of the Familia had helped to secure his election in 1764.

Poland, by 1764, had become one of the most socially and economically backward countries in Europe. Social mobility, an essential ingredient in the development of a wealthy society, was rare. Agriculture declined and, with the exception of Danzig and Warsaw, life in the towns atrophied. A constitution which concentrated political power in the hands of the nobility and excluded the professional and merchant classes had reduced Poland from the great power and centre of culture she had been in the sixteenth century to an almost ungovernable state. The 'Liberum Veto' enabled the most insignificant deputy to cancel the work of a full session of the 'Sejm', the Polish parliament. By the eighteenth century it was being used to wreck all attempts at reform. Frontiers, which provided few natural barriers to invaders, left Poland open to attack from powerful and ambitious neighbours and wars further weakened her economy. Stanisław August set out to develop her industries and modernise her constitution. His sweeping reforms were supported by the Familia but opposed by the more reactionary of the landowners and by the Jesuit order, whose property and control of

[1] *Prince Adam Jerzy Czartoryski (1770–1861). Lach-Szyrma was one of many students sponsored by the Prince when he was Curator of the University of Vilnius and one of hundreds of refugees, in exile after the failure of the 1830 Rising, who were supported by Czartoryski.*

education were threatened. The Constitution of 1791 created a crisis. This freed the serfs, transferred some political power from the land-owning *szlachta* to a growing middle class, and abolished the 'Liberum Veto', the cynical use of which had made a mockery of both royal and parliamentary power and had opened Polish territories to predators. The Constitution would have made Poland the most democratic state in Europe and potentially governable; Catherine the Great of Russia was determined that it should be neither. The absolute monarchies of Europe were already threatened by the French Revolution: to them the possibility that a democracy might emerge in Poland was intolerable. Catherine had had little difficulty in persuading Austria and Prussia to join her in seizing Polish territory in 1772. In January 1793, on the day of the execution of Louis XVI of France, Russia and Prussia agreed to the Second Partition. In 1795 the Third Partition wiped Poland off the map of Europe. Western powers protested but did nothing to help Poland, while the most reactionary of the Polish nobility looked to Catherine to restore their privileges. Stanisław August was forced to abdicate and died, a virtual captive, in St Petersburg in 1798.

The Czartoryskis had joined a movement to resist the Partitions. Though led by Tadeusz Kosciuszko, a veteran of the American War of Independence and a brilliant commander, the Insurrections failed. The Czartoryski estates were forfeited. In order to recover them, Prince Adam Jerzy was recalled from Scotland and he and his younger brother were sent to St. Petersburg as hostages for the 'good behaviour' of the family. The brothers became friends of Alexander, the idealistic Crown Prince, who was alienated from his grandmother Catherine and disapproved of the Partitions. When, as Alexander I, he became Tsar, he appointed Adam Jerzy as his foreign minister.

During the French Wars Poland was invaded and, in 1807, Napoleon created the Duchy of Warsaw out of the Russian portion. Promised a liberal constitution and the recovery of those parts of Poland still under Austrian or Prussian rule, many Poles joined Napoleon's army. They fought in Spain and Italy and, led by King Stanislaw's nephew Prince Jozef Poniatowski, 10,000 marched into Russia in 1812. They shared Napoleon's final defeat, and at the Congress of Vienna Poland was again partitioned. Austria and Prussia recovered territory lost during the French Wars while, out of the lion's share, Alexander created the Congress Kingdom, not as part of the Russian Empire but as his own personal domain. Adam Jerzy became his chief advisor on Polish affairs. Inspired by the British constitution, which he had admired and idealised, he helped to draft the relatively liberal constitution granted to the Poles.

When the young princes, Adam and Konstanty Czartoryski, and their cousin Prince Sapieha set off on their Grand Tour in 1818, Adam Jerzy was at the height of his power and expected to become Viceroy. The young princes were to be prepared to take major roles in the government of the Congress Kingdom. But by the time they reached Scotland Alexander's love affair with democracy was over. Censorship was introduced, the reactionary Grand Duke Constantine became Viceroy and the undermining of the constitution, which led to the Rising of 1830, began. Both Adam Jerzy and Lach-Szyrma played prominent parts in the Rising. On its failure they went into lifelong exile: the Prince to France and Lach-Szyrma to Britain.

But in 1818 the future still seemed full of promise. When his father sent him on his first visit to Britain Prince Adam Kazimierz had written:

> I do not want you to be a light minded person ... I want you to be an indispensable man and a man of charm ... I do not wish you to be a kind of medicine which is extremely salubrious and effective but, Hell's bells, unpalatable.

Adam Jerzy was determined that the princes' education, like his own, should include a period of serious study at Edinburgh University. Lach-Szyrma, their recently appointed tutor, went with them. A more unlikely candidate for the post of tutor to the sons of so distinguished a family would be difficult to imagine. A Protestant of peasant origins, he was born in 1791 in Wojnacy, a village in the area of Mazury on the East Prussian side of the border with Poland. His father, Adam Lach, was a small farmer. While still at primary school Krystyn began to explore prehistoric sites near his home, and the insatiable curiosity which makes his *Reminiscences* so fascinating, became apparent. At confirmation classes, when he was thirteen, the Lutheran pastor, George Schrage, noticed his exceptional ability. Schrage decided to teach him German, which made it possible for him to attend the gymnasium at Königsberg. This was in Prussia but teaching was both in Polish and German. As the son of a peasant farmer, he was socially ostracised by the other boys but his ability was again recognised. When Napoleon's armies invaded Prussia and overran the family farm, his father was no longer able to pay the gymnasium fees. Ignacy Onacewicz, one of his teachers, adopted him and drew Krystyn to the attention of Prince Adam Jerzy Czartoryski.

In his *Letters Literary and Political on Poland*, published in Edinburgh in 1823, Szyrma wrote:

> It ought here to be remarked that activity in all fields of literature has been much fostered and rendered still more universal by the liberality of the house of the Princes Czartoryski, who might be called the Medici of Poland. At their hospitable hearth men of letters, poets and artists found a friendly reception. In short, there existed within the last period no literary character in Poland who had not, in one way or another, stood connected with that illustrious house by receiving encouragement, benefit and support from it ...

With the financial help of the Prince and money earned teaching German to young ladies, he was able to attend the University of Vilnius where he studied classical Polish literature and learned English from Professor Saunders. Saunders was Director of the School of Engraving and lectured on History of Art and on English Literature at the University. Lach-Szyrma was fascinated by folk poetry, music and the Romantic Movement. Familiarity with Macpherson's Ossian probably laid the foundations for his love affair with Scotland. He added the noble name Szyrma to the plebeian Lach, a name given by the Prussians to Polish peasants. When a refugee in England in the 1830s he referred openly to his peasant origins but at Vilnius he was still suffering from his experiences at Königsberg. In 1813 he graduated in philosophy, with a reference from the principal as 'an exemplary young man of outstanding ability and diligence'. To his friend and adoptive father, Onacewicz, he wrote in 1812:

> I desire to give myself entirely to what surprises people most: Ancient History and the study of the English language. With time I hope to be able to reap the fruit of my efforts in England or some other country and prove to the world that a Pole, though his country has lost its very name, can make that name revive by the power of his own genius and that, if not superior, we are at least equal in learning to other nations.

He was 22 at the time. In spite of his Protestant and peasant background Prince Adam Jerzy employed him as a tutor to some of the young princes of the Familia. He spoke Russian, Polish, German, French and Latin and could read and write English. The personality that emerges from the *Reminiscences* suggests that the Prince could not have made a better choice.

Lach-Szyrma and his three pupils reached Scotland when the embers of the Enlightenment were still glowing. The greatest of the original thinkers – men of the calibre of David Hume, Joseph Black, James Hutton, Adam Smith and William Robertson – had died in the 1790s, but the intellectual climate which they had created still existed. No longer perhaps 'A Hotbed of Genius', Edinburgh still merited its description as 'The Athens of the North' and London was a long way away. The new roads created by the turnpike trusts had cut travelling time from Edinburgh from ten days to two but until, in the 1850s, the railway reduced travelling time to twelve hours, Scotland had a social as well as an intellectual capital. In the polite society which opened its doors to the Polish aristocrats the charm which their grandfather had so valued could be exercised and developed by the young princes.

For two years, during the six months of term time, they studied at the University. Founded in 1582 to train ministers for the Presbyterian Church, it had, by the eighteenth century, become famous throughout the English-speaking world for the breadth of its curriculum. By 1820 there were over 4,000 students, attracted by the reputation of its most brilliant professors and by teaching which was both philosophical and pragmatic. Professors' salaries were low and their incomes depended on their ability to attract and hold students. The incentive to teach well was strong. Dugald Stewart, whose classes in Philosophy the Polish students attended, was only one of the academics whose lectures continued this tradition of excellence. Except in the faculties of Theology and Medicine, few students graduated. Religious tests, which had excluded both Catholics and Episcopalians in the 1690s, were abolished in the eighteenth century. Inter-disciplinary studies were normal and students still met in societies for serious debate as well as serious drinking.

Lach-Szyrma was one of the few students who did graduate. He studied medicine, agriculture, philosophy and economics and emerged with a Doctorate in Philosophy. Most students enrolled in any class that interested them and paid a small fee – usually £3 per session - to the professor. Six of the Poles sponsored by the Czartoryskis paid £10 each to receive private tuition from Professor McCulloch on the economic theories of Adam Smith. Several studied classical literature while lodging with Professor Pillans, who held the chair in Humanities. There was no collegiate system and the poorest students might survive in lodgings for as little as £20 a year; to live in the house of a professor probably cost several hundreds. Professor Pillans charged the Poles

[2] *The Palace at Puławy c. 1820. Situated on the banks of the Vistula, ten miles south of Warsaw, the palace became the main residence of the Czartoryski family. In 1782 it was enlarged for Prince Adam Kazimirz by Christian Aigner and Jakub Hempel and, in the 1790s, its formal gardens were transformed into a magnificent park by the Scottish landscape gardener, James Savage. He had been invited to Poland by Princess Izabela after her tour of Scotland. Her* Varied Thoughts on Ways of Designing Gardens, *published in 1805, and Savage's romantic park set the fashion for gardens for the rest of the century. As a centre of culture and patronage, Puławy became known as 'The Athens of Poland'*

£100 each and Dugald Stewart, when Lord Palmerston and his brother lodged with him, charged £400. Lach-Szyrma delighted in an academic environment in which both teachers and students could come from so broad a social spectrum and in which foreigners from every country in Europe were welcomed.

He was no snob. He describes the appalling formality and boredom of 'At Homes' but relished the quality of conversation at dinner parties where he met men like Jeffrey, editor and one of the founders of the *Edinburgh Review*, and Wilson, editor of its Tory rival, *Blackwood's Magazine*. As a romantic, devoted to folk music and poetry, he admired and revered Walter Scott but was not blind to his weaknesses. When he met tenant farmers and crofters' sons at the tables of the aristocracy he realised, from his own peasant background, that in Scotland intellectual achievement could break down barriers of class.

From Edinburgh he visited factories, farms and institutions throughout the south and southwest. This was the Scotland of the 'Improvers', a land of high farming and model villages where industrial and agricultural change had revolutionised the countryside. The destruction by urban sprawl of so much of the farmland of the Central Belt of Scotland was still in the future. He describes with great accuracy living conditions in the New Town, but was unaware that the Old Town, deserted by the aristocracy, was becoming one of the worst slums in Europe. And the landowners who became his friends seem to have been almost untouched by the economic depression which was driving thousands of Scots to emigrate, many of them to Poland, after the Napoleonic Wars.

In Edinburgh he had been interested in the prisons on the Calton Hill and, in Glasgow, he was fascinated by a lunatic asylum, which reflected Dr. Andrew Duncan's humane approach to mental illness. Endlessly curious, he set off after two years in Edinburgh to explore the southern Highlands. From Tarbet on Loch Lomond to Oban he travelled on foot, his guide acting as interpreter, and discovered a world of mountains and lochs in which there were neither roads fit for carriages nor inns to shelter travellers. Familiar with Macpherson's *Ossian* as well as the novels of Walter Scott, he loved the country, but the dire poverty of its Gaelic-speaking people filled him with dismay. Where his interpretation of Highland history is superficial, it reflects the ignorance and prejudice which were general amongst the Lowland Scots with whom he had been associating. George IV's visit in 1822 had made the tartan image fashionable but ignorance of Gaelic culture and history remained profound, and guidebooks of the early nineteenth century were often inaccurate and misleading.

The Grand Tour ended in 1824. During the years when Lach-Szyrma had been an employee of the Czartoryski family he had supplemented his salary by writing. He had contributed articles to the Warsaw, Vilnius and Lwow presses and, in Britain, to English journals. Encouraged by Professor Wilson, the editor of *Blackwood's Magazine*, and assisted by the Keeper of the Signet Library, he wrote his *Letters Literary and Political on Poland; comprising Observations on Russia and other Slavonic Nations and Tribes*. These were published by Constable in 1823. His chief aim was 'the popularisation of Poland'. He had been startled by the ignorance of people in Britain about the Slav nations, 'terra incognita' to the most intelligent and educated of the Scots. He realised that almost all western historians were unable to read Slavonic languages and depended on secondary sources. In the preface to the political letters he wrote:

> Taking all the books ever published ... I find that they chiefly relate to the exterior of the people; as for instance their dress, manners, amusements and mode of living – interspersed with anecdotes, true or false no matter, if they only possessed enough singularity to amuse the majority of credulous readers. Political views, of which there was no lack, commonly ended with heavy sighs on barbarity and slavery The moral features of the nation and still more the literary, as they have appeared in the succession of ages, remained a sealed book.

After a short stay in England he returned to Poland. He was appointed to teach English Language and Literature at the Polytechnic Institute. and, in 1825, became the first professor of Moral Philosophy at the newly founded University of Warsaw. But reaction had set in. By 1830 the policies of Tsar Nicholas I, who had succeeded Alexander in 1825, had driven the Poles to rebellion. With the rank of Colonel, Lach-Szyrma, 'the Scottish Philosopher', became the leader of the Academic Youth, the student insurgents in Warsaw and Cracow, and editor of their daily newspaper. After the failure of the Rising, Warsaw University was closed down. He and his patron Prince Adam Jerzy were exiled for life, the Prince to become leader of the Polish community in Paris and Lach-Szyrma to struggle to earn a living in England.

The failure of the Rising had brought his career in Poland to an end. To his friend Professor Pillans he wrote in 1832:

> As leader of a corps I am excluded from amnesty, if an amnesty proclaimed by a Russian autocrat could deserve that name. . . . And in fact what could I do, returning to Poland? It is impossible that I should know my former places. Universities are shut, libraries are sealed. In witnessing so many noble and patriotic efforts thwarted I would die of grief ... I have come to London in order to continue to devote to my country my services in a Literary way, which is now the only one remaining, and I must think also of gaining means of subsistence ... Several gentlemen here are about to form a committee for the support of the Polish cause, which is also the European one. Could you not form a similar association in Edinburgh?

He was joined in England by his wife Jozefa Dzierzgowska and their two daughters. After Jozefa's death in 1837 he married Sarah Somerville, the daughter of a captain in the Royal Navy, and took British citizenship.

During the long years of exile, and until his own death in Devonport in 1866, he was an active member of a diplomatic and literary community of Poles living in London, working as a journalist and translator. Assisted by the patronage of Lord Dudley Coutts Stuart and the unfailing generosity of Prince Adam Jerzy Czartoryski, he organised charities to support Polish refugees and acted as secretary to the Literary Association of Friends of Poland. He became foreign correspondent for the Polish newspapers *Czas*, *Gazeta Warszawska* and *Gazeta Codzienna*, while the articles he contributed to British journals did something to undermine the misinformation with which the partitioning powers, Russia, Prussia and Austria, were trying to destroy the image of the country they had dismembered.

He spent the rest of his life in England but he never forgot Scotland. In a letter to Alexander Young of Harburn he wrote:

> Although I have been absent from Scotland's coasts my mind is occupied with it more than you are aware of.

The Scotland of the Enlightenment has been well served by its historians. Edward Topham's *Letters from Edinburgh, 1774–75* is an Englishman's picture of upper-class society in the days of David Hume and Adam Smith; Henry Cockburn's *Memorials of his Time* is an insider's view of the same social group in the thirty years before Lach-Szyrma reached Scotland. Lach-Szyrma's *Reminiscences* are a rare example of a foreigner's impressions of Scotland and the Scots in the 1820s and a memorial to what he remembered as the happiest years of his life.

Although his Tour had been financed by Prince Adam Jerzy, the Czartoryski princes of whom he was in charge are scarcely mentioned in the text. Before his own return in 1824 he had twice crossed the Channel; he may then have been escorting the princes back to Poland. To have written about them in his *Reminiscences* might have been socially unacceptable. Instead he concentrated on the Scots, with whom he seems to have related more easily than the English. Like the *literati*, he sometimes referred to North Britain and said 'England' when he meant Britain. But at a time when Poland's existence as a nation was being deliberately destroyed by her neighbours he identified with Scotland, conscious of the threat to her identity still posed by the wealth and power of England. As a romantic, he loved a land of mountain and flood and, though a shrewd observer, he sometimes idealised the qualities of its people. His *Reminiscences*, the first description of Scotland to be published in Polish, was an immediate success. It was published in Warsaw in 1828, at a time when the Waverley Novels and the Romantic Movement had made everything Scottish, from gardeners to governesses, fashionable. A fuller account of his travels was planned but never written. His *Memoir of My Life* has not been translated. It was published in London by his son, the Rev Wladyslaw Lach Szyrma, seven years after his death. It was dedicated to 'My brave countrymen who, in such troubled times, have enriched me with their confidence and care; their memory will stay with me till my dying day'.

Helena Brochocka was working for the Ministry of the Interior of the exiled Polish government in London in 1940. Her previously unpublished translation of Lach-Szyrma's text is from a copy in the British Museum. She omitted the first four chapters of Volume I, which describe the journey from Dover and the brief stay in London. Other omissions have been translated by Peter Piniński, the owner of a rare first edition of the *Reminiscences*. Volume III relates to his stay in England and only short extracts from it have been included in this translation.

Other than Morton's harrow, the only illustrations in the original work were portaits of well-known poets like Scott, Wordsworth and Coleridge. In this translation these have been replaced by pictures from contemporary sources. Most of the sketches of Edinburgh are from J. W. Ewbank's *Picturesque Views of Edinburgh* or T. H. Shepherd's *Modern Athens*, and scenes from the rest of Scotland are mainly from Francis Grose's *Antiquities of Scotland*.

Lach-Szyrma's Scotland

Canal ———
Border —·—·—

INVERNESS

ABERDEEN

Skye

Fort William

Glencoe

Staffa   Mull   Oban   Dunkeld

Callander   PERTH

Abernethy

R. Forth

STIRLING

Dumbarton   Dunbar

Islay   GLASGOW   R. Clyde   EDINBURGH

Hamilton   Berwick-upon-Tweed

Lanark   Peebles

Dumfries

Gretna

0 10 20 30 kilometres
0   10   20 miles

Author's Introduction

THE author surely has no need to inform the reader that, in writing about Great Britain, he is writing about a country important from a multiplicity of perspectives, whose society, from the viewpoint of education, both moral and political, has attained a certain maturity. This will become plain from the succeeding pages.

The present work was intended for publication immediately upon the author's return to his country. He did not think that anyone would consider it appropriate that he should tarry, like Horace, for nine long years, which many seem to suppose would guarantee literary perfection. It is sad that commitments have forced a delay of even one half of that period of time for, were it not thus, the public would already have had this work in its hands for two full years if not longer.

This long delay was the reason why this book was not entitled *Travels* but *Reminiscences*, the last being more accurate since that is how the whole has flowed from the pen. He feels however that a work of this title is not worthless. 'Travels' have no need to be some sort of newspaper, in which only that which is recent is of value. The present should form a link with the past, in other words, with the history of the country in which these travels occurred. Later, when writing about the nation whose character, government and institutions have crystallised to a certain degree, their further maturity will be based upon this very same past, like some immovable geological stratum. From this, events resulting from various causes will invariably emerge for which one will be more or less able to account and foresee. As the author supposes, about such a nation one can never write too late or too hastily. The proof lies in the number of 'travels' written in a rush or, as it were, straight from the highway travelled. How many are the needless details and foresights contained within, and how inadequate the general picture of the nation!

In so far as this author is aware, he has maintained the highest degree of objectivity. He has looked at nothing through the metaphorical magnifying glass, as is the wont of so many tourists. Thus the reader will not find in this text any exaggerated praise for Great Britain nor unfair judgments. The author has chosen a middle path in the conviction that every nation has its good and bad side, being concerned only with the truth. The truth, however, may be badly perceived for unconscious reasons of which nothing is seen, or through being unable to break with prejudices towards which there exists one or another sympathy. Nations gain nothing from falsehood. Indeed it may be seen that the more noble amongst them prefer the mantle of truth for, enveloped within it, its qualities become obvious.

Not wanting therefore to wrong Great Britain in any way the author has been guided in his writing by her greatest poet, Shakespeare: 'Speak of me as I am.' This single sentence he took as his guiding principle and it was ever present in his mind.

Finally, the author knows only too well, better perhaps than even the demanding Aristarchus,[1] the shortcomings of his work. It would not be difficult to put this right but his work must either appear now or never and, as for rhetoric, he has neither time nor will. Neither did he write this as some textbook. He would prefer that it should speak for itself Moreover, he believes in the indulgent tolerance of his readership; that they will deign to judge this work as they might the fruit of moments of respite in which the author, if he failed to please, tried at least to serve. This service he placed above everything else.

Warsaw, May 1st, 1828.

I

The Journey from London: York. Durham. Newcastle. Alnwick. Dunbar. Haddington. Edinburgh. The Parthenon

OUR stay in England should be called a passing through rather than a journey. Six days after our arrival in London we started for Scotland. The weather served us well which was all the more desirable for the appreciation of the surrounding countryside. It must be noted that the sky is seldom really blue in Great Britain, nothing compared with the deep azure of the Italian or even our Polish skies. It is greyish here, mostly cloudy. The clouds move about or sometimes seem to stand quite still as though a fleece had been thrown over them. The British poets call them fleecy clouds. They look lovely in moonlight; the sky then seems all soft. I travelled quickly for the roads are excellent.[1] From time to time we had to stop at turnpikes for the toll to be levied but this never lasted long, for the moment the coach was seen in the distance they made ready to let us pass as quickly as possible. The upkeep of the roads is in private hands and the Government has nothing to do with it.

We passed through several charming and prosperous towns about which, however, not a great deal may be said. In each flourished some industry or handicraft, for such is the main characteristic of all English towns. The canals which criss-cross the whole country enormously facilitate trade and communications; their length is estimated at some 500 miles. Our road took us through Stilton, a place famous for its cheeses, which are known by the same name, and then through Grantham where Newton[2] was first introduced to the sciences. Her inhabitants being fully aware of the fact told us of it. O happy nation that knows its great men! Doncaster, at first sight, appears to offer little to the traveller. It is well built, full of life and has numerous horses at pasture on her level ground. This includes an enormous enclosed area where races are held.

To the right lies York, one of the ancient towns of England with her magnificent Minster, which, in terms of size, might rank second amongst the greatest churches of Europe. According to experts, York Minster is an excellent example of gothic architecture. Particularly remarkable is the size of the columns which support the ceiling and the lancet windows alongside, which are some 57 feet tall but only five feet wide. A music festival is held here every year at which can usually be found, besides numerous citizens and connoisseurs from all parts, artists, sometimes reaching 200 in number. One year they even included the famous Catalani.[3] Performed here are the main compositions of Mozart, Haydn, Handel and Beethoven. At the trumpeting of the words 'Tuba mirum spargens sonum' Mozart's Requiem fills one's eyes with tears. The music creates such an indescribable impression throughout the vast and imposing Minster that it seems the very earth itself is passing judgement on the dead. At York there is also a hospital for lunatics which is said to be exemplary. It was founded by the subscriptions of the Quakers and is also supervised by them. It bears the gentle name of The Retreat. Gone are the bolted doors and rattling manacles; instead there is a beautiful home farm with a garden intended for the use of the afflicted. The sweetness of being able to amble around it, together with the fine diet it provides, is considered an essential principle of treatment. Banished also is the letting of blood, while warm baths are used to alleviate melancholy.

We passed by Durham, a small town said to be the poorest in England; yet in a beautiful setting the massive walls of her cathedral provide a picturesque quality. Of an age contemporary with the cathedral is the castle built by William I and now in ruins. It was, according to Scottish chroniclers, into these very fastnesses that brave Wallace[4] entered, dressed as a bard, in order to decide with Robert the Bruce who was imprisoned there, the destiny of his native land. In this place the passerby may wonder at the high bridge slung from cliffs between whose shady banks flow the waters of the Weare.

The bishopric of Durham is supposed to be the richest in the land, bringing to the bishop no less than £9,000 of income, if not more. A tidy sum and that with little work and fewer still privations! He has beneath him deacons and canons and they too are well recompensed. All live happily doing precious little, like the gods in Homer's plays, with the one difference that the clerics become old and must make way for successors. By virtue of his high rank the Bishop of Durham is also a Justice of the Peace; there is surely no lay position which combines more suitably with the dignity of a cleric.

In Durham there still lives Boruslawski,[5] the famous dwarf from the time of Stanislaw August. He is aged almost 80 but remains in rude health and was still considered to be a notable wit. Welcomed into the homes of the country's foremost families, he was described by them as a count.

The road led further to Sunderland where we crossed by the famous iron bridge. It is formed of a single arch and stands a full 100 feet high, being 236 feet long. Under it masted ships pass with ease. Arriving into the district of Newcastle one might easily believe one had entered the land of Vulcan. Wherever one looks, nothing can be seen but smoking foundries and flaming furnaces in which iron is being smelted. The people rushing around are as black as in the land of Negroes. Everything is done here by machines which are driven by steam. Here too are the famous coalmines whose produce is said to be of the finest and hardest quality. It is extracted in such quantity that it suffices for practically all London. Everything local is connected in some way to fire and coal. Thus it is easy to conceive that this land, whose very bowels are being torn out, can scarcely present anything of beauty to the human eye. I also saw iron roads for the first time. These are in fact iron rails in which run wheels and there is no iron where the horses have to go. Newcastle is also the birthplace of Captain Cook[6] who sailed the globe. Beyond lies the Picts' Dyke[7] which runs from here to Carlisle, in other words to the Irish Sea. In the year 121 the Emperor Adrian ordered its erection so as to keep out the incursions of the northern Picts and Scots from his newly conquered province. At distances of equal measure along the wall stood guard the tough and experienced soldiers of the emperor's legions.

Further along our route we passed Alnwick with its enormous castle, seat of the Duke of Northumberland. It surpasses in magnificence all other such monuments in England, or at least those which are still inhabited, with the single exception of the royal palace at Windsor. Alnwick stands on a promontory above the river Alne and within is divided into three courtyards. Its upper parts are designed in the style of all old castles, with bastions and towers throughout whose interiors stand suits of armour. All in different positions, as though ready for battle, they will certainly not conquer this fortress. Below ground are dungeons dating from feudal times. Today everything has a gentle appearance; no longer violence but benevolence and respect reign supreme. The Duke of Northumberland is universally known for his charity. In the year 1810 he built a school in the town for 100 poor boys.

3

Near the highway, on a hill, we saw a column some 80 feet high erected in his honour by grateful tenants.

Having left Alnwick near Branxton, I visited the Field of Flodden.[8] There is a cross at the roadside, marking the fatal spot where in 1513 James IV, the greatest of all the Kings of Scotland, fell with the flower of Scottish knights. From thence we came to Berwick which is the last English town and lies on the very frontier of Scotland. It was fortified in ancient times and has resisted many an invasion. But today the ramparts are only used by the inhabitants for walking. The river Tweed and the Cheviot Hills mark the boundaries of England and Scotland.

The nearer we drew to Scotland, the more hilly became the landscape and the more varied, for fertile fields and pastures were also seen. The hills became more and more like mountains and their outlines were sharper and bolder. Flocks of sheep were grazing on the steep slopes. In one place we saw Gipsies, busy with their camp which they were preparing for the night. They were lighting numerous fires. The road followed deep valleys and climbed up steep hills from whence the sea could be seen. We saw the ruins of the Castle of the Douglases,[9] lonely among the gloomy firs. A stone bridge, a single arch 120 feet over a roaring stream, seemed to be the only entrance to that fortified place. Further on the views increased in beauty and at night, when clouds passed dreamily over the shining face of the moon, I felt indeed that I had reached the country of Ossian,[10] and that I had breathed the same air as that father of all song did breathe. Near Dunbar the view of the sea is simply splendid. The whole shore is lined by cliffs and their shape is so strange that one wonders what uncanny evolutions of the earth have formed them that way.[11] The heavy threat of the waves, for the sea is very stormy there, is heard at a great distance. A mist like a constant drizzle arises from the foaming breakers.

The fields of Haddingtonshire are pleasant to observe and they are known in the whole of Scotland as the best cultivated. John Knox[12] was born at Haddington. The remains of a 12th century Franciscan church may yet be seen; it was ruined during the Reformation and most of it is roofless now. In the less damaged part, service is still held on Sundays. Driving further I admired the Firth of Forth, Arthur's Seat, and the Calton Hill. I passed through Prestonpans where the Pretender won a victory in 1745. Then through Musselburgh and Portobello, meaningless little towns, known only for sea bathing and military barracks.

To enjoy the finest view of Edinburgh, one should always approach it by the road from Calton Hill. There is no town with more marvellous

[3] *Berwick-on-Tweed. Most of the thirteenth-century castle was destroyed when the railway line from London to Edinburgh was completed in the 1840s.* Grose

and impressive surroundings. The road was cut through the rocks at great expense. To the right one sees the sea and Leith Harbour and to the left Arthur's Seat, 850 feet high. The Salisbury Crags touch it, and at their feet are Holyrood and the ruins of the Gothic Chapel. Not very distant is the churchyard in which Adam Smith and Doctor Gregory are buried.[13] One sees the whole old town and the cathedral church with its tower like a crown. In the background towers a castle on a steep hill; a banner waving over it and clouds often pass across. The least sensitive spectator is bound to be charmed by so many beautiful things. The present British king, when he came to visit Scotland in 1822, also arrived by that road. Seized with admiration, he exclaimed: 'God what a sight'. And I do not wonder at his emotion. Anyone who knows the history and the fate of a great nation must be touched deeply at seeing the places where all this happened.

The suburbs of Edinburgh are not wild and neglected as are those of Paris or London. The approach to the city is through a wide, rich and beautiful street which provides ample food for thought. Nelson's monument, the Observatory, the Penitentiary, the Jail, David Hume's monument, the Picture Gallery, hotels, chemists, the Post Office, the

[4] *The Pease Bridge. The gorge of the Pease Burn is one of the few natural barriers on the east-coast route between England and Scotland. It was bridged for the first time two years before Grose made this sketch in 1789.* Grose

[5] *Tantallon Castle. This fourteenth-century stronghold of the Douglases was surrendered to James V in 1529 and abandoned after General Monk's siege of 1651. The Bass Rock in the distance is a volcanic plug. Used as a prison till the eighteenth century, it is now the breeding ground of over 25,000 gannets.* Grose

Regent's Bridge, over which people pass to and fro, and the Theatre, etc. were passed. How numerous and varied are the types of life represented here. Though all this is contained in a comparatively small space, yet it is so disposed that it does not give the effect of being crowded. It is a place fit for meditation.

Prince's Street, straight as an arrow and almost three quarters of a mile long, begins behind the theatre. A deep valley to the left, over which two bridges are thrown, divides the Old Town[14] from the New, the Scottish from the Anglicised. The former is as old as Scotland herself; the houses are narrow, some eight or ten storeys high, with closes for pedestrians between them. In the latter part, built much later, everything is as in an average English town. The same squares, crescents and even such gardens as could be found in the very centre of London. The streets are wide and the pavements excellent, made of stone cut in the shape of bricks. This gives the impression that they are paved with a recumbent wall. Each stone prepared for paving costs the town the equivalent of one Polish zloty. Some of the streets have a wonderful view of the sea. The houses are much more impressive than in London for they are built of stone, not brick. This stone is quarried near the town. When new it is straw coloured, but it becomes grey under the influence of the air. It contains mica and owing to this it shines in the sun and the houses seem to be stuck with diamonds. The roofs are mostly made of stone shingles. The houses are healthy and dry for the stone does not let damp through. In Scotland, as in England, they are heated only by open fires, but here they are much warmer. Though there are no double windows and no stoves, the walls are much thicker. Watching new houses being built and huge stones being hoisted up, I thought that in Scotland they seem to be making houses for eternity. The very greyness, which covers them in time, makes them somewhat similar to the eternal granite rocks of the Alps.

For the exceptional beauty of its position, travellers compare Edinburgh to the most famous towns of Europe: Lisbon, Naples and Constantinople. But to the Scots, imbued as they are by the poetical spirit which has chosen their country as its home, cold comparisons are not enough. They speak of their native town in parables and with great sentiment. The common people call it: 'The City of Palaces'; sentimentalists, in accord with the ballads, 'The favoured Seat of Edina'; the romantics, led by Sir Walter Scott,[15] 'Our romantic town'. The classicists find that it is like Athens and, disregarding whether or not they will meet with general approval, they call it: 'The Athens of the North'. The

[6] *Princes Street, Edinburgh. Ewbank has sketched the Mail Coach arriving at the east end of Princes Street. Behind it is the Theatre Royal and across the road the Waterloo Hotel and Robert Adam's Register House.* Ewbank

likeness is indeed striking. Like Athens, Edinburgh is beautified by a bay, for the Firth of Forth is certainly worth the Aegean Sea; Leith is good enough to take the place of the Piraeus; the castle on the rock that of the Acropolis. The Parthenon alone seems to be missing but even this is to be erected. The consent of Parliament was obtained in 1822, and during the King's stay the foundation stone was laid, in the King's name, by the Duke of Hamilton, Scotland's first peer and the Grand Master of the Scottish Free Masons. The plan and the dimensions of this Scottish Parthenon have been taken from the Minerva Temple at Athens. It will be dedicated to the memory of Scottish men, and will be called the National Monument. It will be erected on the top of Calton Hill and, as there is not enough room for it, the monument of Nelson will have to go. This is certainly not a pity, as it is nothing but a satire on the lack of taste of the Athenians of the North. It consists of a round tower on a square basement, with winding stairs inside. Having paid, one could go up these stairs to admire the view. In the basement there was a café and several rooms for guests. What a singular idea, for the monument of a hero! How indecent and how ridiculous, thus to make money from such lofty things! Monuments erected to the dead should be solely for the dead. Turned into a means of bringing profit to the living, they are an insult to those departed.

I am told that the foundation stone of a school has also been laid on Calton Hill. Formerly the situation of the High School in the old town was too enclosed and unhealthy. It was impossible to choose a more appropriate place for the education of the young than this spot, so near the future temple of fame and facing such beauty of nature. Genius is sure to develop here, and the future generations will think of this place as one of the most memorable.

II

History of Edinburgh. The Castle. The Visit of the King.
Holyrood. John Knox. Allan, the painter

THE origins of Edinburgh are lost in the distance of centuries. It is said to have been founded in the 8th century by the Anglo-Saxon Prince Edwin. It was called then Edwinenburg.[1] Not until the 15th century were the Councils held there, and it was then that it began to be considered the capital of the country. The old Scottish capital had been Scone where the kings had been crowned. For lack of written documents, little is known of Edinburgh during the Middle Ages. In 1504 the houses were chiefly wooden and it was surrounded by a wall. It could not prosper for long because of the constant English invasions and unceasing internal trouble. But it had suffered most during the Religious Wars. The swords, which for centuries had been wet with blood, had a chance of resting in their scabbards only after the year 1746. Peace brought its blessings and prosperity to Scotland and England.

Because of this, Edinburgh has few noteworthy objects of an earlier date than the 16th century. Most of the relics of antiquity were lost during the Religious Wars. In no other country has the Reformation worked such havoc to science and art as in Scotland. The churches were bared of their ornaments; the convents of their libraries which, at the time, existed only in the monasteries. In the attempts to efface all religious traditions the national ones have been blotted out almost entirely. 'Destroy the nests and the ravens will leave them' was the favourite saying of John Knox. And the population put this advice into practice all too fervently. Altars, pictures, and the tombstones of their own forefathers were then destroyed. There is nothing more appalling than fanaticism.[2]

In fact only the Castle and Holyrood are left from olden times. The ruins of the Chapel in Holyrood look lovely by moonlight. I saw them

[7] *Edinburgh Castle. The Half Moon Battery, built in 1574, encloses the lower floors of David's Tower. This was an L-shaped tower of 1368. The Palace behind was the birthplace of James VI and is probably the site of the Great Chamber of the fourteenth-century tower.* Ewbank

represented exactly like this at a Paris Exhibition (Diorama[3]). The illusion was so great that I had entirely the impression of reality. Such was the daze in which I found myself that the Scottish Maiden, who in the attitude of a Vestal virgin guarded the fire near those ruins, I took for a living person. It makes us wonder, where is art going to lead us in the end? If other things were as truly represented, many would refrain from the difficulties of travel.

Due to the fact that the monuments I have mentioned are so closely connected to the history of the country itself it is not without relevance, as I believe, to relate here the more interesting details thereto pertaining. I will present them in such a state as they were beheld in the autumn of the year 1822, after the departure of the King from Edinburgh. Let us begin therefore with the history of the Castle which predates even the town itself. For it already existed in the year 1093, being mentioned at that time by ancient chroniclers. The Castle is by nature of a very defensive character, due to the steepness of the slopes of

[8] *Holyrood Abbey. In 1128 David I founded the abbey for
Augustinian canons. The church served the parish of the Canongate
until 1685 when it became the chapel of the Knights of the Thistle and
the congregation was moved to the Canongate Church. Only the nave
survived the sacking by Hertford's troops in 1544 and further damage
by protestant mobs in 1559 and 1688.* Ewbank

the hill on which it stands. Sometimes, in unsettled periods, kings of
Scots would take refuge here. It was here that Mary Queen of Scots gave
birth to her son James VI, who, after the death of Elizabeth I, was called
to the throne of England to reign as James I, thus uniting under one
sceptre these two nations of long standing enmity. Within the Castle
walls were imprisoned French soldiers captured not long ago during the

Spanish wars. Amongst their number were even a few Poles.[4] Now the Castle forms barracks for the garrison. Not long ago, in 1818, there was discovered in this place the ancient royal regalia. Such has been the suffering of this people that even their most precious jewels had been forgotten. Their discovery provided a rich field upon which Scottish antiquarians could display erudition. The crown had no mark on it from which one might identify from which century it came; many took the view that it came from those happier days when good King Robert the Bruce ruled over Caledonia. The rest of the regalia, namely the sceptre, sword and silver rod and the chancellor's insignia, presented little difficulty for they bore the mark JVR. It was but an easy matter to guess that this referred to Jacobus V Rex.

When the present King[5] made his entry into the castle in 1822, the first peers of the country carried the regalia, discovered in the Castle in 1818, in front of him. The Duke of Hamilton carried the crown, the Earl of Morton the sword, and the other emblems were carried by other nobles. They were all on horseback in the ancient dress of the country. It was a splendid and even moving sight, for it made one realise to what extent the Scottish nation is devoted to its King. People came from the most distant parts of Scotland to get a glimpse of him and to greet him in the ancient capital of the kings of Scotland. The streets through which he passed were not wide enough, there were not enough roofs or windows to give room to all those anxious to be present. Everybody was dressed in the national attire and full of national feelings. The Guard in front of the Palace was composed of young men of the best Scottish families, in the tartans of their clans. The kilts were then put on after a long interval; it was as if History was raised from the dead to greet the Monarch. The ancient attire looked very strange and wild among the commonplace everyday life. The wildness was augmented by the loud, shrill Scottish music, which accompanied their parades. They all seemed convinced that the best way of greeting the King was to greet him in the full particularities of Scotland, for only tradition can give expression to the truth and warmth of national feelings. When the King appeared to greet the people, the enthusiasm was indescribable. The very sky seemed to shake; so violent were the repeated 'Hurrahs!'. The King's visit seemed one huge festival. The whole time order, peace and happy thoughts prevailed. One heard of nothing else, but illuminations, gala dinners, fireworks, balls and parades in the capital of the Stewarts. The good Scottish People, so well known for being industrious, had then become lazier than one would have thought possible.

I have visited Holyrood several times, but never as thoroughly as when I accompanied Prince Sapieha.[6] The guides seemed to have much more time and patience then. This famous place is built in a square with turrets at the corners, and a courtyard in the middle, but the architecture is nothing special: it is too heavy. The Duke of Hamilton is the hereditary keeper of the Palace where he has the rooms which he occupied during the stay of the King. The whole staff of the Palace is under his orders and many servants are also hereditary. One of them descended in a direct line from the gardener of Queen Mary. History has passed, but its outward forms remain and it could be said that the Court has survived its Sovereigns. The staff were aware that a Polish Prince, a friend of the Duke of Hamilton, was to visit the Palace and they were all waiting in gala dress. The Groom of the Chamber was in a red uniform, court shoes, white stockings and a three-cornered hat. He met us at the gate, a silver staff in his hand, and went before us to the Palace. Two constables, also with staves in their hands, followed us. At the doors of different chambers various officials greeted us. In rooms designed for Ladies there were special women attendants.

We were shown as a great curiosity the rooms in which the Count d'Artois, the present French King,[7] and the Dukes of Angoulême and Berry (the latter murdered later on in Paris) had lived during their exile. The Count, though reduced to the station of a private person, lived as far as possible according to the Versailles etiquette. He ate in state twice a week and received in audience all his courtiers, émigrés as himself.

Thence we were shown into the rooms occupied by the British King and to the throne chamber in which he received. This chamber is preserved exactly as it had been during his stay, and probably will be thus preserved for many years to come, for such memories live long in Scotland. The King received on the 20th of August and he wore a kilt. A countless number of carriages was drawn up in front of the Palace, having brought the Scottish nobles to his drawing room. Huge crowds were standing around watching all this luxury of array. It was not the gala uniforms, which are simple and without special decorations, which attracted such attention but the old traditional dresses of the country. The Chief of Glengarry[8] was surrounded by the people of his clan who ran around his coach with rifles on their shoulders. This personage, armed and fierce-looking, made one think of the motto of his coat of arms: 'Nemo me impune lacesset.'[9] (No one can offend me with impunity.) He was in strange contrast with the civilised and quiet-looking people around him. But this was truly Scottish! A strict etiquette

[9] *Holyrood Palace. The tower in the foreground was built as a royal lodging for James IV and Margaret Tudor. After the Reformation the abbey's conventual buildings were converted into a palace. This was accidentally burnt by Commonwealth troops in 1650 and rebuilt by Charles II's Surveyor of the King's Work, Sir William Bruce, in 1671. During his visit to Scotland in 1822 George IV held receptions in the Palace but stayed at Dalkeith as the guest of the Duke of Buccleuch. Ewbank*

is obligatory at Court. Those who were to be presented had to be dressed accordingly. The ladies had ostrich feathers on their heads and wore dresses with long trains. They had to take special walking lessons not to get entangled in them, for etiquette does not allow a lady to turn her back on the King and so she has to leave the chamber walking backwards. The custom of the country is that the King gives each Lady presented to him an embrace from his throne.

We were taken in the end to the most interesting part of the Palace, that of Mary Queen of Scots, famous for her misfortunes. Her chambers are so tiny and simple that the humblest women now live in better ones; but everything in them is preserved with great piety, as it had been during the life of the Queen. The elderly woman, who was showing us around, pointed to the bed of the Queen and told us: 'His Majesty inspected it and found that it was kept in good order.' We were quite willing to believe her, though we were in doubt whether the blankets on the Queen's bed, badly torn and tattered, were so damaged because of scrupulous cleaning, or perhaps because ferocious visitors tore out patches and bits to keep as souvenirs. Even Argus is unable to stand guard on humans. A portrait of the Queen is hanging in the room but it has no special merit. The art of painting was unable at that time to flatter the beauty of women. There is also a Queen's toilet and a chair and a table on which the basket with her work is resting. She liked to seek distraction in needlework, for her throne was not littered with roses. The portrait of Darnley, her first husband, was shown to us in the next room and his arms and the rest of his heavy armour. Also the hidden stairs through which he came with his armed men to murder the Italian Rizzio, who was then playing on his lute to the Queen and the Duchess of Argyle. In vain did the sobbing Queen try to save him; he was stabbed with daggers and the body, covered with 56 wounds, was dragged out of the room. Up to now the bloodstains are still visible and our woman guide assured us that no earthly power is able to wash them off. We chose the easier course of believing the words of so worthy looking a woman, rather than give ourselves the trouble of verifying the reality of such miracles.

We were led afterwards to a narrow hall, 150 feet long, which was used for Parliamentary Assemblies; new peers are inaugurated here nowadays. The walls are hung with portraits of the kings, beginning with Fergus. These portraits have no merit whatever except perhaps that of being hung in chronological order. The row finishes with James VI. Charles, the last descendent of the Stuarts, who in 1745 gave a banquet in that orphaned Palace, is not represented here. The first peers and peeresses of Scotland took part in the banquet. Fate, unfavourable to him but favourable to Scotland, grudged him the throne of his forefathers. Ever after, Scotland united herself with closer ties to England and drew great industrial and educational profits from that alliance. Charles appeared and vanished like a meteor. With the change of luck the sentiments of a nation change also. Though egoism and wisdom took the upper hand and prevailed over enthusiasm, the purer feelings were preserved in songs and romantic stories. Songs about Charles are still sung in Scotland. Walter Scott has depicted in a masterly way the character of that Prince as well as the feelings, which were then dividing the nation, in his novel of *Waverley*. Many are the romantic stories about Flora Macdonald and the Pretender, or the Chevalier. The defeat at Culloden brought all to an end. The Prince himself would have perished at the hands of his persecutors had it not been for the courage of Flora MacDonald who, at the home of her father

[10] *'John Knox admonishing Mary Queen of Scots' by Sir William Allan. Allan was influenced by Thomas McCrie's recently published* Life of John Knox *which had reassessed Knox's role in the Scottish Reformation. Reviewing it in* The Edinburgh Review *Francis Jeffrey had written: 'We do not hesitate to pronounce it as by far the best piece of history which has appeared since the commencement of our critical career'.*

in Skye, helped him escape by hiding him amongst her train of servant girls, disguised as one of them. Charles Edward Stewart, for the sake of contemporary protocol otherwise known as the Chevalier though to history as the Pretender, died in Rome where his uncle was a cardinal. He married the Polish princess, Clementina Sobieska,[10] from whom Flora Macdonald, according to the romance *Waverley*, received an annual pension.

Having visited the Palace, we went to see the garden of Mary Queen of Scots. There is a sundial in that little garden, but the trees have all been frosted some time ago during one especially hard winter. The Scots, in memory of their Queen, were buying wood from these dead trees at high prices and making it into keepsakes framed in gold or silver. The guide offered me some snuff and told me that his snuff box was also made out of wood of one of the pear trees. It is astonishing to see what an influence such old memories can have. No nation appreciates old traditions more than the Scots.

Having left these sad places to which so much of the past still clings, we went through a narrow lane, the Canongate, to the Castle. This street was once the principal one but now it is inhabited only by the very poor. Our attention was drawn to an inscription in three languages on one of the houses: Deus, God, and God in the Greek alphabet. A small pulpit was carved in stone and a tiny human figure could be seen inside it. It represented John Knox, who had once been preaching from one of the windows of the house.

It is owing to that strange work of art that I made the acquaintance of Allan[11] the painter. He was working on a picture then, a historical one, which greatly excited the curiosity of connoisseurs. But as it was not yet finished he did not permit anyone to see it except his nearest friends. Our guide was one of them. Having entered the studio and having introduced me as usual, my guide, Mr Y.[12] added that I was a Pole. 'A Pole,' Allan exclaimed, 'Welcome! I have spent in Poland some of the happiest years of my life.' I learned that he had spent eight years in Zofiowka, the beautiful country place of Count Potocki[13] in the Ukraine. He was well acquainted with our poet Trembecki,[14] and described him to me as if he wanted to paint his picture: his high forehead, bald head, and his whole respectable looking silhouette. He spoke of him with veneration as of some sacred thing or relic. He heard from me that the man was dead. He used to play chess with him. He inquired after a number of other people whom he had known, but most of all after Count Waclaw Rzewuski.[15]

He took us afterwards to his study where, to prove how much Poland was still in his thoughts, he showed us different Polish arms, national costumes and even a Polish riding whip (nahajka). We spoke a few words in our native tongue but not having spoken it for so long has made him forget it. Nevertheless, he understood everything I said. He was born in Scotland and the Duke of Hamilton, when travelling through Poland, took him back with him. I am not expert enough to be able to judge the works of Allan, but I must say that I liked his last picture immensely. It represented John Knox admonishing the Queen at Holyrood. The expression of fearlessness in the posture and the face of the Reformer was very striking, especially his tight set lips and frowning brow which expressed extreme severity. He was pressing the Bible in his hands with force as though he wanted to squeeze out of it even more reasons for humiliating the Queen. Mary Stewart, her face bathed in tears, her head on her hand, seems half to acknowledge her faults. She does not try to deny them, but her expression makes one wonder who is faultless in the face of the Holy Bible? Who is perfect? Historians state that the tears of the Queen soaked several handkerchiefs on that occasion and Allan depicted her so, with her handkerchief in her hand. Allan is considered to be one of the first-rate painters of the day. To make his works better known some have been engraved on copper. I saw one of such beautiful engravings: '*Les Femmes Circassiennes*' if I remember correctly. His pictures are mostly of Scottish history, for such are the best paid in so patriotic a country. They are praised for their fine conception and the carefulness with which they are finished. He paints only in oils and, as he told me himself, he owes the development of his talent chiefly to Poles who paid lavishly for his early achievements.

III

The Jail and the House of Correction. The Gas Works. The Parliament House. Libraries. Charitable Institutions. National Schools

EDINBURGH possesses many splendid buildings, useful Institutions and establishments worthy of the attention of the foreigner. All this, being the outcome of the superior education of our century, gives a wealth of practical ideas to others.

On March 17th 1823, having got the permit of the Lord Provost, we went to visit the Jail and the House of Correction in Bridewell. Nobody is allowed without special permits, both for the sake of security and to avoid the exceeding curiosity of the crowds. Both buildings are situated on the slopes of Calton Hill, both are surrounded by one wall which, though very high to look at, is not high enough to prevent the prisoners from escaping. The very night before our visit such an incident occurred; two thieves had escaped. It is easy in British prisons, for there is no military guard and the jailer alone is responsible.

The Jail is divided into two sections; in one are the debtors, in the other the criminals. Both parts are equally well guarded and secured. In a country, which has such a great respect for property, that the stealing of a few shillings is punished by hanging, those who do not pay their debts must be considered as greater transgressors of the law than in other countries. The strictness of the law in these things has been very great in these islands for centuries. Tacitus says that, amongst ancient Britons, the one who lost at some game and could not pay became the slave of the one to whom he lost. Who does not realise what being a slave meant in those barbaric times!

The jailer took us round the cells in which those condemned to death were imprisoned. They are not kept together nowadays as they had been in the past, for instead of repentance only corruption was the result.

Each is kept in a separate cell, fitted with iron doors, but the prisoners are not chained. The sound of a voice reading aloud came from one of the cells. The jailer gave us the sign to stop and listen, so we did; it was the voice of a young man, condemned to death, who was reading the Bible. This is given to every prisoner in his last moments. The silence of his cell and the Bible as his sole consolation were more likely to make him repent than any human volubility. This unhappy young man was only twenty-one and there were several even younger, of scarcely fifteen years of age. They were awaiting either capital punishment or Botany Bay. This overseas country is to the Britons what Siberia is to the Russians. A woman was in one of the cells; she had been accused and convicted of having murdered an unknown young man in her house and of throwing his body out of the window. One of the best-known advocates undertook her defence, if one could call that defence which is only intended to make the sentence less severe. Defence, as the last gift of human feeling, is not refused even to the most obdurate criminals. The Court, having listened to the defence and to the witnesses, pronounced her guilty and subject to capital punishment. A verdict of the law cannot be put into force on these islands as long as the verdict of the conscience is not fulfilled. Such is the procedure of the tribunals in which the sworn-in juries take part. The unusualness and the greatness of the crime caused a crowd to attend the Court, for Justice is administered in public and, also in public, the criminals are put to death in the middle of the Market Place. This terrible sight has not yet been withdrawn from public places and crowds gather to witness it. Some of the more daring criminals talk to the people even from beneath the gallows. And the said woman did not wish to leave this world without making some impression and, not trusting her volubility, she wanted to produce some effect by her attire. Feathers were waving on her head and she was covered with a rich shawl.

Some time ago a great number of children used to be imprisoned. It was gathered from their confidences that lack of education caused their transgressions. To prevent such things, numerous schools have been opened in the capital, one even within the precincts of the prison. Ever since, the number of criminals has decreased every year. Lack of knowledge is the source of all evil. The Jail we visited is erected on the ruins of the former one, the Tollbooth,[1] with which the readers of Walter Scott must be well acquainted. When that prison was demolished, the beautifully sculptured entrance gate was given to Walter Scott and now adorns his country place at Abbotsford. Those allowed by fate to visit

[11] *Trinity Collegiate Church, Edinburgh. Founded in 1460, it was dismantled in 1848 to make way for the extension of the railway from Haymarket to Waverley Station. Many of the carefully numbered stones were stolen before the remainder were re-assembled in Chalmers Close in 1872. Behind the Church are the Governor's House and the House of Correction of the new Jail.* Ewbank

the Bard in his home are also enabled to see those ancient remains.

Within the precincts of the prison walls is the house of correction, the Bridewell. It is a semi-circle seven storeys high. On every storey there are balconies separated like boxes in a theatre where the prisoners work; their cells are behind. In the very middle of the semi-circle is a tower in which the gaoler resides. Through long narrow windows he can observe unseen how the prisoners behave during their work. The whole courtyard is covered by a skylight, supplying light to the prisoners. A big furnace erected in the courtyard heats the whole building during winter. There is a pulpit in the middle and benches on which the gaolers sit during the services. The prisoners listen, from behind bars from their respective storeys, to the sermons, which are generally adapted to their condition. Each of the prisoners has a Bible in his cell. The reading of the Bible is considered to be the most effective form of correction. Length of imprisonment depends on the seriousness of the crime. Some prisoners

[12] The North Bridge from the Calton Hill. The bridge was completed in 1763, providing an essential link between the Old and what was to become the New Town. In the foreground is the Jail and in the distance 'The Earthen Mound'. This was built from some two million cartloads of material excavated to form the basements of New Town houses and was not completed till 1830. Ewbank

spend only a few weeks in the house, others several months, but nobody more than two years. Everybody gets work for which he is fitted or to which he is accustomed. Money gained by the sale of objects made by the prisoners goes to a common fund from which all the expenses of the establishment are covered. There are several machines which facilitate difficult work. We saw one for making corks but it was not active at the time. There were 184 prisoners on the day of our visit. It is curious that there are always more prisoners in winter than in summer and always more women than men. On this day, there were forty more. The gaolers complain that they are the most difficult to manage and impossibly noisy. Corporal punishment is not used at all, for practice has shown that it only debases human beings and does not improve them. If they refrain from their bad habits it is only from fear, and at heart they remain as wicked as ever. The reduction of food, confinement in the cell and solitude are the usual punishments used. The latter is considered the most severe. Prisoners are flogged only for attacking a gaoler. But even then he resorts to it only in self-defence.

It was with relief that we left this place of crime and guilt and heard the heavy door shut behind us. The impressions made by these two places were very different. In the House of Correction I felt nothing but disgust; it echoed with shrieks, ribald laughter and jeers. The prisoners, especially those newly arrived, seem to make the very thought of repentance impossible. And yet time, the great Healer, and a sensible way of treating them do achieve much. In the prison, on the contrary, I felt pity and respect. The deep silence, broken only from time to time by sighs of sorrow, gave to the place a strange solemnity. The human soul is often great even in its lowest and it never can leave other human beings unmoved.

The gas works are not distant from the prison. They are situated lower than the town which is of great use as the gas reaches the upper streets the more easily. It is distributed underground in iron pipes and branches out everywhere. From out of the main ones come those of smaller dimensions leading to street lights and private houses. On all their floors, each corner, according to the owner's wish, may be lit by gas light. The total extent of all this pipe work comes to twelve English miles. One has a diameter of twelve inches and is capable of producing the same amount of light as a million candles. Some parts of the city, which are further away from the factory, are better illuminated than those nearer. This is due to the slower flow which exists there. Too rapid a rate, such as must exist in the proximity of the factory itself, hampers lateral distribution. Theatres, artisans' manufactories and shops are all gas-lit. In shops various shapes determine the amount of light, that of a star being the most common and indeed the most effective. This is simple enough to make and it is sufficient to make the appropriate holes in the pipe's end. One may use up as much gas as one wants, and for just such an amount is one charged. The greatest discomfort thus far lies in the fact that one is obliged to light and extinguish the gas at regulated times, for no one may have gas at any time except these. Yet even this inconvenience has been resolved by the inventiveness of the Scot. Now, no matter how much or when, one may at all times obtain gas. Artificial devices have been introduced into homes which use gas and they, being linked to the distribution pipes, constantly relay back to the factory owner information as to how much gas is needed and where. In relation to this, so does the consumer pay. This is a new invention which, at the time of my sojourn in England, was still unknown,

No traveller could fail to find in Edinburgh something to interest him. A lawyer can find nothing more thrilling than the Parliament House, especially when the sessions of the Courts of Law take place there. The entrance is adorned by Scotland's coat of arms and by two huge figures, representing Truth and Charity, and the inscription: 'Stant his Felicia regna.' A huge hall, 120 feet long, contains the statues of the defenders of Justice. Watching large numbers of lawyers in their black robes and big wigs, passing by, or speaking to the crowds, one can get some sort of idea of what Forum Romanum must have been like. But also other thoughts are awakened. It is here that the most active and the most educated classes of society gather, for such are the Scottish lawyers. Here speaks the witty Jeffrey,[2] the eloquent Gladstone, the deep Murray, well known for his learning and, what thrills the foreigner even more, it is here that one can see Walter Scott. He has a job which brings him £2000 a year, and so little work that he writes his novels here during the sessions. Not only has Walter Scott this very lucrative office but also his estate of Abbotsford; he was, therefore, not much affected by the bankruptcy of his publisher.[3] A couple of new novels will soon make up for what he has lost, especially as the originals are published in England, and in Leipzig and Paris simultaneously, thus enabling him to triple his money.

The same building contains two Libraries: that of the Advocates and of the Writers to the Signet. The latter contains many books about Polish History and Literature. Some of these are in Latin, others in French, English, German and several even in Polish (Niemcewicz, Naruszewicz, Krasicki and others).[4] The Latin writings of Copernicus[5] and the old Polish History of Dlugosz are among the most remarkable. A better arranged library could not be found. Luxury and comfort are combined here. The chief hall has a double line of columns and above a gallery filled with books. On both sides in the windows there are small tables and chairs, and everybody can read and write as if in separate little rooms. The tables are immovable, made of iron and empty within, so that in winter they are used as little stoves and are heated by the air coming from pipes under the floor. Neither of these libraries is public. and to be able to use it one must have a letter of introduction from one of the lawyers. Books are not allowed to be taken home, only in exceptional cases a special permit is given by the director. For a foreigner wanting to study English Literature, to try to get such a permit seems the best thing to do, especially as there are no public libraries in the city and the hiring of books in bookshops is much too expensive. But as a rule foreigners experience great kindness and I, for instance, during

[13] *Heriot's Hospital from the Castle Hill. George Heriot was a goldsmith and moneylender to Anne of Denmark and James VI. He followed the Court to London and the fortune he sent back to Edinburgh financed a 'Hospital' where the sons of impoverished merchants could be educated. The school was designed in 1628 by William Wallace, the King's Master Mason, but the building was not completed till the end of the century. It is now a co-educational school.* Ewbank

my stay in Edinburgh could enter both Libraries and take home as many books as I pleased. I owe deep gratitude to the Librarians, Mr Irving and Mr Napier,[6] who not only helped me with extreme kindness to find the most noteworthy works, but also gave me much wise and enlightened advice. Both these men are known for their published writings. Mr Irving has written about Buchanan,[7] a Scottish Latin poet, and he mentions our Sarbiewski[8] appreciatively in his work. I do not agree, however, with his statement that the Latin of Buchanan is better than that of Sarbiewski.

The Advocates' Library, though considered to be the largest, has no more than 80,000 volumes. It increases daily, however, thanks to the privilege of receiving at least one free copy of every work printed in Great Britain. Several British libraries enjoy this privilege: The British Museum in London, Kings' Inn in Dublin, and seven Universities: Oxford, Cambridge, Edinburgh, Glasgow, Aberdeen, St. Andrews and Dublin [Trinity College]. The publishers consider this privilege to be

[14] *The Tron Kirk, Edinburgh. The wooden tower of the seventeenth-century Tron Kirk collapsed in the great fire of 1824. The old Tollbooth, whose door is now built into Scott's house at Abbotsford, stood between the Tron (the public weigh bridge) and the High Kirk of St Giles. In the foreground is one of the wells to which water was piped from the reservoir on the Castle Hill. In 1674 the Town Council had paid £2,950 to Peter Bruschi, a German engineer, to bring water from Comiston to the city.* Ewbank

very hard on them; especially if expensive editions have to be offered and so many of them are published.

Edinburgh possesses a number of Charitable Institutions; I will mention some of them. The most prominent is the Infirmary[9] where, according to statistics, 2,381 poor patients have been treated. The city gives £5,000 for the maintenance of this hospital. It also serves as a clinic for the students of the medical faculty. To supplement the charity exercised by this Hospital, various associations work together with it, like The Society for the Treatment of the Poor Sick in their own Homes, The Society for Vaccination against Small-pox and The Society for the Treatment of the Eyes. Owing to the sharp winds, sore eyes are extremely frequent, and it would be difficult to find a country with more blind people than here. For those unfortunates who have already lost their sight forever, a special spacious house is provided in which they learn to weave baskets, to make nets, stockings, straw or horse hair mattresses, and other work suitable for them.

All Charitable Institutions bear the name either of Hospitals or Asylums, but it must not be understood that the hospitals are designed only for the sick. Any house in which an orphan or an invalid or a pauper finds shelter can be thus designated. For instance there is an orphanage called 'The Orphan Hospital', and the Gillespie Hospital, where several poor men and women are boarded, and a school for a hundred poor pupils is also founded here. Watson's Hospital is intended for children and grandchildren of merchant families that have become poor. There is also a Merchant Maiden Hospital, maintained by various donations. Girls from 7 to 17 are brought up there. They are taught, as in the other schools, a little French, drawing, music and needlework. Many on leaving the Hospital become housekeepers in rich houses, many find even better positions. When leaving the Hospital they receive 10 guineas. At the time 50 girls were studying there. An even more ancient and not less important foundation is the Heriot's Hospital, meant for 180 poor students. Most are prepared for trade or handicrafts but some adopt a scientific career. Those leaving the institution do not cease to be under its protection. For the first five years they receive a sum towards their maintenance. For instance those who go to the University receive £30 a year during the first four years. Students on leaving the Institution receive an outfit of new clothes and a beautifully bound Bible with which they are sent out into the world. After many years of kind care, an orphan can nowhere be more beautifully provided for. This Institution was founded by George Heriot, a son of an Edinburgh goldsmith and himself a goldsmith at the court of James VI. The income of the Institution is more than £5,000 a year. The Magdalen Asylum gives shelter to those unhappy creatures who, having deviated from the path of virtue, show compunction and a desire to change their life. The present King during his stay in Edinburgh gave a generous allowance to this Institution. It is meant for 50–60 persons. The statistics of 1822 show that during the 23 years of the existence of the Institution, 432 girls have been received there. Out of these, 140 became good house servants, 81 were reconciled to their families, 12 married, 8 died and 33 have remained for a longer stay. In all the larger towns, humanity has erected such institutions.

It would be difficult to give even the names of all the Welfare Institutions, much less go into details and particulars about them all. But no misery, infirmity or suffering has been overlooked. Not only has charity united people in the effort of carrying help to the needy, it has also armed them to destroy evil in the very beginning. Societies have been formed to prevent begging in the streets and nakedness. Houses have been opened to facilitate earning, and to provide cheap clothes for the poor. One of the most successful is the old age fund, where workers put by part of their weekly income and afterwards receive it back with interest. If only such institutions could be started in our country as they are planned to be. Public charity, the church funds, and private donations maintain most of the institutions for the infirm and the poor. If one of the establishments is in sudden need of money, a good preacher undertakes to explain the necessity to the public and supplies are immediately forthcoming. The funds of the Biblical Society come also from such sources, for the ignorance of the Holy Bible is considered with reason to be the greatest moral deficiency.

No country has so many schools in which the poor can be taught; the supervision of these belongs solely to the founders. Scottish women do a lot to run them efficiently, and many a daughter or wife of the richest laird fulfils the duties of a village teacher or schoolmistress. I did not believe it at first, but I have seen it myself. Thus, humanity unites the rich and the poor by a lovely tie. What kindness of feelings, what a brotherhood of classes such an attitude must develop in the future.

It can be stated as a whole about Scotland, that misery is being fought there by means of education and by opening the eyes of the poor to the profits a man gets from being industrious and laborious. This kind of education is very advanced in Scotland and has reacted successfully to the misery, which can be softened in England only by enormous taxes, and in Ireland is simply shocking. This activity by itself shows plainly that the Scottish people are more hard-working and industrious than the English and the Irish. Well educated, they know how to adapt their ways of living to their means, they are practical and quiet. This high level in itself becomes a source of prosperity. As examples of everyday life show, a Scotsman will soon become rich in England; but an Englishman will not become rich in Scotland, and as to an Irishman, he is poor wher ever he goes. The high educational standards and the iron endurance of the Scots will be surpassed by no one.

IV

*The University. Examinations. The Income of the Professors
of Edinburgh. The programme of the studies. The Students
of Theology. The Auditoriums. The Ancient Literature.
The Library. The Museum. The Botanical Garden.
The Observatorium.*

THE University of Edinburgh[1] is not as ancient as that of Oxford or
Cambridge, or the Scottish ones at St. Andrews, Glasgow or Aberdeen.
It was established in 1583, during the reign of James VI. The style of its
architecture is not Gothic as in the older Universities. It is built and
arranged after the German plan. Its prosperity is owing not to the
generosity of Monarchs but chiefly of private persons who, loving some
special science, gave donations for the promotion of its study. The
present fame of the Edinburgh University is due to the exceptional men
who taught there. Adam Smith[2] and Blair[3] lectured on rhetoric, Monro[4]
and Gregory[5] taught medicine; Playfair[6] mathematics; Dugald Stewart[7]
and Thomas Brown[8] philosophy; they are well known in the scientific
world by their writings. Now Wilson[9] and Leslie[10] are lecturing and
their innate genius seems to intend them for the widening of human
knowledge. A great splendour also surrounds the name of the University because of the numbers who attended it and afterwards worked
most usefully and successfully in various walks of life. I say 'worked', for
it must be stated to the glory of this University that, great though the
development of the heart and mind through ideas might be, it has always
been the aim of the University to adapt learning to life and make it
practical.

As to the undergraduates, special rules bind them which are different
from those of other universities They have nothing to do with each other
except at lectures. They are not as in other British universities bound to
wear a special dress or to live in colleges. Nor are they supervised by the

[15] *Edinburgh University. Founded in 1582 by James VI, the University had expanded dramatically in the eighteenth century and had outgrown its original buildings. The foundation stone of Robert Adam's New College was laid in 1798 but building stopped during the French Wars. It was 1820 before it was completed to William Playfair's design. The South Bridge was built over the Cowgate to link the University, and the southern developments of the city, with the New Town.* Ewbank

university authorities. Notwithstanding this freedom, which in another country might have proved harmful to the young, one does not hear about fights, potations or duels as in the German universities. One is simply astounded to see the quietness and the order with which everything happens within and outside the University. This must be partly put down to the great respect which is felt for the Professors, partly to the habits of self-control the young men acquire in their homes. Partly also to the point of honour binding them, proud as they are of their nationality, and partly also to the mixing of students of different ages. The very young must check their exuberance in the face of the elderly and because of this they themselves often become as serious as old men. Here elderly men are not ashamed to attend lectures together with the very young. A foreigner watching white-haired old men besides striplings makes a mental note that, in this Athens of the North, education is not finished early in life. The audience is especially large at the beginning and the end of the year, for the lecturers are especially eloquent: at the beginning to make people more eager to learn and, at the end, to make the learning sink in. It is then that one can see among the audience the best-known men in the country. They are brought here either by personal friendship for the lecturers or by sheer love of learning, never by shallow curiosity. The sight of these great men present here, as if to set a good example for the young to follow, cannot but awaken lofty ideas and great respect for the place of science. From this the professors derive their popularity and are so much respected that, even in their old age, they are always gratefully remembered.

As far as tuition is concerned the undergraduates are very independent. Those who would attend the lectures simply have to become enlisted in the *Album*; they pay five shillings and receive a little note with the words: 'Ciris Bibliothecae Edinensis'. This gives them the right to use the Library and serves instead of the matriculation obligatory at other Universities. With this card the undergraduate goes to the Professors whose lectures he wishes to attend. Nobody asks him for his school certificate. This is the explanation of the great numbers attending the University; there are as many as 4,000. The undergraduate is allowed to attend lectures free for the first week after which, if the test is successful, he is enlisted under the Professor. The students of Theology and Medicine have more precise rules. All the other faculties are attended by people who simply do so for love of learning. They are independent and no one is interested in what sort of progress they are making. There are no yearly examinations and the medical students pass only one examination, which gives them the right to practise and the ring of wisdom. The thesis they defend is short and has to be printed. The defence is seldom public and generally takes place in great secrecy. The final examinations have to be passed in August. About 150 students take the medical degree every year. All this leads one to suppose that among the worthy ones a great number of incapable sons of Esculapius must sneak through. Nevertheless, this does not prevent the Edinburgh School of Medicine from being considered the best in Britain. As in all other faculties, the personal assiduity of the students counts most. Besides the professors who lecture in public there are also private teachers who help the students to acquire knowledge. Undergraduates have meetings at which they can discuss scientific problems at their leisure. They write essays until perfection is reached; no wonder that the University prides herself that many eminent men have studied here.

Nine faculties have professors appointed by the Government, and the town council chooses the others. The salary attached to the faculties is not large, and it depends on the generosity of the founder of the faculty in question. The lowest are £100 and the highest £200, which is very little for so expensive a country and, in any case, a rather poor pay for talent and learning. Nevertheless the professors are far from poor: on the contrary, thanks to other incomes, their posts are considered very lucrative. Their greatest income comes from the students who have to pay three or four guineas a year to be able to attend the lectures. In Edinburgh, where the number of students is so great, this constitutes a great sum, especially for those professors who teach well. Mr Hope,[11] for instance, who was teaching Chemistry, had 500 pupils, thus he had 2,000 guineas a year beside the regular income attached to his faculty. Taken together the sum is so large that only the first Government officials in other countries can dream of having such incomes. It is true that his were the very best attended lectures, but nevertheless many of his colleagues had *almost as many students.*

Studies begin in October and finish in April, which means that they last only half a year. In summer only some of the subjects are taught. The undergraduates are not at all overworked and have plenty of time for individual studies. They form societies and discuss important works, write essays, argue with each other and thus make great progress. This system develops their faculties of independent thinking, which can be given by no other teaching. In their discussions they are very fair to each other, their civility is exemplary and equality is respected. Because of this the student societies have a strange aspect of maturity. One of the members is chosen to preside. More important societies have their own libraries and all the periodicals referring to their respective studies. The names of the members are enlisted in a special book and many a name of great fame can be found there.

To those of my readers, who will be especially interested in so famous a University, I enclose some particulars. It has four faculties: Theology, Philosophy, Law and Medicine. Art has not yet found room there. The Chancellor is called the 'Principal' and he is chosen for life. There are no deans. Nobody is responsible for the progress of the undergraduates; they are left entirely to their own devices. The programme of the lectures is announced every year on a small sheet and it is entirely left to the professors how they choose to deal with their subjects. The long and learned 'Prolusiones', as seen in the German universities, are not known here. Oxford and Cambridge never announce any programme at all. For

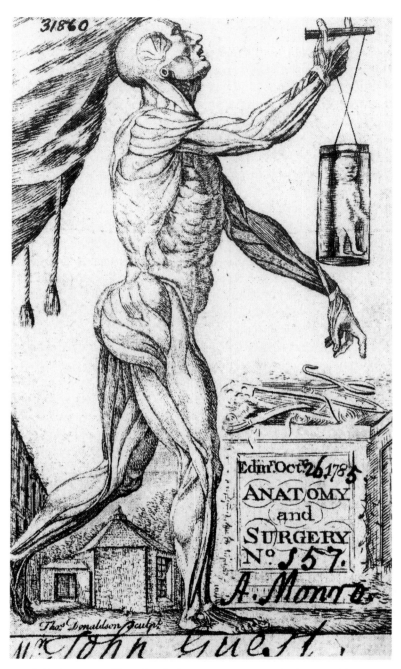

[16] *Anatomy Class Card, 1785. On payment of a fee, usually £3,
students were issued with a card which would admit them to lectures for
a year. Five shillings went to the University Library and the rest to the
professor. During his two years at the University, Lach-Szyrma studied
medicine as well as philosophy.*

those interested I enclose the programme of the year 1824 at Edinburgh University, entirely as I have copied it:

1. FACULTY OF LITERATURE AND PHILOSOPHY

SUBJECTS	PROFESSORS
Humanitas (Latin Literature)	Pillans.
Greek Literature	Dunbar.
Mathematics	Wallace.
Logic	Ritchie.
Moral Philosophy	Wilson.
Physics	Leslie.
Rhetoric and Art	Brown.
Universal History	Hamilton (Baronet)
Natural History	Jameson.
Botanics	Graham.
Agriculture	Coventry.

2. THEOLOGY

Theology	Ritchie. (Doctor of Theology)
History of the Church	Meicklejohn. (Doctor of Theology)
Hebrew	Brunton. (Doctor of Theology)

3. LAW

Civil Law, Institutions and Pandectic	Irvine.
Scottish Law	Bell.
Public Law	Hamilton.

4. MEDICINE

Dietetica, Materia Medica, Pharmacology	Duncan. (Junior)
Practical Medicine	Home.
Chemistry and Chemical Pharmacology	Hope.
Theory of Medical Science	Duncan. (Senior), Alison.
Anatomy and Surgery	Monro.
Practical and Theoretical Gynaecology	Hamilton.
Legal Medicine	Anyone from the Faculty.
Clinical Surgery	Russel.
Military Surgery	Ballingol.

As we see from the above the Medical and the Philosophical Faculties have the best professors. Medical students can get private tuition from professors whose certificates have the same importance as those of the University professors. These are called: Lecturers. The students of the Law supplement their studies by attending the Courts of Justice, where they have the opportunity of listening to famous advocates; the students of Theology frequent the churches, where they listen to the best preachers (Chalmers,[12] Alison,[13] Thomson[14]). They work longer than all the other students to prepare for their future profession. They will be preaching to people; this requires much effort and eight years of study. During the first four years the young theologian is obliged to attend classes at the university for subjects like Latin and Greek Literature as well as Mathematics, Philosophy, Logic, and Physics. After gaining the certificate (passes) in these subjects, he can be admitted to the Divinity Hall. Here he spends another four years studying Theology and the languages which he will require in order to teach the Bible. However, since these courses take only one year, there is no need for him to attend the classes for the remaining three. He simply pays the customary fee to the professors, which is obligatory, and is free to do whatever he likes with his time. Poorer students are usually engaged as tutors in wealthy families while they continue reading theological papers to prepare for professional work.

After eight years each candidate has to present himself to a committee of ministers for the final examination. If he gains a pass mark, which is usually the case since the examiners are rather lenient, he receives a Licence to preach in public. He can now look for vacancies in the ministry. The procedure is the same in all Scottish universities, whether in Glasgow, Aberdeen or St Andrews. Young people trained at these universities are renowned for their sound knowledge and good behaviour. Any neglect on the part of the future minister would not be forgiven in Scotland. It is generally admitted that the Scottish Clergy are better educated than the English; the way they are taught is different. The lower clergy, the curates, need not have university training. They are generally taken from the ranks of village schoolteachers, recommended by an influential patron. Higher clergy, on the other hand, are trained by the universities of Oxford and Cambridge so that they can become dignitaries of the Church, with financial rewards which are not available to the lower orders.

The auditoriums, although spacious, are still being enlarged and often have skylights. On entering one I have always been impressed. The undergraduates sit on benches rising in tiers one above the other. They all wear caps, which they only take off on the entry of the Professor. The professors wear gowns and lecture from chairs. They sometimes sit, sometimes stand for greater effect. Some of the students use shorthand for noting down the lectures. But it never occurs here, which is so frequent in Germany, that the lectures thus noted down are illegally published. The undergraduates applaud each lofty thought or beautiful sentence by clapping hands or thumping on the floor. This, if lasting too long, disturbs the lecturer. The professors try to adapt themselves to their audience and take every opportunity of pleasing it. Even those who translate the Ancients try to combine eloquence and power of speech. The Professor of Latin Literature, an expert Philologist, whilst translating, used to find numerous comparisons between the Ancients and the national Literature, and he thus held the interest of the listeners. He also taught Roman and Greek Geography in a delightful manner, often referring to the present state of these famous places. He quoted various travellers, but most of all Lord Byron's poems; for this great poet loved these places and breathed in their atmosphere until he died. A lecture like this perfected the taste and feelings of the listeners and killed all boredom, which accompanies stiff, dry learning. At the time of my stay in Edinburgh, Wilson, a well-known writer of several poems and novels, was also famous for his lectures. It was he who had succeeded Brown as Professor of Philosophy. His lively imagination, his new ideas and his eloquence, flowing like a powerful torrent, were very impressive. So too was his personality which was so very striking that it attracted crowds of listeners. Dr Hope, Professor of Chemistry, having attended one of his lectures, was heard to say that this was the best he had ever heard, which was saying a great deal as Dr Hope was the oldest of all the Edinburgh professors. The opinion of such an eloquent and well-known man (and a good writer too, for I have certainly not read anything better than his *Introduction to Chemistry*,) did a lot to encourage the young Professor. Personally I did not agree with Dr Hope about everything. I was shocked to hear him saying during one of his lectures, in which he had been quoting only English works on Chemistry, that: 'One can also take advice sometimes from a few French scientists. Several of their works are as good as the English'. And this in such a matter-of-fact and indifferent voice, as if Lavoisier,[15] Fourcroy,[16] Verthollet[17] were not even worth mentioning! What conceit and unfairness! But it is not only the British scientists who are blind to everything which is not their own country's special achievement.

[17] *Dr John Hope in the Physic Garden, Edinburgh. The Garden had been founded in 1667. Kay has sketched Hope, the Professor of Materia Medica, talking to one of the gardeners. John Kay.*

During Latin and Greek Literature, I was fully aware of the drawback of insufficient grounding at school, apparent in some of the students. The professors were obliged to divide the undergraduates into classes: two in Latin and three in Greek. This of course prevents the subject being tackled really properly. A method is even adopted which has been entirely discarded at other universities, being only suitable for schools. The professor makes the students translate in front of him and corrects their mistakes. The translating was passable as a rule; nevertheless, it was necessary to ask them about cases, origins of words, etc. Nobody goes so far as to talk Latin; they do not find it necessary for in Great Britain one learns in one's own language.[18] Besides, nobody except themselves would be able to understand their Latin for, pronouncing it in their own way, they make it as incomprehensible as Chinese to other nations. English universities murder Latin even more than the Scottish ones, for the Scots pronounce it more in its usual way. Not withstanding this, the Classics are extremely well taught there, and the knowledge of them is considered to be essential to serious education. The very affinity of English with Latin makes it even more so.

Connected with the University are several useful establishments; the Library is one of the most remarkable. It contains 50,000 volumes. I have been shown such invaluable documents as that of the Betrothal of Mary Stuart to the French Dauphin and the Protest of the Czechs against the burning of John Huss[19] in 1417. This was sent to the Council of Constance and 150 Czech and Moravian seals were attached to the document. Nobody quite knows how it came here.

The Museum, or the Natural Science Study, is also in the University building.[20] The great collection of birds, which was bought from Defresne in Paris, is very remarkable. There are 4,000 specimens. The tickets cost half a crown, and this money is used to pay the interest of the sum borrowed to augment the collection. The visitors are so numerous that in a few years the sum will be re-paid. There is also an anatomical Museum founded by the grandfather of the present professor of Anatomy, the famous Munro. The Faculty of Anatomy is hereditary in this family, but the capabilities are not. The University possesses too a Mineralogical Museum. Dr Balfour founded the Botanical Garden[21] in 1670 but it can scarcely be compared with medium continental botanical gardens. But as a rule Scottish gardening is of a high level and is considered as one of the first. This is the merit of the Horticultural Society, which lavishly rewards good gardeners for first-rate products. I was present at one of its yearly meetings which was combined with a dinner. It was a real pleasure to examine the various treasures of Pomona, the more valuable for being reared by human care. Never in my life had I seen such enormous grapes and gooseberries. Many people say that French grapes are neither as big nor as good as Scottish ones. The Scottish gardeners are also considered the best, and they are sent to England and even to the Continent. The harshness of their own climate teaches them how to deal with plants with the greatest care. They know how to make the most out of the soil and the climate. But though vegetables and flowers are a great success, fruits are hard, sour and tasteless. They often have no chance of ripening for lack of sun. The best apples obtainable in Scotland come from France and are called 'French Apples'. Lemons and oranges come from Italy and Spain. Whole shiploads of them arrive and one can be bought for three pence.

The Observatory on Calton Hill is built on a rock and thus has the firmest foundations, as well as a wide and unhampered horizon. But I have neither heard of astronomers, nor of cases of curious research in Scotland. Astronomy is not studied at Edinburgh University[22] and it does not seem a science fitted for that country. The eternally cloudy sky is seldom starry and sparkling as in Poland. This is the reason why Britain possesses only four Observatories, whereas there are more than fifty on the Continent.

V

*Examinations in High Schools. Lower Schools. Schools of
Handicraft. Scientific Societies. The Trade in Books.
Periodicals. Meetings of Scientists and Scholars*

HAVING given some idea of the University of Edinburgh, it would be
appropriate to give some attention to the schools. At the time of my stay
in Scotland, there was one High School and a second was being
planned.[1] The High School had four forms and four teachers; the
Headmaster was the fifth. About 800 pupils attended it and paid one
guinea a term; there were five terms in one year. Out of curiosity I once
attended examinations of the highest form where the well-known
philologist, Carson, was teaching (he was Headmaster). In the Latin
language there were Horace, Virgil Terentius, Tacitus and Livy, whilst
in Greek were Homer, Sophocles and Heroditos. St. Mark was even
translated from the Bible. In the list of lectures I saw the names of yet
more writers. The very list of the classical writers studied showed that
more time is given to them here than in Poland. Buchanan was
translated; he is to the Scots what our Sarbiewski is to us, but I would be
glad if so much time and attention were given to him as is given to
Buchanan here. Sarbiewski is certainly more appreciated in Scotland
than with us. Authors take his rhymes as titles to their books; teachers
give them as subjects of essays and compare him with their best authors
like Milton and Cowley.[2] One of the Cambridge University professors,
John Walker, was translating Sarbiewski's poems into English and he
was to publish them beside their Latin originals.

The method of examination, which one might equally take as one of
teaching, is as follows. First of all a student is called out, whereupon he
recites a passage of a given author. After having done so he analyses its
word order and then translates, during which the teacher gives not the
slightest help. In order to ascertain whether the pupil understands

everything, only later does the lecturer put questions concerning the syntax, metre and smallest properties of the speech. The students seldom erred in their answers; they answered swiftly, confidently and boldly. It could be observed that precision plays a great role in education. Of the students' progress one could judge easily, as the texts to be translated depended neither upon them nor their teachers but were chosen by one of their guests. Neither did they translate in sequence but at random. Sometimes students were tested on writers whom they had not read at all.

The translating of the classics during examinations was mingled with the reading of written essays. In a country where the need to speak in public arises so often, elocution is not neglected. I have known parents who employed actors to teach their children to speak. One seldom meets an Englishman who does not know how to read aloud. All gesticulation is laughed at here as ridiculous and the whole expression must be conveyed by the inflections in the voice. An Englishman speaking in public has to be immobile as a statue, otherwise he would be considered as lacking in dignity and common sense. A sensible people must be addressed in a sensible way; passions have no influence here. I have once witnessed a Spaniard delivering a speech to the Scots. His wild gesticulations had awakened uncontrolled laughter even before he had a chance of opening his mouth. It is one thing to address people who listen for amusement, as in a theatre, and quite a different thing to address them on a Council. Here if one wants to have any influence at all, one must speak to reason and not to passion. People, when their own affairs or those of their country are considered, weigh each word carefully and the signs of uncontrolled enthusiasm in the speaker can do him more harm than good. In this land of cold reason all discussions are quieter and far less stormy than I would have thought possible. Already the youths in schools learn how to obey the voice of reason and to stifle all passions. This is really taught to perfection. Dionisius, the Tyrant himself, could not have managed his school in Corinth better than Carson, the headmaster of the High School. When the Lord Provost who was to be present at the examinations arrived, the Headmaster greeted him with the coldest and most distant of bows, just acknowledging him by the slight inclination of his head. He showed no more enthusiasm towards other guests. This indifference was by no means a sign that he was unable to be more civil, only that his idea of what the dignity of a teacher in front of his pupils should be was so great. He simply thought that it is better to be too distant than overdo politeness. He did not believe in exaggeration. The pupils all sat motionless; he was the only person who moved about. When fellow students showed their appreciation of some of their friends' especially good essays, by thumping or clapping, Mr Carson only lifted his hand and immediate silence followed. His hand seemed then the trident of Neptune, the lifting of which calmed the most violent breakers. His countenance was marked by the utmost severity. Only once was it lighted up by the shade of a smile when, at the Lord Provost's request, three pupils were translating *ex tempore* Tacitus and Livy with great success. On that one occasion tenderness and emotion triumphed over cold reason. I have observed it in all British schools that notwithstanding a great kindness, iron discipline and order prevail. Good citizens of a country are prepared at school.

I discovered to my great astonishment that little time is given to mathematics and science[3]. All attention is turned to the moral side of the education; this can be said also about English schools. No languages are taught except Latin and Greek. The young people are educated solely on the ideas and learning of their own country. They know everything about their Government and social institutions. I was very surprised when during the examinations, when the classics were finished with, questions about the British Constitution were asked, and the Roman and Greek and the present British Governments compared. The pupils all knew this by heart and recited so mechanically that it gave me the impression of assisting at a lesson of Religion and hearing the Catechism and the articles of the Faith repeated. If impressions received in one's childhood last the longest, classical education must form the national character of the British. Until he dies a Briton turns his thoughts to the two most civilised countries of ancient history and, comparing them with his own, he learns to despise all others and to be prejudiced against them. The geography of Greece and Rome as they were in the times of their glory is studied in the utmost detail, whereas the geography of modern countries is painfully neglected. Although the Greeks and Romans of old exist no longer, the British visit with enthusiasm the countries in which they lived. These places remain sacred to them, and that explains the constant journeys of the British to Italy and Greece and the numerous references to them in their literature.

Elementary schools also give classical education. They are differently arranged, according to the wishes of their founders. These arrangements, though often unsuitable for the present day, have one great advantage and this is their unchangeability. This makes up for a lot of inconvenience. They are all under the immediate supervision of the Town Council.[4] All

British educational institutions are autonomous, and no government department supervises them. As they have been founded, so they exist, and if any ameliorations are made at all, they are only superficial ones. At every turn one meets here the forms of life of more ancient periods.

Sunday Handicraft Schools for the Poor have been created in great numbers from voluntary contributions; every year a report of their progress is issued. Once I attended a meeting of the Governing Body of the School, composed of men and women. The women, who were responsible for the girls' schools, rightly attend these meetings but they did not speak. Before 1823, Scotland had 1,433 Sunday Schools. Since then that number had increased by 200; 78,000 pupils attend them. For the two million of Scotland's population, this is a surprisingly large number, especially if one remembers that besides the Sunday ones there are numerous other schools. There is certainly no country in which education is so much cared for as in Scotland.[5] The dream of King George III that each of his subjects should be able to read the Bible, if not yet entirely come true, will be so very soon. Frequently one sees elderly folk attend the Sunday Schools and learning to read.

In 1821 the first School of Arts [6] was opened. These schools are founded from contributions of craftsmen, and all things useful in handicrafts and industry are taught there. By now most of the industrial centres of Great Britain have such schools. Mr Dupin[7] has introduced them a few years ago to Paris and it is only to be hoped that other countries will follow. Nothing improves industry as much as the education of the workmen. The English philosopher is right when he says that: 'Knowledge is power'. Happy the country that knows how to increase this power: 452 craftsmen seemed anxious to prove the truth of the philosopher's saying by attending these schools from the very start. In hours free from work when in other countries, sitting and drinking, the workmen learn vice, here they learn instead the theories of Newton in Physics and Davy in Chemistry. A Library attached to the school enables them to take books home and there work at the subjects for which they had insufficient time at school.

Edinburgh also possesses many societies for the advancement of knowledge. One of the best known is the Speculative Society, founded some sixty years ago, where young people learn to debate and form their opinions about moral, political and literary questions. All branches of learning have such Societies, but the most numerous are the Religious ones, which either spread good ideas and the knowledge of the Bible among the poor, or try to convert to Christianity the Jews or the wild

[18] *Francis Jeffrey (1773–1850). Jeffrey's political and legal career was restricted until the Whigs came to power in the 1830s. He then became M.P. for Perth and Lord Advocate. An outstanding writer and critic, his most important work was as one of the founders of the* Edinburgh Review *in 1802 and, until 1829, as one of its editors.*

nations in Africa and Asia. During my stay the efforts of these societies were chiefly directed towards the Russian Tartars.[8] The help of the Sultan Katagerry was eagerly hoped for. He had been converted to Christianity during his travels in Scotland, married a daughter of an Edinburgh citizen and promised to assist the endeavours of the society on his return to his country. The Royal Society[9] is the most important of the scientific ones; most eminent men of Great Britain seem either to have belonged or now to belong there. Hume, Robertson, James[10] and Adam Smith were all members. There is also a society for the cultivation

[19] *Archibald Constable (1774–1827) by Henry Raeburn. A bookseller and publisher of outstanding importance, Constable published* The Scots Magazine, The Edinburgh Review *and* The Encyclopaedia Britannica *as well as many of Scott's novels. Scott was involved in the bankruptcy of both John Ballantyne and Constable, having been a partner in the firms which had printed or published his work.*

of Scottish music, which gives a reward every year to the best piper. For Scottish music is chiefly that of the bagpipes. The competition is held in a theatre and is combined with Scottish dances. The cultivation of traditions and costumes is undertaken by another society called the Celtic. The youth of the best Scottish families belong to it. They are bound to attend the meetings and banquets wearing kilts and clan tartans. This society is a sort of cheerful club and undertakes only pleasant functions. The chief activities are feasts, during which plenty of good food and drink is served. National songs are sung and speeches made in which their forefathers' deeds are recalled. Walter Scott presides generally and as the poet and historian of Scotland he stimulates the spirit of the revellers. He even has frequently to administer justice when the young men, heated by wine, try to renew the ancient feuds of the clans. These, not unlike the powerful houses of Poland, were eternally quarrelling and fighting. Often swords are drawn out of their sheaths during the meetings of the Celtic society. It once happened while I was present. A descendant of one of the clans hostile to the Campbells, after these had already left, began singing something deriding them. One of the friends of the Campbells jumped on the table with his naked sword and tried to kill the singer. He also threatened to kill anyone who would not agree that the song was all libel and lies. A great turmoil started and only thanks to the intervention of the friends of the Highlander was his wrath at last appeased.

It can be judged by the trade in books to what extent Edinburgh is cultured. Books are provided here not only for England and all the countries of Europe, but also for all the parts of the world where English is spoken. The Edinburgh editions are in no way inferior to the London ones; print, paper, bindings, illustrations are all of the highest quality. All the works of Walter Scott are printed here by Ballantyne,[11] and published by Constable.[12] According to the theory of Adam Smith, who first inaugurated the idea of the division of labour, printing is separated here from publishing. The next best publisher is Blackwood,[13] and both have a say in politics. Constable is a Whig and publishes all the works of his party, while the Tory Blackwood those of the Tories, except the books of Walter Scott,who, though a Tory, is very ambivalent where his publishers are concerned. There are reading rooms at both the publishing offices and partisans assemble there to read newspapers and books. Both these publishers deal more in wholesale than retail and are in contact with the biggest firms in London. Two best-known bookshops are those of Millet and Laing. The first has everything new in store and as his shop is in Princes Street, the smartest part of the city, his is the haunt of the elegant world. Laing possesses all the old books and editions and is frequented by those to whom the new vellum volumes bound in Russia leather mean nothing, but who are after the half moth-eaten works of the Elzewirs, the Robertses, and the Alds.[14] Books in Great Britain are very expensive, partly because everything is expensive, partly also because the British editions are so luxurious and the tax on paper high. One must be a rich man in England to possess a library. Those who are less well off hire books, and this can be done even in the smallest towns. Or else several people buy books and after

A Nasmyth delt

[20] *Engraving from the title page of Walter Scott's* The Monastery. *Book production had become a major industry in Scotland by the late eighteenth century. The 1822 edition of* The Waverley Novels *was published in board and cloth by Constable and printed in Edinburgh by James Ballantyne & Co.*

W. Archibald sculp.t

having read them resell them and buy new ones. People have got so used to reading that they find it impossible to do without it. During the winter season there are two sales by auction at which books can be bought cheaply. A book is considered second-hand if even one of its pages has been cut, and then its price is much lower. Books to be sold are sent to Carfrae and MacLachlan, who arrange the sales. Catalogues can be seen beforehand.

Edinburgh has 44 printing houses with 150 printing presses. In 1822 there were nine daily papers and periodicals. The best daily is *The Scotsman*[15] and the most respected scientific one *The Edinburgh Review*,[16] which is known all over the world. In former days Britain also had good papers like *The Spectator, The Rambler*, and *The Mirror* which chiefly ridiculed the national faults and aimed at the improvement of morals and the amelioration of taste. They certainly did a lot but, being engrossed in only one topic, they had soon exhausted it and even the uneducated began to find them boring. Their day was past. A new period dawned, a period of daring research, of extraordinary discoveries and of profound science. A reversion of points of view, of morals and of taste followed. Minds were turned away from the superficial and the outward and occupied themselves with the core of things. More and more books appeared and the need was felt for a paper that would criticise them and keep the cultured citizens in touch with the progress made by their century. It was thus that *The Edinburgh Review* started. It gives criticisms of everything noteworthy published in the country and abroad, and embraces all branches of science and learning. Great possibilities opened for talented writers. The Review has a different method of dealing with the books it analyses than those used up to now. Instead of praising it gives severe criticism. No extracts of the works are quoted and the whole attention is centred on finding some new aspect of the work and, if it is entirely devoid of original ideas, to give it some meaning.. The style is brilliant, full of humour and satire, more witty than biting. A few men, independent, and writing for the love of science rather than to earn their livings, publish this review. Mackintosh[17] and Brougham,[18] well-known members of Parliament, are among them. Jeffrey, the lawyer who was editing it for many years, has now been succeeded by MacCulloch.[19] This Review is an organ of the Whigs and is opposed by a Tory paper, *The Quarterly Review* published in London by Gifford[20] and also by the *Blackwood Magazine*, published in Edinburgh, by Wilson and Lockhart.[21] There is also the *New Monthly Review* edited by the poet Campbell and *The London Magazine*, praised for its originality (Coleridge and Shelley write for it). *The Literary Gazette* writes about new books with more wit than truth. There are many strictly scientific papers, as well as those which are devoted to Religion, Medicine or Industry.

In no other country does literature pay as well as it does here. Messrs. Mackintosh and Brougham have been paid £50 to £60 for each page of printed matter. Huge sums are paid, especially to better-known authors, for larger works. Hume got £5,000 for the manuscript of his second part of *The History of England*; Robertson[22] £4,500 for his *History of Charles V*. For the least valuable of his books Walter Scott receives more than anyone before him and everything he publishes is rather snatched than sold. 16,000 copies of the *Lady of the Lake* have been sold in four months for £7,800. *Rokeby* brought £9,348 in three months. But as to the actual sums paid to him by the publishers great secrecy was maintained for a long time. People were even wondering whether it really was Walter Scott who was the author of the novels ... He acknowledged them not long ago. Nobody quite knows what the reasons for hiding his identity could have been. Some think it was fear of severe criticism, others that he thought the novels unworthy of his pen, but it is most likely that he simply wanted to sharpen public curiosity and thus ensure for himself an even better sale. For a long time he was called 'The Great Unknown', though everybody felt sure he must be hiding under that name.

In a city as prolific in writings as Edinburgh there must, of course, be much first-rate literary talent. The great and learned world of the Athens of the North is not as inaccessible as it might seem at first sight. It is however impossible to make the acquaintance of anyone without letters of introduction and it is not every foreigner who happens to have such. This difficulty can be solved, however, owing to the fact that the most eminent men take an active part in the social life of the country. One meets them in the Courts of Law, in Libraries, in University Halls, as well as at banquets, everywhere in fact, where either brain or social talents are needed, for they are the soul of everything. Thus the traveller, though unknown to them, can observe them in all the glory and splendour of their active lives. This is good even if one can by no means obtain personal contact with them though, of course, it does not make up for the advantages of meeting great men and enjoying their society. I was very lucky indeed, for I had the opportunity of seeing them in the midst of their families and intimate friends, when they enjoyed some leisure after the labours of their vocations, as well as when they were applauded by the crowds. I listened to their conversation and observed the train of their thought. Finding myself so near to greatness. I felt as if I myself was rising and attaining to it. So strong is its influence that not only does it enlighten, lift up and encourage, but it also gives confidence. The sight of human vice on the contrary saddens one, for it revolts all the noble instincts of man. It kills all the capabilities as if by the touch of death. I have been impressed to observe how real greatness unites with simplicity, the profoundest learning with modesty. I became convinced that pride and jealousy are unmistakeable signs of mediocrity. When I remember the charming hospitality shown by these eminent personages to me, I cannot check my enthusiasm, nor my gratitude and admiration. The manner in which a foreigner is introduced to them is noteworthy and brings credit to the Athens of the North and to the hospitality if its inhabitants. This generally happens at dinners or evening parties. They are far too busy in the daytime and one can easily become indiscreet by taking up the valuable moments of such a man, to whom they are his greatest treasury. The best way is to see him at one of his friends' houses. It is quite sufficient to have letters of introduction to one or two of the more important houses; these will introduce one to others. They will give one all necessary information about new institutions and establishments and get permits, through their friends, for visiting these places. It is to that truly Scottish kindness and hospitality that I owe all my friendships and the intellectual profit of travelling. As some of the people whom it was my privilege to meet are of worldwide fame, it will certainly interest my readers to hear more about them.

VI

Dugald Stewart. Jeffrey. Williams. Horner. A Dinner Party with Pitt. Sir Walter Scott. Hogg. Wilson. Leslie. Oliver and Muir. The Tenants. MacCulloch. Agriculture. Morton's Machines. The Smithy of Mr A.

IT was at Craigcrook, the country place of the lawyer Jeffrey, that I first met Dugald Stewart, the Nestor of all living philosophers. His works are translated into all the European languages. We were asked to a dinner party there soon after he arrived. Poland is acquainted with the philosophy of Dugald Stewart, thanks to Jan Sniadecki.[1] This profound writer fully appreciated and has expounded them in his writings. Since the works of Stewart have been published the world began to appreciate the qualities of Scottish philosophers. His last book is the History of Modern Philosophy, which may be taken as an example of how such books should be written. He is now living in a country house given him by the Duke of Hamilton,[2] a few miles from Edinburgh. Such is the fate of philosophers that fame comes to them rather than fortune. Stewart, from what I could judge, looked when I saw him about 75 years old (1820). He is neither tall nor short, strongly built, serious looking, with pronounced facial features, and his Scottish nationality is extremely apparent in his looks. He is most taciturn. I was placed next to him at dinner and he kindly insisted that I should visit him at his house. However it did not come off, alas, and even now, as I write, I am sorry to have missed such an opportunity. Jeffrey, Stewart's friend and disciple, was very different in looks. Short, slight, dark, with a small face and a protruding forehead, with black lively and fiery eyes, he looked much more like an Italian or a Frenchman than a Scotsman. He talked a great deal, concisely and brilliantly, either about the writings of Madame de Stael,[3] whom he hated, or of the case of the English Queen,[4] which stirred everybody at the time. Whatever he talked about, he expounded in a

[21] *Dugald Stewart (1753–1828). Stewart was living in
retirement at Kinneil House when Lach-Szyrma met
him. He had been an outstanding teacher of whom
Henry Cockburn wrote: 'To me his lectures were like
the opening of the heavens'. He shared the Chair of
Mathematics with his father Matthew before becoming,
more appropriately, Professor of Philosophy in 1785.*

masterly way and, during the whole dinner, nobody spoke but himself.
If one heard some other voice, it was only a sort of entre-acte to give him
breathing space. He has great innate capabilities developed by much
learning. A son of a poor doctor, by hard work and talents he not only
became famous but also rich and lives in a very comfortable way. He is a
skilful writer, a good critic, one of the best Advocates and the most
popular speaker. Nothing of importance happens in Scotland without
his being consulted. For a long time he edited *The Edinburgh Review* and
the best articles about poetry and literature were from his pen.

Williams[5] the painter was also present at that dinner party. He had just returned from his travels in Greece. The personal qualities of this man give him the right to be remembered, as well as his great talents. He wrote a very good book: *Journey to Greece.* Leonard Horner[6] was also among the guests. He is the founder of the School of Arts, and there is scarcely an institution, for welfare or education, which he would not help.

The Tory Party gives a subscription dinner every year to the memory of the famous Pitt, whose ideas are their own. I was present at such a dinner and it was there that I met Sir Walter Scott and the poet Hogg.[7] The Marquis of Huntly was in the chair; he is the son of the Duke of Gordon, a family which is related to that of Prince Czartoryski.[8] It was my first public dinner and I had never attended such a big one before. I was very much impressed. There were 800 guests. The Rector of the University, the Rev. Baird, said grace before dinner and then the toasts were drunk. The first was to the memory of Pitt, in whose honour the dinner was given, then to the King and the Royal family, then to our Jedrzej Zamoyski.[9] It is customary for the one who proposes a toast to give his reasons for doing so; this time it was only out of hospitality. The more important toasts are drunk standing, the lesser ones sitting with three loud shouts of Hip! Hip! Hurrah! The guests twirl their upraised glasses in front of them. The more numerous the shouts, the more important the toast. The toasts to the memory of the honoured dead are drunk sitting and in silence. This is a touching way of paying homage in the midst of the gay banquet. After each toast music is played, and sometimes appropriate national songs are sung.

Late at night, when the Marquis of Huntly had left, Walter Scott was unanimously called to take the chair. He likes to remain to the very end of the banquet. In a short speech, the poet made his acknowledgements for this honour and he sat down amid loud applause. Under his direction, the company became much gayer and the revellers shouted songs at each other. Most of those were against Whigs and Liberals, who on that day were holding a dinner in memory of Fox.[10] One of the Scottish lairds, Bothwell, was conspicuous for his great wit. A year afterwards he had a quarrel with a Whig, and was killed in a duel. At last it came to the turn of one of the poets present, Hogg. After some waverings, he responded to the call, but at the fourth or fifth verse, he got stuck and could not go on. Then Walter Scott, wishing to help out his brother poet, addressed the company: 'The Ettrick Shepherd, our esteemed Friend, is unaccustomed to sing to someone else's lute, he has his own!' General applause followed. Hogg was an ordinary shepherd in the Ettrick Hills before he became a poet. His poem, 'The Queen's Wake', about Mary Stuart's arrival in Scotland from France, has made him known to the world and brought him out of obscurity. This poem is romantic to the highest degree, as are all his other works. He has not received a good education and everything in his writings is due to inspiration. His all too vivid imagination, which makes him often swerve from the path of reality, has such freshness and novelty, that it appeals even to those reared on classics. This simple country bard is sought out by the choicest society and liked because of his gaiety and originality.

There is nothing especially striking in the appearance of Sir Walter Scott. He is passably good-looking, strong and has a pronounced limp in one foot. He generally carries a stout cudgel on which he leans. By a strange coincidence, Britain possessed two lame bards at once, for Byron also limped. Sir Walter's forehead is high, his hair sparse, fair and already going grey: his features, thick, heavy and blurred, his grey eyes small with long eyelashes; they light up when he speaks. His upper lip is out of proportion, the lower part of his face common-looking; in one word, Walter Scott is not what my imagination painted. His way of speaking is exactly the same style as that of the novels ascribed to him, and this alone would be proof that he is their author. He is extremely fond of society, especially conviviality, and his conversations at meals, where good cheer is provided, is at its very liveliest. He is extremely simple in intercourse; a child could converse with him. He has no trace of pride, no trace of exaggeration. But he is accused of slight snobbishness. The accusation is just for, writing about the feudal age of chivalry and lords and vassals, he prefers to conform to the former, as most people certainly would do, these being the nobler. He is rightly called the poet of chivalry. He loves song and music and had his daughter specially taught, so that she could sing him Scottish ballads. He in fact started his literary career by assembling these ballads and publishing them (*Border Minstrelsy*) He began late, for he was about thirty then. He is not one of those geniuses who develop early. At present he is well into his sixties, and no longer writes poetry, only novels. *Hallidon Hill*, a kind of drama, was his last poetical work.

One day between Christmas and the New Year, a time when everybody enjoys themselves and even the faces of the Athenians of the North brighten, I found myself among many talented men, in the house of Professor Wilson. The host himself is famous for his writings. Besides

[22] *'The Ettrick Shepherd'. This portrait of James Hogg, dressed as a shepherd, was published in the 1820 edition of his work. Hogg was then an establishment figure and a regular contributor to* Blackwood's Magazine. The Private Memoirs *and* Confessions of a Justified Sinner, *on which his reputation now rests, had been published anonymously.*

him there were: Dr Brewster[11] and Leslie, both of European fame for their natural science research works. The painters Haydon[12] and Watson [13] were there and also the famous writers, Galt [14] and Lockhart, the son-in-law of Walter Scott. There were also several noteworthy poets and travellers whose names I no longer remember. They did much to enliven the company. I have never before been between so many famous men and listened to such interesting conversation. The 'symposies' of the Greek philosophers could not have been more enthralling. The dinner was indeed what is sometimes said about dinners in Scotland 'The feast of reason and the flow of the soul'.

The conversation was about literature and music, painting and all sorts of subjects and topics, but everything was tackled with masterly skill, for masters were speaking. Many poetical matters were also discussed and the flow of talk never faltered; it went on from 5 pm. till midnight, never losing its natural ease and its important interest. Wilson, so eloquent in his writings, is perfectly delightful in society. He is imbued with the spirit of poetry, to which he has sacrificed all his youth, and with the philosophy to which he has given his latter days. He expressed his lofty ideas with fire in a beautiful form. He scarcely needed to explain his thoughts, they were flowing so naturally. Nevertheless, his poetry and likewise his prose are characterised not so much by a boldness of vision as by a delicacy of feeling and idiosyncratic charm of elocution. In conversation he is complex but concise and shows more fire. His main works are *The Isle of Palms* and *The City of the Plague* This is a dramatic illustration of the terrible pestilence of 1655 which turned London into one great cemetery, with grass-covered squares and deserted streets whose silence was broken only by the terrifying voices of the undertakers hauling away their grim load with the words 'Bring out your dead!' His works are published as prose in the form of romantic novels in which he does away with the customary picture of the various social estates of Scotland; peculiarly bucolic are the following: *Margaret Lindsay, The Forester* and *Lights and Shadows.* The most recent of his works is entitled *Principles of Moral Philosophy*, a subject presented in his lectures.

Leslie is a crofter's son. When he was still in the Highlands he was already known for his mathematical abilities and many people came to talk to him. Among them was the philosopher Dugald Stewart. He gave Leslie one of the most difficult problems of arithmetic to solve. Leslie, who was then grazing cattle in the fields, asked him: 'How do you want me to solve this? From above to below, or from below to above?' This meant: synthetically or analytically. Stewart asked for both ways, whereupon the boy, lifting his eyes up to heaven, which he does even now when faced with some extra difficult question, concentrated and solved the problem out of his head, surpassing all expectations. Stewart then took him under his special protection, sent him to school and taught him personally. Leslie is now a very famous Professor of Physics in Edinburgh University and has already made important discoveries in his special branch. His lectures are conspicuous for the broad Scotch with which he refuses to part, as if he wanted to retain it in memory of the days when he was a crofter. But he is not the only professor who speaks in broad Scotch. The famous Hume[15] and Robertson of Edinburgh University spoke it, though they wrote perfect English. I heard

Leslie, during one of his lectures, call our Copernicus a Pole, which is not always done by other scientists as there are so many false notions about that great man's nationality. When I was taking my leave from Leslie, before my return to Poland, he told me a most interesting thing, that there was once a scholarship at Edinburgh University, meant for two protestant Poles.[16] It had been founded by one Brown, a merchant from Dantzig. I undertook to find proofs of it in the University archives but I was obliged to leave before I could do anything. Leslie is short and stout, his pupils have no difficulty in drawing his portrait: a round globe, over it a smaller globe, two dots for eyes, two lines for legs and the inscription: 'This is Leslie'.

Thanks to Professor Pillans,[17] I made the acquaintance of one of his pupils, a Mr.Oliver, tenant of Lochend, near Edinburgh. I used to think that this class of people lived like our peasants, in simplicity bordering on misery, but I am now able to state that things are different. They not only have the means but also know how to live well. Freedom of the soul and body reigns in their houses, which makes one think that there is nothing surpassing the quiet and gay country life.

The tenant gave us dinner, juicy, succulent, clean and wholesome, a true dinner for men. The host was unmarried. We were nine, the very best number, for some wise man has said that at a really good dinner there should be more people than Muses, and not less than Graces. This number had been chosen by the tenant, I do not know whether accidentally or on purpose, for a man who, like himself, reads Virgil and Cato could have very well made that choice grounded on his learning. The guests were not at all 'rustici' but very 'urbani'. There were plenty of things to talk to with men like Pillans, professor at the University and an eminent philologist; Maclaren,[18] the editor of *The Scotsman*; Morton,[19] a brilliant agricultural engineer whose many machines have received patents; MacCulloch, after the death of Ricardo the best economist. He taught political economy to the Poles then in Edinburgh and afterwards left for London. There he did his utmost to change the deficient corn laws and to introduce free trade which, of course, is the best for England. A certain Mr. Muir, a tenant, was among the guests. He talked about agriculture, not like a farmer, but like a professor, only with less conceit. He told me that our Polish Count Pac, when travelling in Scotland, spent three days in his house. He praised Polish lavish generosity, which many of his friends had experienced, and could not get over the fact that Count Pac[20] possessed such enormous estates. He also remembered what the

Count had told him, that in some of these estates it was impossible to find one single stone, and that from his country house an avenue, straight as an arrow and bordered with trees, led right up to the Prussian frontier. All this seemed incredible to the Scotsman, whose own country is all hills and where there are certainly more stones and rocks than soil.

Everybody was in the best of spirits during dinner; Port and Madeira were served beautifully in carved glasses and toasts were drunk. The first proposed by our host was to Lord Moray, the owner of Lochend; the second to the famous Ricardo,[21] the defender of agriculture and of a sensible economic system in the country. These were followed by toasts to the guests in turn. According to the national custom, which seems shocking to the foreigner, they were drunk when one of them left the company for a moment. His praise was added, shouted so as to make him hear it in the place in which he then was. This dinner lasted from 4 pm. to 3 am. The host had reason to be pleased with his guests, though they departed much too hilariously.

Besides the pleasure such gatherings give they also bring some profit. Thoughts on politics, morals and literature are exchanged and I know few things more interesting than listening to people who have led active lives giving word to their inner thoughts and relating what they have experienced. Only then does one fully realise how empty and meaningless are the conventional exchanges of the world. During that particular dinner, the conversation dealt chiefly with the agricultural and economic problems of the day.

During the wars with France Britain was obliged to take many people from industry and return them to the land. Owing to this the country is now self-sufficient. A quarter of wheat, which formerly was 100/-, costs now only 65/-. Pastures have been turned into fertile fields, the agricultural methods have greatly improved and new labour- saving machines have been invented. The cheapness of the agricultural products is a sign of improvement; nevertheless, it may cause people to turn away from a not very lucrative occupation. Poland is very much in the same position as Britain. There too there was a time when the prices were four times higher than they are now. The English tenants, who have contracts made for 24 years and not for three as ours do, find themselves ruined. They are bound to pay the same rents as at the beginning of their lease, whereas the prices of the things they sell have so much fallen. Some of the owners understood the difficulties of their tenants and lowered the rents; Lord Moray did so for Mr Oliver. The price of the land is very much fallen and the products of the land are so superfluous that many fields are being turned back into pastures. There is little hope of trade between Poland and England (in corn). The landowners and the tenants are against it; only the industrialists and workmen are for it because the prices of commodities would then be lower. But they have no say in Parliament, which is composed chiefly of landowners. These are not always capable of acting against their own interests. It is difficult to expect that the law forbidding free trade should be repealed and yet only free trade could stop the harm and open new roads for possibilities of international trade. As long as this does not happen the only objects of trade between England and Poland will be hemp, flax and timber. Our corn trade must turn to those countries which use their own labour in industry, not agriculture. Or else we must develop industry ourselves and thus increase the numbers of our own consumers. Ten years ago England had 2,544,000 families, out of which 896,000 lived from agriculture, and 1,129,000 from industry. There were 519,000 families of the very rich and of the very poor who were also to be fed. What an encouragement for agriculture to have so many people to feed!

I have been especially struck by the truth of one of the remarks about political economy, that the food required by a workman is no standard of his real needs. His clothes, living abode and all the other necessities must be taken into consideration. Each country has its own standards of requirements. The food consumed by an English workman constitutes only one third of his general needs and the food of the noble and wealthy only one hundredth part. So small are our real physical needs when compared with all the others, which are not essential ones. The richer the country, the more needs of the last kind there are. In a very poor country there is no room for imaginary necessities; the wild tribes need nothing but food, drink and the most primitive of clothes.

Mr. Oliver rented 154 acres, for which he paid £1,500 a year, but the income from land is such that he was not a loser. Of course it was Mr Oliver who had to pay for all the agricultural machinery, tilling of the land and farm labour. However, such is the value and income of land! I knew a citizen of Edinburgh who had a market garden in the city with a surface area of just one acre for which he was paid £1,000 sterling. The details such as Mr Oliver gave concerning his farm are as follows: the cost of agricultural labour varies according to the season, normally one pays from three to three and a half shillings a day, which increases to five at harvest time. He doesn't keep any cattle; the only animals being horses, which are used for ploughing. Hay and straw he sells in town, which is more advantageous. Dung he buys in town, paying for one wagon load (drawn in a two-wheeled one-horse vehicle) eight shillings. To the question 'How much grain does wheat produce?' he had no answer. Value by grain is unknown in this country. When I explained our farmers' way of reckoning the quality of land he gave as his answer, after considering the matter for a short while, fifteen at most. He did not consider ours a sufficiently accurate measure, productivity being too dependent on effort put into cultivation. Oats and straw he estimated at eighteen to twenty. One acre of potatoes brought him about £50 sterling a few years ago, but now the price has fallen to £24. Turnips are now priced equal with potatoes. The cost of farm products and, in particular, foodstuffs in Edinburgh, scarcely varies from the price in London; the navigability of the Thames and its easy accessibility prevent excess inflation. In the neighbourhood of London rental cost of land is no dearer than near Edinburgh. There are places no more than seven miles from London where you will not get more than £4 sterling for an acre. In Westmorland and the mountains of Scotland, where the land is poor, even that amount cannot be had. Such barren ground is used for pasture. Of the 27,794 square miles which make up Scotland, barely one half is arable, and it is reckoned that there are only 58 inhabitants per square mile.

A few days later I went to see Mr.Morton's agricultural machines. I saw there ploughs of his invention as well as those improved by him. One plough was made entirely of iron, only the handle being of wood, with one blade but yet turning the earth from the furrow onto both sides; the second with two blades, which together made two furrows with earth turned to all sides; this latter is designed for ploughing on steep slopes and thereby halving the effort. There was an interesting machine for topping potatoes and turnips in the shape of a plough with a sharp blade and, on its side, two sharp sickles for removing weeds. Indeed it is used exactly like a plough. The whole furrow is immediately cleared of weeds. Only the raised surface is trimmed of its redundant foliage. It may be used everywhere. It is only necessary, just as in England, to sow the potatoes and turnips, not in strips, but in rows of piled earth divided by a deep regular furrow. I also saw a machine for breaking up unploughed ground of clay soil. It is in the shape of two wheels without a rim, mounted with sharp iron spoke; it is attached to a plough and by its rotation forms of the freshly turned earth two raised piles on either side of the furrow. However, the most interesting of Mr Morton's inventions, which might very profitably be used in our country, was a so-called revolving harrow designed not only for the breaking up of soil but

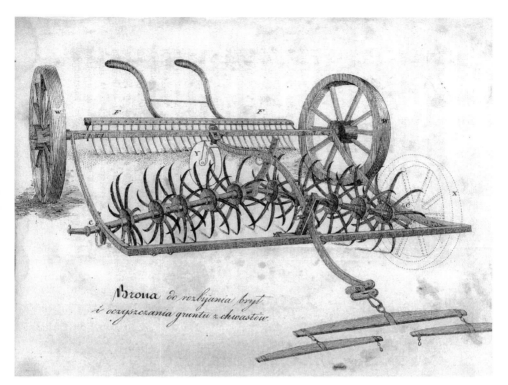

[23] *Morton's Revolving Harrow. Thomas Morton (1781–1832) was a shipbuilder whose inventive skills extended to carriages and agricultural machines. Several Scottish engineers were contracted by Polish landowners to copy these, and other machines invented in Scotland, in factories set up on their estates. This illustration was taken by Lach-Szyrma from J. C. Loudon's* Encyclopaedia of Agriculture.

also the simultaneous clearing it of weeds. I attach a drawing of it showing its construction. The two supporting wheels are marked W. The barbed wheels which revolve on the axle marked C are for the tilling and breaking up of the ground's surface. That part of the machine marked R is mounted on the shaft and can be either raised or lowered, thus constituting a regulator both for the direction and also for the depth to which the barbed wheels are to penetrate the earth. F indicates the iron harrow for clearing the ground of weeds and is attached to the machine by way of two iron rods. When the revolving harrow must be removed to a different site, the wheels at W are removed and placed on the forward axle marked C, as indicated by the superimposed shadow drawing marked X. The machine is made of iron, for only that material may give the desired result, since the breaking up of hard ground requires both a heavy weight and strong barbs Though being some 72 feet in extent, one pair of horses will suffice to pull the machine since it is only slightly heavier than a plough producing a furrow of a similar depth. When working the hardest of ground a third horse may be added. And to manage the whole, only one man is required. The harrow is used on denser soils, particularly clay ones, when, after ploughing, drought may bake the ground and make it unsuitable for sowing. By drawing this machine once or twice across such a field the earth's surface is not only broken up but also cleaned of weeds. One ploughing during the autumn and the application of this machine in springtime prepares the ground far better than three ploughings and a traditional harrowing. These only rake the surface and leave the roots of the weeds and grass in the ground. Mr Morton's harrow turns and cleans to a depth of seven to eight inches. Its use in springtime has this further benefit that the plough no longer buries itself in snow-softened earth, as is usually the case during springtime ploughing, but remains on the surface. Neither does it remove the dampness from the soil, so essential for the good germination of the crop. Moreover this machine saves at least half the work which would otherwise have been expended. In Scotland it costs £18 sterling, which is certainly not cheap; indeed in these parts people are complaining of the cost. In our country, as I understand, it would be nowhere so dear. It was, however, at that time a new invention in Scotland, although fully tested. Nearly twenty tenants signed their names in attestation of its usefulness, as a result of which Mr Morton received an exclusive patent for the manufacture of such a harrow. This much I may with certainty say about its benefits. I leave the matter to the better judgement of amateurs of agricultural invention, as well as the calculation as to whether the cost is merited by the profit derived.

Mr Morton has also made important improvements in the field of carriages. To the ordinary two-wheeled gig drawn by one horse which, upon striking a stone, would rock too violently and break its springs, he has added an elongated axle so that the wheel has room to move laterally. So that the gig can avoid stones more easily, he has made the axle so that it can pivot. Hubs, which hitherto have been wooden and finished with iron, he has made entirely from cast iron. The problem of spokes falling out of such iron hubs is avoided by the simplest of methods; their ends are soaked in water whereupon they are immediately hammered into the hub, forming the tightest of seals between wood and iron. Carriages of Mr Morton's manufacture do not require lubrication, for on the inside of the axle is a hidden container filled with lubricant, providing a constant supply to the moving parts. He makes wheel rims in two ways:

narrow ones for hardened highways and wide ones for agricultural usage, for carrying material from fields and meadow so that they should not become stuck in soft soil. I also saw many machines for sowing: for each type of seed there was a special one. The most commonly used machine for sowing was constructed in this way: simultaneous with the sowing the corn was covered, growing in, as it were, little trenches. Nothing was wasted, which is not the case when traditional harrowing is applied.

One particular invention demonstrated Mr Morton's inventive genius. However, it is no use to us, as it can only be used by those countries with a seaboard. It is a machine for pulling ships ashore when in need of repair. This will do away with the need for expensive docks. From these arise the inconvenience that only where there is deep water may ships be brought into them. The aforementioned machine has this inestimable benefit for navigators that, at any place, a ship may be hauled ashore and its whole apparatus may be brought with it. On distant sailings, to which the British are accustomed, what could be more useful? In England this machine costs £1,500 sterling; but where wood is abundant it would cost less. Such a thing would be more than useful on the Baltic coast, especially as all along its shore repairs are hampered by the shallow depth of water. This constituted the summit of Mr Morton's inventiveness.

The same day I also visited the Smithy of Mr. A. and his foundries. I watched how long pipes were being made, meant to conduct the water for many miles to the town. What the old Romans did from stone and bricks is now made from iron. I wonder which of the works Posterity will find more wonderful? Prior to pouring the molten iron into the mould, lying at an angle, a fire was lit at its upper end so as to rarefy the air. Molten iron was poured from the furnace to the vessel in a stream which was as liquid as water and glowing as fire itself. From two sides, bellows fuelled the fire in the furnace whose degree of heat was so high that there is no known way of measuring it. The bellows were driven by a steam-operated machine which at the same time fulfilled other functions such as sanding and polishing wheels. Black coal is used for the furnaces and the hardest is rhe best quality. Newcastle supplies this fuel because Scottish coal is too soft. Cast iron is brittle and mediocre by comparison with forged; thus it is mainly used for water pipes, being seven times cheaper. As is generally known, iron works in Britain are of a higher standard than in other countries This may be put down to a better quality of ore and hard coal. Nevertheless, British products are mainly to be recommended for the quality of material, durability and strength rather than for the excellence of their design, in which field the French stand in first place.

VII

Painting. Exhibitions of Haydon and Williams

Great Britain for a long time did not produce famous painters. Most of the pictures in galleries and wealthy houses are foreign. Apparently the English did not seek fame in these fields. Their national Muse speaks like Virgil's 'Excudent alii spirantia mollins aer ...' Until the time of Henry VIII there is nothing noteworthy in the field of painting except for antiquarians. Henry was the first to collect pictures, but the generosity of that King and his descendants had more to do with foreigners than with the English. He himself greatly encouraged Holbein,[1] and his daughter Elizabeth, greedy of fame to the point of being lavish with her portraits, recompensed Zuccharo[2] and other Flemish portrait painters. Charles I, not only a patron of art but also a connoisseur, used to send his own works of art to Rubens for correction. It was he who got Vandyke to England and also the famous Raphael cartoons. Though these pictures must have awakened taste and the love of painting, this period produced no painter. National painting began some fifty years ago at the end of the 18th century. Sir Joshua Reynolds was the founder and the President of the King's Academy of Painting. Then came West,[3] Barry[4] and the painter of caricatures, Hogarth. They laid the foundations and painting, helped by the country's wealth, developed splendidly. If today Wilkenman and Boss[5] saw the progress made they certainly would not deny to Britain taste and talent. There are many painters nowadays in London: Philips,[6] Wilkie,[7] Shee, Westall, Turner, Calcott and Thomas Lawrence.[8] In Edinburgh the most famous portrait painters are Raeburn[9] and Watson; Williams, Nasmyth[10] and the Rev John Thomson are painters of landscapes. Allan[11] and Haydon and Martin[12] are historical painters. The works of all of these have their special character, which makes us realise that there is already an English School of painting. At the beginning, a great tendency to

[24] *William Allan, by William Nicholson, 1818. Allan is in Circassian dress. During the ten years he had spent in Poland under the patronage of Countess Zofia Potocka he had travelled extensively in the Near East and was fascinated by the Orient. On his return to Scotland in 1814 he became the leading painter of Scottish history.*

allegory could be traced, idea meant everything and less importance was attached to the form and technique. The same could also be said about sculpture. This can probably be put down to the literature, which is full of allegory. The more recent painters aim at the simplicity of the Italian School, though not at its colouring. Perhaps the climate of Italy is more propitious to painting, for much depends on the quick amalgamation of colours, when they dry quickly. Perhaps also in a bright and sunny atmosphere no such sharp lines are necessary as in England, where everything is veiled by mist; only very bright colours can be seen distinctly in Albion. Whatever the reason, one thing is certain, that present-day English paintings are so garish in colour that they almost seem to be illuminated. This great brightness, which seems to emanate from a sort of haze, is the chief characteristic of the English School.

All English artists paint portraits, and they are incomparable in the art in which they acquire great practice, thanks to the encouragement they get from their countrymen. In former days, a painter called Kneller[13] used to say: 'Historical painters raise the dead to life, but themselves have no chance of living except after death. I paint the living instead and they enable me to live'. This practical outlook has been generally accepted and no country has as many portrait painters as Great Britain. Most of them are so good, that one can state with truth that this branch of the art has been really much perfected here. Sir Joshua Reynolds got £50 for painting a head only, and £200 for a full-sized portrait. It is a huge sum but gladly paid, for everyone is generous where his dear ones are concerned. Owing to that passion for portraits, Thomas Lawrence, the founder of the Academy of Arts, has made a considerable fortune, lives like a Croesus, has the title of a Baronet and not one of the living painters is better off than he. But an object which, to the individual, is of the greatest interest chiefly from vanity, or because of the amount of money spent on it, is seldom of such an interest to posterity. Portraits, unless very well painted or representing eminent persons, are soon forgotten. Historical pictures are of a far greater importance and it is chiefly on them that the greatness of the art school depends. Haydon and Williams, and especially the former, have contributed to their country's fame in that field. The works of both have been exhibited, for it is the custom for artists to travel from town to town with their works, and exhibitions bring them more profits than the selling of their pictures. Learning and art in Great Britain are on such a high level that they are able to exist independently. They no longer need the protection of the Government and of the wealthy, for the whole nation cares for them.

[25] *'Kenmore, Perthshire' by Hugh 'Grecian' Williams. Williams' watercolour of Kenmore was painted before his visit to Greece and the publication in 1820 of his* Travels in Italy, Greece and the Ionian Islands.

Let us give some attention to the exhibitions. From all the pictures of Haydon, his *Entry of Christ into Jerusalem* was the most admired. To give more interest to his work, the painter has added three modern personalities. They observe the wonderful scene with mixed feelings. Newton, a firm believer, looks at Christ with unshaken faith, as if he was saying: 'Thou art the Son of God incarnate'. Wordsworth, a living English poet, who has introduced into poetry a Christian Platonism, watches Him with deepest respect and humility, very apparent in his attitude. Voltaire stands by with the jeering face of an unbeliever. What an unforgivable anachronism! Some might say that the anachronism could certainly not have escaped the attention of such a great artist as Haydon, but could he without anachronism demonstrate the influence of Christ on all the ages? Would it be possible to concentrate in one picture the changes worked in human souls and in nations by His teach-ings? Where a high aim is in view and where genius dwells in regions forbidden to the crowds, who will dare to drag it down from the heights of inspiration to the vulgarity of strict School prescriptions? Why cannot ideas united in our brains be put together in a picture? It is a privilege of genius to gather thoughts dispersed all through the centuries, and make them understandable. Ideas and feelings are the links without which everything would be disconnected, broken up and poor. 'The Judgement of Solomon', the 'Resurrection of Lazarus' and 'Macbeth' are the other more conspicuous works of Haydon. He paints religious subjects, as did Michelangelo, Raphael, Rubens and most of the old masters.

The exhibition of Williams was just as interesting. It consisted of views of Rome and Greece. Haydon wanted to represent the feelings awakened by Christianity and Williams the immense world of the extinct ancient power. Both seemed to exhaust all the wonders of art and wisdom. The pictures of Haydon are oils and those of Williams, watercolours, so well done that not only the colours but the very atmosphere seemed to be transferred to the picture. It is a pity that these colours are not lasting and with them the art of the painter will fade away. Greece and especially Athens supply a wide field for Williams's talent. His painting of the Parthenon brings back the memory of Lord Elgin, a Scottish peer who has brought to England most of the bas-reliefs with which this temple was decorated. They are now placed in special rooms at the British Museum and are called The Elgin Marbles. Public opinion was very much divided about this busi-ness. Sculptors and painters, who now had ample patterns for imitation, were delighted and thought Lord Elgin[14] had done a great thing for their country. But disinterested lovers of art, who considered the deed from the higher point of view, were more stern. They thought the stripping of the Parthenon of its decorations was nothing but a shameful looting, dishonouring the man of poor taste and weak reason who descended to such a deed. Monuments of the kind cannot be transported; their charm lies in the combination of surroundings, light and climate. It is one thing to look at the bas-reliefs as they were in the Parthenon, with all the enchantment lent by atmosphere and past memories clinging to them, and quite another to contemplate them hung on walls in a darkish and inadequate Museum, at no proper distance and maimed as they have been during their long journey. There everything had its reason for existence and meaning and formed one whole; here everything is in pieces, almost in ruins, without any sense or order. There everything was seen and understood at once, for greatness is most easy to understand; here in broken fragments, sight and mind get tired and thought loses its thread. In a word, these remains brought to England are no longer what they were in Greece and Italy, where the common people, even through looking at them, developed their taste and perception. Here, those treasuries of Phidias and Praxiteles are called by the English: 'Stone shop of Elgin'. For the English carry wherever they go their commercial and industrial points of view. Alas, in this case the judgement of the populace is only too just. But notwithstanding all this, one has to admit that perhaps it is as well that these priceless gems are safe in London. For during the last war of the Greeks and the Turks, when Athens passed from hand to hand, the furious god Ares might not have spared the temple of his sister Pallas, and they might have perished altogether. These sad events, however, which could not have been foreseen, cannot change our judgement on the deed of Lord Elgin. Though events do absolve him *post facto*, what he has done remains shameful and nothing can save him from Minerva's wrath. The looting of the temple horrified all the Art lovers of the day, and the Greeks watched it being done with tears in their eyes. Lord Elgin defended himself by the written permit of the Turkish Government which, of course, did not care a whiff for Greek monuments. In his *Journey to Greece*, Hobhouse[15] tells us that there is a deeply carved inscription on the eastern wall of the temple, an inscription that is meant to last forever; it ranks the Scottish peer with the destroyers of the world's civilization:

> Quod non fecerunt Gothi,
> Hoc fecerunt Scoti.

In his *The Curse of Minerva*, Byron[16] also brands the deed:

> Daughter of Jove! In Britain's injured name,
> A true born Briton may the deed disclaim!
> Frown not on England, England owns him not.
> Athena! No! The plunderer was a Scot.
> And thus accursed be the day and year,
> She (Caledonia) sent a Pict to play the felon here.

I hope my readers will not bear me a grudge for this rather long digression. But it throws light on the ways of thinking and the character of the people about whom I am writing. The delight felt at the sight of all these classical remains shows plainly that the public here thinks, with Cicero, that the pleasure of seeing famous places is not solely due to the splendid monuments and works of art; more comes from the memory of great men, where they lived, walked, sat or talked. It is even pleasant to meditate over their graves. Such an attitude of mind is worthy of a cultured people.

VIII

The Edinburgh Society. The Celtic Ball. The Theatre.
The Reading Room. The Concerts. Yaniewicz. The Interior
of a House

THOUGH Edinburgh has a well-developed trade, it cannot be considered as one of the industrial cities, consequently the inhabitants are devoid of that special spirit which is considered to be alien to good taste and generosity. On the contrary, Edinburgh, as the capital of Scotland and the seat of the Government [1] and of learning, is also the seat of the best society. London itself is put in the shade by it. There is an exceptional equilibrium among the different classes headed by the most cultured set. Education, which spreads all through the country, raises the humblest people to higher standards. The greatest charm of society life in Edinburgh is its national character. Perhaps no other nation is quite as devoted to their national traditions as the Scots. Neither education nor contact with other nations has been able to weaken that. Old sagas, legends and songs are preserved like a sacred flame, which warms the hearts of the simplest men. The past, thus united by a beautiful bond with the present, becomes real. The former outline of the Scottish character, daring, great but somehow uncouth, has now acquired the polish of the cultured ages. The past has been worked out into a fine ideal. This ideal feeds talents, pens and brushes. Living types, fitted into the forms of life in the past, can be met daily in the social intercourse in Edinburgh. One can discern, peering from under the cover of civilisation, the wild age of Rob Roy or hear, in the tunes of the harp, the tenderness of Ossian's century.

The Scots love to recall the memories of the past. And there is a strange charm in the contemplation of ancient customs, so different to the present ones. I observed this at the Celtic Ball given in 1821 by the Celtic Society. One thought oneself back in those times when Scotland, divided into clans, was led by their chieftains. The costumes, the dancing, the music, even the supper were all specifically national. The whole world knows that the Scottish national costume is a peculiar one. Men are dressed 'sans culotte'; a short little kilt, well above their knees, covers their nakedness. They have broad swords hung across their backs, swords and pistols at their belts, a knife, and flint and steel in a small bag. Their caps are round, navy blue with stripes of checked red and white and a goose feather stuck in them. The chiefs wear an eagle's feather. Instead of shoes they have sandals tied Roman wise. Each wears a sporran and a plaid hangs down from their backs. This in olden time was used by day instead of a coat and at night as a blanket. One discerns by the pattern of the tartan to what clan a man belongs. The whole costume reminds one of Roman dress as seen in pictures. The national costumes of women do not, except for their garish colours, attract such attention as those of the men. They wore white dresses checked à la Walter Scott. Silken tartans were thrown over their shoulders; heather was in their hair and heather garlands adorned their dresses. Married women wore small round velvet caps. The effect was extremely picturesque and, as only those belonging to the very first families were present at the ball, it was all very sumptuous and rich. Five hundred people were present. The sight of such a splendid and in its way unique gathering made one return in thought to the century of Wallace. The ball began about nine to the shrill sound of the bagpipe. The bagpipes were played in the battlefields in the old days, and are used now in the Scottish Regiments. The Irish pipes are softer in tones but they also tear the ears of the listeners. Most certainly these instruments are meant rather for the battlefield than the drawing room. One of the Scottish Chiefs, who came from the Highlands especially for the ball, opened it, dancing with the Countess of Morton. While dancing he addressed the young men present with the words of an old song:

> Come lads and view your partners well,
> Wale each a blithesome roguie

Whereupon the 'lads' rushed towards the ladies. Only national dances were danced and especially their Reel. But it seems to me that the ancient Scots must have been most certainly more given to wars than dancing, for they do not seem to have introduced any variety or charm to their dances. Their chief dance is nothing but a sort of wriggling, while standing in the same place. It gives no chance whatever to a dancer keen to show off his gracefulness. After special entreaties on the part of the

[26] *William Macdonald. By the 1820s Macpherson's* Ossian *and Scott's writings had made everything Scottish fashionable throughout literary circles in Europe and North America. William Macdonald was an officer of the Highland Society, one of whose dinners Lach-Szyrma attended.* Kay

ladies a few French 'contre-dances' were allowed towards the end. But the Quadrilles were strictly forbidden. Waltzes are simply considered as horrid and indecent. The ball ended by a banquet of Scottish dishes, with plenty of the famous oatcakes, which have given Caledonia the name of 'land of cakes'.

Such a ball, however, is an unusual event. As a rule balls are given every week in winter and are open to all, subject to certain qualifications. These balls are called: 'Assemblies'.[2] They are neither splendid, nor well attended. The spirit of the country is rather alien to such public rejoicing. Women keep away from them because of their education, which imbues them with the love of quiet home life and modesty; men because they are too busy to seek such futile amusement. Some are against such festivities because of their stern Puritan Religion, which more than any other objects to balls and theatres, simply condemning them all as inimical to Religion. Because of all this, one would look in vain here for those joyous, happy and carefree crowds which one meets at the Continental balls. All the spirit of joy and freedom is also killed in Great Britain, by endless formalities, which are scrupulously observed. Dress according to fashion; dance only with a lady with whom one is well acquainted etc. A foreigner who has no partner is introduced to the patroness of the ball and she finds one for him. Not to apply to any of the sacred rules would be an unforgivable mistake. Every ball must have patronesses who have a keen eye that decency and order should be respected. They are well-known ladies and the dignity of Patroness is bestowed on them in turn.

The theatre, though more frequented than the balls, is also not as popular as might have been expected, judging by the wealth and good taste of the inhabitants. Numerous people scarcely know from hearsay what theatre is. No one has as yet seen a Quaker or a Methodist in the theatre and, as these are many, their influence is felt. The Edinburgh Theatre[3] is humble. The entrance is adorned by the statue of Shakespeare supported by the muses of Tragedy and Comedy. Inside, although smaller and much less frequented than the Warsaw one, the Edinburgh Theatre is adequately arranged. It is crowded only when one of the famous London actors comes to Edinburgh. The first performance I saw was Sheridan's *School for Scandal*; there is no better comedy in English. The translated repertory of the Warsaw theatre is available here. Comedies and dramas are the most popular, the latter being chiefly taken from Walter Scott. Each of his novels has been adapted for the theatre. How our own literature would be enhanced if 'Janof Tenczyn',

'Ruszczyc Pojata' or 'Lojetek' were similarly adapted to the stage.[4] That kind of drama is most admired. The Scots have here a taste for the Germans. Nothing French except one or two of the gay farces goes for long in either the London or the Edinburgh theatres. The dramas of Kotzebue[5] are accepted, but French tragedies do not exist for them. During all the years of my stay, I did not see one single translation of Corneille or Racine. Shakespeare alone is constantly given and of course, up to now, nobody has ever equalled that tremendous genius. Also Otway's *Freed Venice* and Douglas Home's[6] tragedies are sometimes represented. But Dryden, Young, Congreve, and Addison are already quite forgotten and the works of the young writers, Maturyne, Milman and Croly, were unable to get a hold in the theatre. Lord Byron's *Cain* and *Sardanapalus*, which were meant for the theatre, proved to be better for reading and have never been represented. It is generally said that it is easier to write a good tragedy than a good comedy. But the state of things in England seems to deny this as, for ten successful comedies, scarcely one tragedy can be found.

The Edinburgh Theatre possesses several good comedians but badly lacks tragic actors. Mrs Siddons is perhaps the only eminent dramatic artist. She is the niece of that Mrs Siddons who was called: 'The Tragic Muse of the English Theatre'. Her niece seems to have inherited her talent and would be capable of acting in the best theatres of Europe. In appearance and in age she reminds one of our Ledochowska.[7] She is inferior to her in her rendering of strong and violent emotions but superior in soft and tender sentiments. She is incomparable in romantic tragedies. But she could not equal the Polish artist in classical dramas, where it is not enough to feel deeply one must be able to rise to a certain degree of superior dignity.

The concerts and reading rooms are more frequented than the theatre, for they are more in keeping with the severity of Scottish ideas. As far as I know, the reading rooms are known only in Scotland. Some well-known actor collects an audience and recites for it pieces from the best authors. Sometimes he quotes by heart, sometimes he reads from a book, acting very slightly and without the exaggeration of the theatre. I have listened with great pleasure to several declamations. Two hundred people were present at one of them. Women, men and children come, for the choice of topics is very strict and nothing that might have a double meaning or be even slightly insinuating is ever allowed. The best writers such as Shakespeare, Milton, Addison, Sterne, Cowper, Campbell, Byron, and Wilson are chosen. Tickets are bought as for the theatre

[27] *The New Assembly Rooms. The Assembly Rooms followed the upper classes around Edinburgh. When, in the 1760s, they started to desert the Old Town for George Square, the Rooms moved from Old Assembly Close to Buccleuch Place. Ten years later the Earl of Moray raised subscriptions to build on a site given by the Town Council in George Street. In 1818 William Burn added a portico to John Henderson's building of 1787 and a music hail was added in 1843.* T. H. Shepherd

and, as in the theatre, beautiful thoughts are given loud applause. In some of the reading rooms all newspapers and periodicals are available. Subscribers pay £1 for three months. One of the reading rooms is in the Waterloo Hotel,[8] in the big drawing room in which banquets are also given.

All musical performances at that time were led by a Pole called Janiewicz.[9] He lived in Edinburgh for a long time and used to give concerts for the poor in the Musical Society Hall. He was director of this Society. These concerts brought in sometimes as much as £1500. It is partly to him that Scotland owes the development of musical taste. He plays the violin to perfection and is also a good composer. He has done much to popularise Polish music, which he has published in special books. I have often heard in Scotland our Krakowiaki and Mazurki,[10] variations on our national melodies and especially the grandiose polonaise of Oginski,[11] played almost by every young girl who learns music. Listening to them in so very distant a country, I had sometimes the impression that melody makes distance disappear.

As Janiewicz is a well-known man and brings credit to the country that gave him birth, I think it is fair to give some more particulars about his Scottish life. Part of it I have heard from his own lips. Janiewicz was born in Wilno and was discovered by King Stanislaw August who heard him play in Warsaw. He was sent abroad by that monarch for further musical education. He spent nearly three years in Italy and was in Paris during the whole French Revolution. The sad changes which had by then occurred in his own country caused him to remain in Paris, where he lived by the exercise of his talent. His income must have been considerable since he was in a position to lend (as he told me himself) one of his countrymen, Mr C., a Lithuanian whom he met in Paris, 2,000 Polish red zloties. The loan was formally receipted but his heirs were instructed not to recover the money on his death. From Paris Janiewicz went to England and twice made a fortune in London, enough to live comfortably for the rest of his life. But he indulged in business and twice lost his money. Over and over again he re-started earning by his violin and invariably was successful. What can be accomplished by talent! When I met him in Edinburgh he was on his way to a fortune for the third time. People knew him to be a Polish noble and this helped him a good deal, for good birth means much even to the Whigs of Edinburgh. He speaks good French and English but both languages with a strong Polish accent. This is the more astonishing as by this time he had entirely forgotten Polish. If even a musician endowed with a delicate ear

[28] *'Sedan Chairmen'. The wealthy had their own sedan chairs but, till the mid-nineteenth century, a taxi service was provied by chairmen, often Highlanders, who waited for custom at the street corners of the New Town.* Kay

cannot lose his foreign accent, then how conceited are some of our countrymen who consider themselves to be perfect in German or French. Janiewicz is married to an English woman and has two daughters. They are both talented; the elder gives piano concerts and the younger plays the harp beautifully. He is short, strongly built with a round face and a kind manner; on hearing something touching, he is moved to tears. He loves all memories of his country and is very particular that his name should be pronounced in the proper Polish way. To make the English do this he has had to change the first letter 'J' to 'Y'. It shows how talented Janiewicz is that Catalani, when in England, entrusts to him the leading of the orchestra wherever he is to sing. He finds it impossible to find a better leader.

I have asked Janiewicz whether the British are musically gifted. He answered that though fond of music and not grudging money for it, they do not show much talent. He must be right, for there certainly is no other country where such execrable theatre orchestras would be tolerated and also so few concerts given. And yet it is difficult to find a girl, of even very limited means, who does not try to murder some tune on the piano. They mostly play ballads and dance tunes. Those who attempt sonatas are looked upon as marvels; the harp is seldom played. In the country of Ossian I have heard it only twice. Organs are much more common and can be found even in middle-class houses. They adorn the sitting rooms and are in keeping with the religious spirit of the nation. Their tones are especially soft and delicate, and I will never forget how lovely the ballad about Zolkiewski[12] (by Niemcewicz) sounded, when Miss Janiewicz played it once to me. Music in Great Britain has not the encouragement it gets in Catholic countries. In the Church of England only the organ is used during the services. In Scotland, where there is not even an organ, only singing which has nothing in common with harmony. Calvinism forbids all musical instruments in churches. Though the Scots love music they can make no progress in it if they cannot use it for Religious expression. Besides, music has no status if it is taught only to women. The men, though during banquets fonder of singing than those of any other nationality, are certainly not musical and look down on music as on something unworthy of their manhood.[13] They are simply stupefied to see my countrymen play the piano. This explains why musical societies are unable to exist and that, up to now, Britain has no well known composer excepting Bishop.[14] Handel, the Kramers[15] and Janiewicz are foreigners and, of course, they play mostly foreign music. Reis,[16] Beethoven, Rossini are the most fashionable now.

Having said so much about Janiewicz, I feel I must repeat a joke he told me which proves that with music one can speak to people. Having come to London for the first time, our countryman had lodgings in the western part of the town. To make the acquaintance of the local artists he had to pay them calls. He started to do it at once, and having called on the whole lot, he hired a cab to take him home. A strange conversation then began between himself and the driver:

The Cabman	Where do you want to go?
Janiewicz	Home
The Cabman	I know that much, but where is your home? – and he glared at Janiewicz, taking him for a Frenchman.
Janiewicz	That's not the point, mon ami, Where is my home? I think but cannot remember. (He spoke broken English and French.)
The Cabman	What do you expect me to do then? – asked the Cabman with a jeering laugh.
Janiewicz	Eh bien, I see that you are a gay little bird. Dites-moi, do you know some music?
The Cabman	What has this to do with your home? (He glared even more.)
Janiewicz	Ecoutez mon ami, listen... (He began to hum.) Do you know this?
The Cabman	Yes, it is 'Marlborough'.
Janiewicz	That's it, that's it, take me then to Marlborough Street, my home is there. (The tune he hummed, was the well-known 'Marlborough s'en va-t-en guerre'.)

Besides the above-mentioned social entertainments there are of course parties in private houses. They are called by various names according to their degree of splendour. Many of them, because of the large numbers of guests, are very like the public assemblies. But I will speak of these later on; now I would like to give an idea of what a Briton's home is like. An Englishman's home is not only his castle, as the saying goes, but a very lovable abode. No wonder the inhabitants profess such love for quiet home life, seeing the comfort with which these homes are arranged. The houses, generally two storeys high, are as like each other as if they had been built according to the same plans.[17] The inside of the houses are also very much the same. Each storey has three rooms, a larger one in front and two smaller ones at the back. Very few houses are planned differently. If there is a third floor it is generally designed for garrets or

[29] *George Street, Edinburgh. Ewbank's drawing of George Street shows the gas lighting which so intrigued Lach-Szyrma. St Andrew's Church is on the left and the Assembly Rooms are on the right. In the distance is the memorial to Henry Dundas, Viscount Melville, 'The uncrowned King of Scotland'.* Ewbank

for servants' bedrooms. But as a rule these live in the basements where the kitchen is also to be found. Behind the house are the stables separated by a narrow lane, or a strip of garden with a few trees, used generally for drying linen. In the suburbs there are little gardens in front of the houses and these are full of flowers. The houses are separated from the street in the city by an area, a sort of ditch seven or eight feet deep and surrounded by iron railings with a little gate and steps leading down. The servants go through here to their basements, while the masters have another entrance. Though the outward appearance of these small houses does not promise much, a delightful order reigns inside, a degree of luxury and comfort which, in another country, would have been considered exaggerated and wasteful. Immediately on entering the lobby one steps on felt or on carpet. If it rains, a woollen rug and a brush are attached to the door, on which to dry one's feet. The stairs and all the rooms are covered with carpets and the sitting room is most luxuriously adorned. Mahogany furniture covered with rich materials or, in everyday life, with chintz wrappers, is so arranged as to be easily reached from all sides. In winter all floors are covered with heavy carpets and the muslin curtains are changed for woollen ones. All walls are painted in oil. Each room has an open fire and coal is burnt there all the winter. A little spade, shovel, poker and tongues are placed beside the fire. Stoves are unknown. On the marble mantel-pieces, chandeliers, mirrors and flowers are placed. On both sides of the mantelpiece spring bells to ring for the servant are arranged. Besides the curtains the windows have also white linen or cotton blinds. Beds have in winter curtains of red wool and in summer of the whitest linen or muslin. Only hair mattresses are used and not feather ones but, in wealthy houses, the bedding is often made of eiderdown. The birds supplying these feathers live in Iceland and this soft and warm down is extremely expensive. In the evening the hall is lit by a lamp hanging from the ceiling. The curtains and blinds are drawn for the night except when a party is given, when the light is allowed to stream out of all the windows. This custom betrays vanity. In London, where distances are very great, it is customary to drive to a dinner party but in Edinburgh, where the fashionable society live almost next door to each other, the ladies allow themselves to be carried in sedan chairs which can be hired on the corner of every street. The doors of the houses are locked for safety, day and night. On entering the houses in Edinburgh, you ring if you are the master and knock if a servant; in London on the contrary, by some queer caprice of fashion, you knock if you are the master and ring if the servant.

IX

The Customs. The Dinner Parties. Evenings and Balls.
The Scottish Women. Conversazione. The Gala Dress.
The Way of Greeting. The Titles. What is a Gentleman?
The Order of the House

EVERY nation has its customs which have been formed during centuries and it takes centuries to change them. The ancient Scottish customs would have been thought in our age too stern and too wild. In old-fashioned houses one still sees some remains of them, but they are like expiring torches and of more interest to the historian than to the traveller. The present Scottish customs are more like the English, which have been by now gladly accepted by most of the European countries. They are best seen in every day life and during receptions at the houses of the rich. Poverty is always inclined to stand stubbornly in the same place and keep to tradition, while wealth induces changeability, imitation of others and awakens vanity.

The fashionable dinner parties some fifty years ago took place at about 4pm. Today they have been changed to six or even seven. One is invited to dinner a week or two beforehand. The hour is mentioned, but it should not be taken too literally; one can be a quarter of an hour or even half an hour late if one does not want to come first. The guests gather in the reception rooms, where the host and hostess are waiting for them or, if they are too early, newspapers have to amuse them for some time. The tiny English houses make it impossible to entertain more than fifteen guests at a time. When dinner is announced, the hostess asks for the arm of the guest whom she wishes to honour most, and everybody else follows in pairs, or sometimes the ladies go first and the men follow. One cannot offer one's arm to or address a lady to whom one has not been introduced. She would consider it as impertinent and bad manners. If one is rather distant in one's behaviour this is thought right; all daring is taken as bad form and a sign of frivolity. The dining-room tables are generally oblong, covered with snowy linen. They are adorned with flower pots, lemon and orange trees and, if these are disposed all over the room, the guests have the impression of dining in the garden. The light of the crystal chandeliers reflects itself in the crystal and silver. The topmost place is occupied by the hostess, the places to her right and left are most honoured, especially to her right. The host sits at the opposite end of the table. Guests either sit as they like, or as they are told. It is usual to have ladies at each side. Only at the dinner table has one the opportunity of getting acquainted with one's neighbour. The first step towards it is made in the anxiety of anticipating her wants. This is considered to be the duty of the man sitting next to her. The first glass of wine is drunk as a rule to the health of one's neighbour, and it is generally then that the first words to her are spoken.

Dinner consists of three courses. The first dishes are already on the table when the guests arrive and, when everybody is seated, the menservants take off the covers. There are one or two kinds of soup, fish, fowl, ham, beef and roast mutton and, for vegetables, cabbage, spinach and potatoes. The soup is ladled out by the hostess, the fish and meat carved by the host and the servants hand it round. Other dishes are dealt out by the person in front of whom they happen to be placed. To do this well one should have some practice, which is why this duty is not at all pleasant to foreigners, who seldom are acquainted with culinary anatomy. However, one can always eschew this disagreeable task by choosing a place in front of which less complicated dishes are standing. It is likewise very tiresome that one has to ask everybody in turn what they want; if it is partridge or a chicken, whether they like a leg or the breast or a wing, and if a joint, whether well done or underdone? One must give to everyone according to their taste, which is not an easy task for a foreigner to whom the customs and the language of the table are alike unknown.

The meat is fat, juicy and carefully prepared but for foreign taste underdone. The fish are excellent but boiled only in water, even without salt. Butter and other sauces are served in crystal bowls left on the table. Everybody helps himself as he pleases. The vegetables, though also of the best quality, are spoilt by cooking. They too are only boiled in water, without salt and generally half raw. Lettuce alone is eatable, the best kind I have ever seen, not growing in heads but in long leaves, sweet and juicy. Everybody seasons it for himself with vinegar, oil and mustard. Some eat without any seasoning at all. Potatoes are cooked in

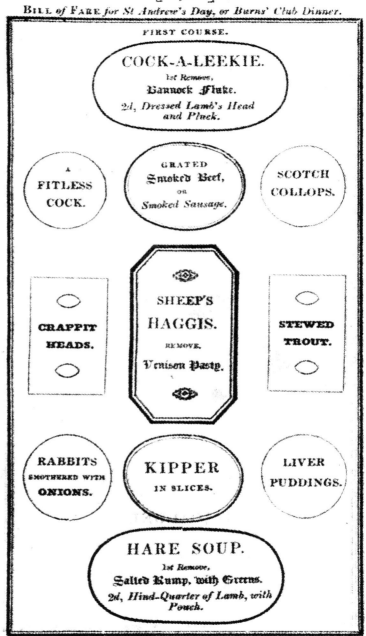

Bill of Fare for St Andrew's Day, or Burns' Club Dinner.

FIRST COURSE.

COCK-A-LEEKIE.

1st Remove,
Bannock Fluke.

2d, Dressed Lamb's Head
and Pluck.

A
FITLESS
COCK.

GRATED
Smoked Beef,
or
Smoked Sausage.

SCOTCH
COLLOPS.

CRAPPIT
HEADS.

SHEEP'S
HAGGIS.
REMOVE,
Venison Pasty.

STEWED
TROUT.

RABBITS
SMOTHERED WITH
ONIONS.

KIPPER
IN SLICES.

LIVER
PUDDINGS.

HARE SOUP.

1st Remove,
Salted Rump, with Greens.

2d, Hind-Quarter of Lamb, with
Pouch.

[30] *Table Setting for 'A Dinner of seven dishes for a St Andrews Day or Burn's
Club Dinner'. Margaret Dod's* The Cook and Housewife's Manual *was
published in Edinburgh in 1826. The setting is for a dinner at which guests sat
down to a table laden with dishes and were expected to serve others from*

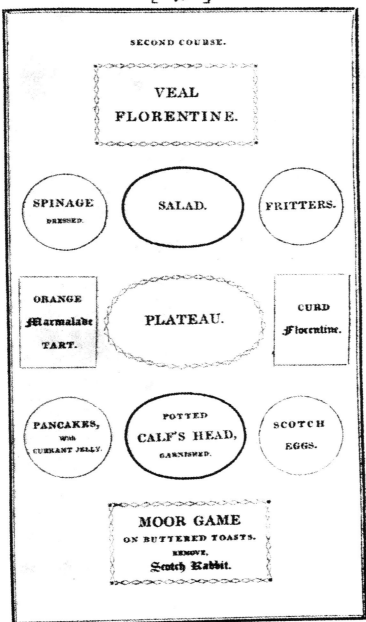

whatever was in front of them. Dinners 'à la Russe', at which servants, working from side tables, served more courses but fewer dishes, came into fashion later in the century.

steam and are delicious but served all dry, without any sauce, and so much liked that they are served even at recherché dinners. Game and fowls are also cooked in the plainest possible way. The hares are not stuffed with bacon as in Poland; the chicken not roasted but simply boiled. Sometimes to make them less uninteresting they are served with ham. All this composes the first course, which is the foundation of the dinner.

The second course consists of game, fowls, pies, cheeses, sweets, cakes, jam and puddings. The famous plum pudding is sometimes served; it is like the one made in Poland, only it is boiled much longer here, four to five hours, and this makes it harder and drier. The longer it is boiled, the better it is said to be. It is served hot, straight from the fire; and a sauce of butter, or sugar and wine, goes with it. For the haste with which it is eaten it is also called: the Hunting Pudding.

The third course is dessert. Apples, pears, nuts, figs, dates, almonds, raisins and oranges are all left on the table in great profusion till the end of dinner. This is not short, but generally lasts through the greater part of the evening.

As to drinks, there is a great variety of these in Britain. The poor have small beer and table beer is drunk also in the best houses. In some places it is brewed at home and then it is delicious. Towards the end of the first course, port and ale are handed on trays. Wines mostly used are: Madeira, Sherry, Port wine, Claret, Burgundy, Rhine wine and Champagne. The three last ones are given only in wealthy houses. A kind of champagne is made in England from gooseberries and is so good that it is difficult to distinguish it from the French one. To make the wines stronger, alcohol is added, for weak wines are not liked. The merchants, aware of this, send over the drinks thus prepared. A lot is drunk, but without compulsion. In better society, excess of drink has greatly decreased lately. Nobody drinks by himself, always with somebody else. Inviting people to take wine, one says: 'May I have the pleasure of taking a glass of wine with you?' If the person accepts (as she is bound to), then one asks whether she prefers red or white wine. Then both persons hold up their glasses, bend their heads and say 'Your good health!', then, looking straight into each other's eyes, they empty their glasses. This must be repeated as many times as one is invited to drink, were it with all the guests in turn. A simple 'thank you' would have been considered an offence. Sometimes three people drink to each other's health together; this is a sign of a special friendship. Some time ago people used to drink to the health of everybody present, pronouncing their names as they drank; the custom is retained today only in middle-class houses and it is much better that it is dying out. How can a foreigner remember the names of everybody?

Before the tablecloth is taken away, which happens when the second course is finished, bowls of water are given to everyone wherewith to wash their mouths. Many exaggerate this love of cleanliness so as to almost wash their faces. The young, however, and the ladies are very decent. The ladies especially scarcely dip their fingers, sometimes only touch the water with them and wipe them with the napkin in so elegant a manner that it is a pleasure to watch. Everything done with decency is almost a virtue. France when compared to England is very dirty. The British are unable to forgive the French for spitting on the floor or into the chimney and for spreading in front of everybody present huge handkerchiefs all soiled with tobacco. The famous Johnson could never forget the disgust he felt when once, travelling in France, somebody put sugar into his cup with his fingers. In Britain things are either served with special utensils for taking them, or else on a plate. I often wondered how things are handled in the kitchen, but one does not think about what one does not see.

When the tablecloth is taken away fresh decanters of wine are brought in and small coloured napkins are put in front of everybody. They protect the mahogany table from being rubbed and also are meant to wipe the glasses if the wine should overflow. The drinks of Bacchus in two or three kinds are then handed round. Everybody takes whatever he likes, invites no one, and passes on the decanters. When the glasses have been filled several times and the conversation becomes more lively and free, the hostess gives a sign to the ladies to retire. The men get up respectfully and remain standing until the ladies have left the room. When they are gone the host takes the hostess's chair and raises a toast to the ladies. The toasts proposed with appropriate sentiments begin to get out of fashion, for people like to be free of all restraint, but at public dinners and in intimate company they are still used. The sentiments expressed are dictated by the heart and by the moment, in accordance with the circumstances:

> Win the hearts and never lose them.
> A sensible freedom to the whole world.

Not all the sentiments however are lofty; some are jeering, aggressive or even vulgar. Each person before drinking has to repeat the sentiment uttered by the toast given. The longer one remains at the table the more one drinks, the more lively and fiery the conversation becomes. The wine loosens the tongue and silent Britons become talkative. It is then that:

> On digère, on raisonne,
> On conte, on rit, on medit du prochain.

The last accusation, however, is not true here, for it must be said to the credit of these islanders that they do not indulge in backbiting, and personal honour, and especially your neighbour's, is more respected than anywhere else. If sometimes they attack each other in the newspapers this is only for political reasons for, owing to her constitution, this country is divided into many political parties.

The greatest variety prevails in the after-dinner conversation. Learning, literature, travels, as well as the most ordinary topics are cleverly

[31] *Royal Circus, Edinburgh. The cost of establishing and maintaining the private gardens, which were an important feature of life in the New Town, was usually shared by the owners of the land and the proprietors of the houses and flats surrounding them.* Shepherd

related. Politics are also mentioned especially in the Whig houses,[1] which seem to be small parliaments. The topic has no charm for a foreigner, at least until he becomes better acquainted with the form of British Government and with the country's internal relations. In Tory houses there is less of politics and more amusement. The Whig houses are more interested in learning. Both parties, however, have the deepest respect for other people's convictions and appreciate principles even in their enemies. This is an unmistakeable sign of high educational standards and the finest trait in the British character. The principles of each man are the result of long thinking and experience. Offending them is a painful business, the more painful that the wound caused is a moral one. The more cultured a nation, the more respected are the principles of others. Barbarians neither have principles nor are capable of respecting them.

An hour or an hour and a half after the ladies have left, the hostess sends word that tea is ready. The gentlemen then join the ladies and immediately their gaiety changes into respectful gravity, this being the result of the esteem they have for the fair sex. The eldest daughter or some cousin of the hostess plays the role of Hebe, infuses that Chinese drink and distributes it to the guests. Coffee is also served but not with rum, as in Poland. Then one of the ladies sits down to the piano, plays and sings. About one o'clock the guests begin to take leave except on occasions when dinner is followed by a dance. Then new guests arrive every moment. One does not say goodbye to one's host and hostess, but if one leaves earlier than one should, it is called 'taking French leave'. The dances last till one or two at night and are followed by a cold supper. On Saturdays the hostess takes leave of her guests punctually at midnight when Sunday, the day most carefully observed, begins. Of course there are many who are less scrupulous and think that this is exaggeration. The clergy and the more old-fashioned houses regard all this with an unfriendly eye, putting down this loosening of morals to the all too frequent journeys abroad. Paris has a specially bad name.

The evening parties are sometimes called assemblies or public balls. To participate in them one must buy a ticket; there are also routs, at homes, and conversazioni, which are given in wealthy private houses and to which one must be invited. There are subtle differences between each of them. Though pleasure is their aim, this is not always to be found where one looks for it. Music, dancing and whist are the chief entertainments but, as not everybody likes these things, many come only to show off their wealth or witness the display of it, or simply to do things as they are done in the upper classes. The person who has attained the incomparable happiness of being able to frequent those spheres, or the one who has been born into them, receives from time to time an invitation stating that: 'Mrs N.N. of such and such an address will have the honour of receiving a small party on such and such a date'. Or simply that she will be At Home. Such an invitation is always written in the third person, as if by a secretary and is not signed: 'Mr and Mrs F. present their compliments to Mr and Mrs K. and request the pleasure of their company to dinner on Wednesday next at seven o'clock'. Such an invitation is sent a month beforehand as if to give time for guests to prepare for it and not to accept an invitation elsewhere. When the month is over, one goes to her who has deigned to announce by such circular that she will be at home. (As if she had been elsewhere all the time!) The house is not difficult to find, even if dark night makes it impossible to read the number. Light streams from all the windows, carriages drive up, it seems as if the whole population has assembled to behold the lady who inhabits her own home so very seldom. A footman in a rich livery asks for one's name at the door and, having heard it, repeats it very loud so that other footmen standing in rows on the stairs should hear and repeat in turn. As one ascends the stairs, one's name and title precede one, shouted from mouth to mouth, until, especially if it is a foreign one, the name is changed and the title alone remains. As all the doors generally open wide to titles, it is easier to pass everywhere with one. Thus, accompanied by one's title alone, one enters the drawing room. The footman standing in the doorway is well trained and knows what to do on all occasions; the greater the title, the louder he pronounces it. One could make a special scale of the rising tones of his voice which increases in volume crescendo: whispering 'Mr.', speaking 'Sir', announcing 'Lord', exclaiming 'Count' or 'Marquis' and shouting 'Prince' or 'Duke'. At the announcing of each title, the eyes of all present turn towards the newcomer as if to appreciate him accordingly. This way of entering a drawing room, as if meant to make any one feel shy, does not have that effect on the British. On the contrary, their appearance, with their innate cold aloofness and composure, is the very thing for such an entry. I never could get over my astonishment at their extreme gravity, which gave to all the assembly a special serious quietness. Having entered the drawing room, they do not bow. The hostess greets everyone in the same distant and polite manner: 'I hope you are well?'. The guest mumbles something in reply, and without any further attempts at politeness, for civility is considered French false coin, he joins the

[32] *The Drawing Room, 31 Moray Place, Edinburgh. This watercolour of the drawing room in a house rented by Count Arthur Potocki in 1840 is the only known illustration of a late New Town interior. The furnishings are almost identical with those supplied for 3 Moray Place, in 1825, by William Trotter. Covers shown protecting the Brussels carpet and silk-upholstered rosewood furniture would be removed before a formal reception.*
Aleksandra Potocka

company. What applies to one guest is tirelessly repeated to all and there are often as many as 300. The well brought up hostesses must be trained in very great patience to be able to bear it. The more splendid the reception, the more crowded it is, so that superfluous guests remain standing on the stairs and landing until they leave and go to some other equally crowded gathering. Sometimes there are several on the same night and one cannot help thinking that the best plan would be to return home at once and go to bed. The whole thing is only superficial splendour and outward show and it really would not make any difference to anyone if the guests went for a few minutes to all the assemblies, so as to be seen, or did not go at all and not even say thank you for the invitation. All the rooms are lavishly decorated with flowers and brilliantly illuminated. In the dancing rooms all the carpets are removed and the floors painted in strange patterns. Men and women are splendidly dressed and women with great sumptuousness. Ostrich feathers wave on their heads and they shine with precious stones and jewellery. At first the scene is enchanting but very soon boredom prevails over all other feelings. A human being needs more than show and superficiality; soul should approach soul and contact and interesting conversation are what really matter. Without this one feels as lonely as in the desert but, alas, the stern English etiquette kills all possibility of freedom. If you try to address people to whom you have not been introduced you may easily get into trouble. They will turn their backs on you or answer in rude, sharp sentences. A sensible host tries to remedy this, entrusting the foreigner to one of his friends who tells him all about the social customs, so that at least he is not deserted and lonely. It is always more pleasant not to be only a spectator but to play some role on the stage of life. Balls are less crowded as a rule, for there must be room for dancing. The company is also more select. It was fashionable at that time to dance very slowly so that dancing was little different from walking. This custom added to the natural gravity of the Britons combined to make a whole which, with the best of good wills, it would have been difficult to call 'amusement'. But nevertheless, at such parties friendships between the young begin and future matches are arranged, under the attentive eye of the parents. Such evenings are almost the only possibility the English young people have of meeting. What is started by chance is worked out to a happy ending by the agreement of both sides. This is why such parties are usually given in the houses which have grown-up daughters.

The maidens of Caledonia are more daring in their movements and attitudes than the maidens of Albion. Their facial features are not as regular as those of English women, but more expressive and animated. They are slim but a little too manly and they have a way of walking with long strides, which deprives them of the delightful grace of French-women. They are more like the serious Juno, or the daring Diana, than the delicate Hebe. Their feet, like those of the above mentioned goddesses, are too large. This is perhaps caused by thick and heavy shoes which they are obliged to wear because of the wet climate. Their skin is more healthy than delicate, their eyes like those of Polish women, dark or grey ones; the latter are considered as a proof of wisdom like those of Minerva. Some are wise indeed and even learn Greek and Latin. They speak better French than the English women, though their knowledge of the language is also chiefly reduced to understanding. French books are not popular with them either, for they consider French ideology to be alien to their national character. But they are well acquainted with their own literature, write poetry pretty frequently and read lots of it. Literary women are called 'blue stockings'. I met a Mrs Grant[2] and a Mrs Baillie,[3] both writing tragedies. Girls draw, paint, try to play and sing, and dance badly. They go nowhere until they are seventeen and do not appear even at meals. They have no time to learn social talents and when they marry it is too late. They do some needlework, but this is rather aimless and manufactories do all these things much quicker and better. The daughters of lawyers, advocates, Writers to the Signet, and as a rule the middle-class women, are better educated. The middle classes also produce the most talented people. Unmarried women have much freedom in Britain. They go to dances, for rides on horseback, for walks with their friends and are even seen in town without the accompanying servant. In Edinburgh, walking with a footman behind is scarcely known. What Goldsmith said is generally found to be true, that: 'a virtue that needs guarding, is scarcely worth guarding'. With their parents, the daughters behave more like friends than children; there is more affection than respect in the intercourse. When they marry, they become devoted to their homes, are modest wives and good mistresses of the house.

There is another kind of evening party met only in London. These are called 'conversazione'. They are given on Sundays to make up for the theatres, dancing, music etc that are all forbidden on this day. The aim of these assemblies is talks between friends, travellers, scientists and artists. Such social entertainments, which enable talented people to take part in really interesting conversations, are the highest ideal to which only great culture can lead society.

To dinners and evening parties attended by women one comes always in full dress, which is black or navy blue tails, black silken stockings and court shoes, and a black or white waistcoat (on no account can a waistcoat be coloured). The kerchief on one's neck must be white, fresh and tied in a fashionable way. This is not an easy thing to do: dandies consider that an hour is not enough to tie it as it ought to be. If one wants to mix with the upper classes, it is absolutely essential to know all the exigencies of fashion. A sign of ignorance or slackness would be taken in a young man for lack of education, or even an offence. Certainly the most sensible course to take is to dress and behave according to the customs of the set with which one lives. If one mixes with the industrialists and the middle classes, one can more easily indulge in some neglect of the adopted ways, but if one has to do with the upper classes this would be an unpardonable sin. One must bend one's knee to the Majesty of Fashion and beware of offending her in dress, manners or speech. Everything vulgar makes a man as if non-existent in the eyes of the great world, and can even exclude him from it once and for all.

The manners are very simple and speech delicate and without exaggeration. No low bowings, no expressions which, if not humiliating, are at least vain and futile like the ones used sometimes in other countries, as: 'I kiss your feet', 'I fall at your feet', or 'Your most obedient servant'. Such expressions, though everybody knows that they are meaningless, should not be tolerated in any sensible nation which understands that words should not contradict thoughts. With advancing education every nation in turn shook herself free from these ancient forms of expressing respect. Instead of exaggeration and humility, words of real regard and respect were adopted. No country has less of these superficial forms of politeness than Britain, nowhere are they so much despised. Nowhere is there such true and real politeness. Hats are not taken off either to one's equals or to one's superiors; a servant does not even take it off to his master. The hat is only touched, as soldiers listening to orders do. If one meets friends, one waves one's hand to them or slightly inclines one's head. Only very intimate friends shake hands. One also shakes hands with one's host or guests. The words of greeting or farewell are very simple. One says farewell to one's intimate friends for this is the more poetical form, and the tone of voice must express whether the words are dictated by cold fashion or by real feeling. As in bestowing gifts, when the manner either increases or lessens their value, so it is with greetings or goodbyes. The conversation is also very simple and not complicated by regard due to people. In a conversation between friends, all titles are dropped, and one simply says 'You'. How convenient this is. We have not got a corresponding word in Polish, though most languages have it, and we are bound to use long complicated forms, addressing people in the third person, using titles, which we scarcely are able to understand or to remember, and which leave us out of breath, stop the natural flow of thought, spoil the terse beauty of the language and enchain the words most disagreeably. At a meeting one addresses the audience 'Ladies and gentlemen', while one says in France: 'Messieurs et Mesdames'. In which of the two countries, then, does more of the real spirit of chivalry still remain?

The word 'gentleman', so often met in English, applies to people in all walks of life. The King himself tries to earn that title. If refused to anyone, it deprives him from being accepted among honest men. A gentleman must possess some attributes of honour, and also some fortune, for he should be independent. The latter statement is proved by such expressions as 'He lives like a gentleman', 'He dresses like a gentleman'. If one is told 'He will do it for you like a gentleman', this would mean that he would not swindle you. Nevertheless it does not dispense you from rewarding his troubles. But even the richest man without a code of honour will not be a gentleman. The poorest try to live up to this title, those who do not attempt it are not even fit to be flunkeys. 'Gentleman' is so much a national word that it cannot even be translated. Simond [4]says with reason, that to try and translate it by 'Monsieur' would be a parody. 'Monsieur' is anyone in France who is dressed better than a commoner. 'Gentleman' implies good birth, though by no means as an essential attribute. One can be a gentleman, though not by birth. 'Monsieur' can be ridiculed and even have a double meaning, but not so 'gentleman', who is a noble of nature's own creation. A dignified, virtuous and almost perfect man was called in Polish 'Dworzanin' and our conception of him is almost identical with the English idea of a gentleman.

There are some things among these Islanders which are so fickle and changeable that they pass as quickly as fashion but there are others, so deeply rooted, that they persist in guiding their steps. Order and method are among these. There is a special time for everything that is done: for town life, country life, luncheon, dinner, calls, and walks, even the buying of ribbons. Special hours also bind the servants in their household work if the whole routine of the house is not to be broken. Each object has its special place, which it occupies for ever afterwards. Even the manner of laying the tables is strictly the same in most of the houses. The servants have no need to be taught, for before entering the service they are specially trained. This is why everything in English houses happens silently, with the regularity of clockwork. The servants have but to be left alone and they will do everything by themselves, without any fuss or ordering about. These qualities of theirs make it possible to keep only a very few. It is simply difficult to imagine how so few can do so many things. In the boarding house in which I lived in London, we were 21 guests and three families. Only two maids did the whole work and everything was done in the most exemplary way. Footmen are only employed in very rich houses, for their wages are considerable and besides, one has to pay a tax for them to the Government. The entire maintenance of a manservant with his clothes amounts to more than £40 a year. Everybody tries to have women servants, whose wages are only £12 a year and for whom one does not pay taxes. The Government's motives in this distinction between men and women servants are that a woman being of the weaker sex needs protection, and this is why it is best that she should work in private houses, whereas a man can always make himself more useful in the country.

These regular habits, which work marvels in households, are also preserved in life outside. The traffic is one-sided and those who do not conform to the regulations have to pay fines and damages. Rules also apply to pedestrians. Meeting a fellow pedestrian one has to keep to the left to let him pass. I had a funny experience once. It is my habit to keep to whichever side of the street I may have started to walk on. I simply give others the chance of passing me on the other side instead of beginning to dance a contre-dance or a minuet in front of each other in the street. Walking once through a deserted suburb of Edinburgh I met a sailor. Keeping to my habit, as the pavement was very narrow, I stood against the wall to let him pass. But he also stood against the wall, and as if wondering at each other, we both began to stare into each other's eyes. I did not understand what this meant at first, and deciding to break stubbornness, by stubbornness I leant against the wall in an even more determined manner. The sailor was the first to speak: 'You took to the wrong side', he said. Understanding at last that he was right, I then let him pass between myself and the wall. These regular habits are of great importance: they are the same in life as diet and restraint are for one's health.

X

*The Climate. The Illnesses. The Population. Trade.
The Food. Markets. The Food of the People. Fuel.
National Entertainments. Sea Bathing. Restalrig*

THE latitude of Edinburgh is almost exactly the same as that of Riga. Notwithstanding such a northern position the climate is moderate because of the nearness of the sea. Extreme frost does not torture one in winter, or heat in the summer. The changes of temperature are so sudden and so frequent, that one hour is scarcely like another. In the most glorious sunshine it is dangerous to go out without an umbrella. The east wind brings rain, fogs and snow and is extremely unpleasant and unhealthy. The west wind on the other hand is very mild and kind to vegetation. There are no distinct differences between the seasons; spring is unpleasant and lasts a long time. In 1823 fires were lit daily in May, it was so bitterly cold. British spring has none of that intoxication and fragrance which accompanies ours. Neither has one that feeling of having become younger oneself, so much everything around seems to be reborn, renewed, growing and living. Summer begins only in July and from August to October the weather is a little more reliable and it does not rain quite so often. But in general it is more cold than warm. In that year 1823, on St. John's Day (June 24th), hoar frost covered the fields. This instability of weather, the winds, cold and rain make the harvest come much later. The wheat harvest began in that year on September 20th and there are years in which it does not ripen for lack of sun. In the hills, where it is even colder and rainier, the more delicate corn is not sown. In winter, if the frost reaches 8-10 centigrade, it is already considered to be very cold. It never lasts longer than a few days and often such warm days follow as in spring. This makes the Scottish fields and gardens always green; laurels, geraniums, jasmine, syringa and ilex, which freeze out in Poland, prosper here all winter, green and unprotected.

[33] *Calton Hill and the Nelson Monument, Edinburgh. Designed by Robert Burn in the shape of an inverted telescope, rooms at its base failed to attract the retired seamen for whom they had been intended. In 1816 these were leased to a caterer. The ball at the top dropped at 1 pm, giving a time signal visible to shipping in the Firth of Forth.*

Notwithstanding all this, the air of Edinburgh, as of all seaside towns, is healthy. The inhabitants live to be very old, and the numbers of people being born are greater than of those dying. Illnesses like black death, leprosy, and mange, so often mentioned in the history of Edinburgh, are now non-existent owing to the high hygienic standards.[1] Order, better lodgings and the progress of medicine have done much. Great cities, however, are not the best for health. A few years ago typhus, a kind of nervous fever, claimed many victims from among the workmen. Scarlet fever, measles and whooping cough are as frequent as everywhere else. Ever since the introduction of vaccination, the once fatal smallpox does not play such havoc. Influenza is the most frequent malady. It is a kind of heavy cold which owes its name to the belief once prevailing that it is due to the influence of the stars. Nervous persons are especially prone to it, chiefly women. It generally attacks people when the east wind blows and, on the contrary, the west wind seems to cure it. This is why the sick await it with great impatience.

According to the statistics of 1821, the population of Edinburgh was then 138,225 souls: 62,089 men and 72,137 women. There were 14,038 more women than men in Edinburgh alone. This predominance of women strikes one's eye. One can take any ten families one would chance to remember and already the prevalence of women is remarkable. This is why girls must be much humbler than elsewhere to try to get husbands. Scottish women are very prolific. It is quite usual to see ten or fifteen children in a family. Part of the population of Scotland, partly because of this, is always obliged to leave Scotland and seek its fortune in England or in the colonies. The whole world is full of Scots. There are so many in the United States that their influence is felt everywhere.

Though Edinburgh is not a merchant city, its trade is very considerable. Linen, muslin, carpets, glass, and paper are exported and groceries, coffee, tea and sugar imported. Furs, timber, flax and hemp come from Poland and Russia. Polish oats and starch are considered the best. And though oats grow in Scotland and starch is also made there, the best qualities are called 'Polish oats' and 'Polish starch'. Fishing brings a good income. Expeditions to Spitzbergen are made for whaling. Herring are caught off the seacoast and in the bays. This trade has its centre at Leith, a port a mile or so from Edinburgh. The statistics of 1823 show that 6,210 different ships left that port during a year, manned by 21,130 sailors.

The food market of Edinburgh is a curious sight. I have nowhere seen one better arranged and better supplied. Everything needed for the maintenance of so large a population can be found in one place. It is situated between the old and the new town in a valley on the slope of a hill. Each commodity has its special place there. Vegetables, beef, mutton, fowls, game; everything is sold at separate stalls and large stone steps lead to them. One can get the most delicious vegetables, for which the Scottish gardens are famous. Gooseberries, strawberries, currants are also plentiful. One can also buy as many fowls as one wants: wild geese, wild duck and Solan geese which are a speciality of Scotland. They are caught on one of the islands, the Bass Rock, on which they nest.

They are brought to market in June and July during the Edinburgh races. Then of course they sell best. They can be procured till the end of September. Later on, they migrate overseas and return in May. They live on herrings. In autumn and winter all sorts of game and fowls can be obtained. The most popular shoots in Scotland, for which many people come even from England, are for blackcock, game and grouse. These are found on the moors. The Polish kind of capercailzie and some of our other birds (jarzabeck-tetrao bonasia) are unknown in Scotland. As I was writing this, I was told from a creditable source that one of the peers has applied to the Polish Forestry Department asking for 30 pairs of these birds, to try and rear them in Scotland. Hare are also plentiful but, as the game laws are very strict, they are brought to the market stealthily. The Scots eat rabbits as well and make of them a black soup with potatoes, as good as hare soup, but the flesh of the rabbit is not good. Besides the butchers who sell beef, the fish market is very well supplied. At dawn fisherwomen come from the seaside villages; they carry on their backs huge creels of fish. The variety is great for sea and river produce plenty. Every month brings new kinds: salmon, trout, perch, turbot, and cod are the most common. The last is caught year round and can be dried. In summer there are great quantities of herring, which are eaten fried. They are fat and delicious, but when salted not as good as the Dutch ones. Eels are also caught but because of some superstition, the common people in Scotland find them disgusting. Praise of these silent sea creatures exposed to view is loudly shouted by the fisherwomen. They speak of the fish as Anthony did of Caesar, and if people refuse to believe what they say and disparage the wonderful qualities of the fish, then they get mercilessly pelted with mud and lashed by the sharp tongues of the women. The oyster women surpass even the fisherwomen in their shrill volubility. The Scottish oysters are bigger than the French ones. They are caught from September till May. They are served with lemon and pepper and port. They are best when some of the seawater is still in their shells. Seashell fish are also very much appreciated. Lobster is highly praised but its flesh is too sweet and it is almost impossible to eat without mustard. Polish crayfish are far superior. Crabs, which are cheaper than lobster and very plentiful, are a dish much praised by the commoners. Generally only their claws are brought into the market: the males are best eaten in spring, the females in autumn. There are also shrimps, little larger than many bugs; some consider them an exquisite dish and even eat them with their shells. They taste like our crayfish.

[34] *'Our gudeman's a drunken carle' by Walter Geikie (1745–1837).
Lach-Szyrma tended to idealise the Scottish working classes. Geikie paints a
different picture.*

Quantities of luxurious food are provided for the rich by the earth, the
air and the water, but the tables of the poor are not as varied. Some time
ago, the bread of the common people was made of barley and the worst
kind of wheat and oats. The Highlanders still bake flat oatcakes. In
towns, however, wheat bread alone is used. Though the workmen are
much better off than they used to be, yet many cannot afford meat. Their
everyday food consists of oats, potatoes, meat and broth. To make a
change they eat herrings which, when in season, are very cheap. Ale is
their favourite drink and it is better brewed in Scotland than in England.
England on the other hand is the land of porter. Scottish porter is

weaker and not so much drunk. Among intoxicating drinks, whisky is the principal. It is made from barley and the best is brewed in the Highlands, whence it is smuggled through, for there is a monopoly on whisky.[2] It smells of peat. Some drink it mixed with hot water and sugar and then it is called toddy. In middle-class houses it is given after dinner instead of wine or coffee.

Coal[3] is the only fuel. Coal is indeed a great blessing to countries deficient in forests. Britain possesses numerous mines; the county of Galloway alone, which has none, must import it from elsewhere or else the inhabitants must burn peat or straw. The richest mines are near Glasgow and Hamilton; a new canal unites Glasgow with Edinburgh, and because of this the price of coal is three times cheaper now. But coal has not been always known in Scotland, and there was a time when heather and wood were the only fuel in Edinburgh. The writer Aeneas Silvius[4] makes the first mention of coal in the 15th century. This is what he says:

> I saw beggars in rags around the church. The passers by gave them, instead of alms, stones for which they humbly thanked them. These stones for some unknown reason, either because of the sulphur they contained, or because of some other ingredients, had the quality of burning when lit. In districts devoid of forests they are used as fuel.

Though, as a rule, the character of the Scots is less gloomy and heavy than that of the English, nevertheless the Scots have also few popular entertainments and show no need of such. One does not see in Scotland, as one does in France, Germany or Poland, happy crowds, dancing and rejoicing together on feast days or in the little towns during the fairs and markets. All this is too frivolous to attract the Scots, whose serious upbringing disposes them for graver occupations. The great feasts of Christmas, Easter and Pentecost are unknown here. Sunday alone is observed and, according to the teachings of their religion, must be spent in meditation and not rejoicings. Visiting a friend or going for a walk is quite sufficient a diversion and on weekdays everybody is busy and no time is left for amusement. The whole nation is so active and laborious that even the common people are ashamed to do nothing. The humblest workman tries his hardest not to be lazy. The love of work is developed by family life. Those who have no families of their own try to live with somebody else's. They quickly acquire the love of good habits and virtues, and a dislike of intemperance or being homeless tramps. Except

[35] *Fishmarket Close, Edinburgh. Deserted by the upper classes, the tenements and closes of the Old Town rapidly became one of the worst slum areas in Europe.* Ewbank

perhaps a few sailors who, for the roughness of their habits, are considered to be the lowest class of society, I can assure my readers that during my stay in Scotland I have never seen a drunkard wallowing in the streets. If it happens that somebody gets a little tipsy he is careful enough not to be seen in public. So deeply moral and orderly are the instincts of that nation that the fathers of families, busy all the week earning their living, are glad to spend Sunday in their family circle and are not given to going to inns.

The New Year is one of the gayest days for the Scottish people. Then even the most restrained Scotsman must have his daft day. In olden times people relate that the day was even gayer but it is still full of merriment. Slightly intoxicated crowds await midnight in the streets, wishing each other a happy year. One sees people with bottles of whisky in their hands, generously distributing it to the crowds, hoarse with joyous yelling. Women that night keep to their houses and do not appear in the streets. As in Russia on Easter Day, it is customary here to kiss passers-by in the street on New Year's Eve. The Scots however apply that custom only to women who, however careful, cannot always avoid such tributes of civility. The rejoicing crowds sometimes stop the passing carriages to salute the most distinguished ladies by kissing them, after which they are safely escorted home. But New Year's wishes are not as solemnly remembered as in Poland, and New Year cards are not sent.

Equally gay, though not for the elderly but only for schoolboys, is St. George's Day. This is celebrated as the King's birthday, though neither the King, nor his father, was born on that date. Then all the mail coaches pass through the streets in gala and the drivers wear beautiful new liveries. The schoolboys dress a straw doll in rags and shoot at it with revolvers. The doll is called John Wilkes,[5] and the only achievement of the day is that very frequently one of the schoolboys has his eyes burnt out by the shooting. From morning till night the noise goes on and crowds gather in the streets. There is no service in church on that day for, if there were one, gaiety would have been subdued. In this country joy does not go with praying. This solemn day ends with a ball for the smart set and fireworks for the common folk. In 1823 the fireworks were a huge success for the night was quiet, fine and dark.

St. Valentine's Day is for the Scottish women what St. Andrew's Eve is for the Polish. Names of men and women are written down on pieces of paper, mixed in an urn and then drawn out at random. Those whose names come out together are meant to marry within the year. This gives opportunity for jokes, smiles and blushes or even swoons, for where love comes into play people are most credulous, ready to believe all nonsense. Many young men and women spend a sleepless night then. The next day packets of anonymous letters are being carried about to every house in which a beloved one lives. These letters, generally rhymed, are full of sighs and exclamations. Most of them are probably written for fun but I would not venture to say that some were not true.

The Scots have their special national entertainments and these are games: golf and curling. There are various games clubs which encourage high standards of proficiency and, by the introduction of rules and order, assist in its attainment. Sea bathing is one of the pastimes dear to the Scots and this is not only pleasant but also very healthy. Some bathe in the sea to cure diseases, others to prevent them. In winter one bathes in warm seawater in special buildings and in summer in the open sea. To make bathing pleasanter there are little houses in which one is driven out into the waves. These little houses in which one undresses are extremely well equipped with everything needed. There are benches under the walls, a little table, a mirror, racks, coat hangers and a boot-

[36] *The North Bridge, Edinburgh. By the 1820s the meat and fish markets had moved from the Old Town to the area under the North Bridge. The morning's catch was carried from the fishing villages of East Lothian by the fishermen's wives and sold from door to door or from open stalls in the market.* Shepherd

jack. One descends steps to enter the water; when one has finished bathing, a boy with a pony arrives and drags one back in one's bathing machine to the shore. One pays either each time or for the season.

The bathing season begins in June, even before St. John's Day. It is best to bathe when the tide is at its highest; high water occurs twice every 25 hours; one must go to bathe an hour later every day. The time has to be chosen not only for safety but also for warmth, for the tide passing over heated sands grows warmer. The tide flows in so swiftly that it gives no time to save oneself. The sea is at its coldest when it ebbs, for the water from the surface, heated by the sun, recedes first and the cold from the bottom remains. It is best to bathe during a wind, if not too violent, for the shock given by the breakers is beneficial to the nerves and the water is much warmer. As the waves are sometimes higher than the tallest man and can knock anyone down, it is a good plan to draw in your breath, shut your mouth firmly, turn sideways to the coming wave and try to plunge through, head foremost. Seawater is salt and bitter and

[37] *Restalrig Village. By the nineteenth century steam was beginning to replace water power in mills on the Water of Leith. In 1814 the inhabitants of Stockbridge complained that the amenities and advantages of their village as a growing suburb of Edinburgh were threatened by 'the nuisance due to the copious emission of very foul smoke from the chimney of the steam mill erected beside the water mill'. Andrew Kedslie, the miller, apologised but continued to fire his boilers. His neighbour, Henry Raeburn, took him to court, claiming that his wife's washing was being damaged by soot. Kedslie pleaded the cause of progress and won his case. The offending chimneys are in the background.* Ewbank

if swallowed makes you sick. It is supposed to be very harmful to consumptive people. Though colder than river water, it is not as dangerous as the latter. In fact it may be compared to some strong drink which, though cold at first, makes one feel warm afterwards. One remains in the sea no longer than 20-30 minutes.

Sea bathing is advised for skin diseases and for nerves but it is also helpful in other instances. I have heard the story of a man called Abraham Bzowski[6] whose right side was going bad. He began to spit blood and the doctors thought his lungs or spleen must be diseased. They said he would die. The man, however, took to sea bathing and miraculously recovered. Remembering him and suffering for several years from some strange pricking in my right side and also spitting blood from time to time, I decided to try the same remedy. I took rooms in the small village of Restalrig, only a mile or so from the city, and every day for two months I bathed in the sea. The pain in my side stopped altogether. I can say that sea bathing has probably saved my life. I quote this to encourage those suffering like myself. I must also add that I used to swallow, although with disgust, a little of the seawater on entering and on leaving the sea. This was to give the ingredients helpful to health a better chance to work from inside as well as from outside.

I shall always remember that village of Restalrig. It lies between orchards in a pleasant valley; from one side it has a view of Arthur's Seat and on the other the sea. Just in front of my house were the ruins of a Roman Catholic Church destroyed during the Reformation. In the middle of the churchyard there was an obelisk to the memory of the Earl of Moray, who was Regent of the country during the reign of James VI. A little further away were the barracks for the army, for in Scotland the soldiers are not billeted, as with us, in country houses. In the evenings one heard excellent music coming from there; it brought credit to the taste and musical culture of the commandant. The Scotch Greys Regiment[7] was quartered there. It distinguished itself during the Battle of Waterloo. Napoleon, when he saw them advancing, is said to have exclaimed: 'Ah, ces terribles chevaux gris!' It is this regiment which decided the fate of the battle which decided the fate of Europe. Charging, they shouted: 'Scotland for ever!' One of the superior officers of that Regiment prided himself on having known Prince Joseph Poniatowski.[8] He used to repeat that, in Spain, the coloured banners of our Uhlans were the nightmare of their cavalry. When speaking of the Polish cavalry, he always exclaimed: 'Damned fellows!' When he trained his men to fight with their spears he used to teach them strokes à la Poniatowski. He said he knew nothing more perfect than the Prince's ways of fighting.

XI

Walks. Duddingston. Craigmillar Castle. The Southern Parts. Dalkeith. Roslin. Hawthornden. Lasswade. Lord Rosebery's Castle. Sea Fishing

PEOPLE often say that the most important trait of an animal is not as interesting as the least important in a human being. Believing in this, it pleased me to observe the Scots in the minutest details of their everyday life. The most meaningless features thrilled me. I liked to deduce which of their habits was due to their upbringing, to religion, to tradition handed down from generation to generation and, last but not least, to their happy disposition which preserved them from laziness but cultivated virtues, diligence and wealth. I often observed the Scots' manner of going for walks.

The walks of such sensible and laborious people must needs differ from those of other nations. Many people are amused by nothing except uproar and noise but not so the Scots. Dissipation and levity is not in their character. They are too busy not to be serious and too well educated not to need some food for the brain and imagination. This is why everything a Scot does is always sensible and well thought out. The beauty of Scotland, with her hills, lochs and sea, inclines one to dreaming and sentiment and develops nobility. National memories are attached to many places and are recorded in history. Through reading, which is popular even among the very poorest, the common people learn all about their country and afterwards, wherever they go, they find themselves surrounded by memories. This broadens their vision and feeds their thought.

This is also the chief reason for Scotland being the country of poets and novelists. The fertile genius of Walter Scott finds there an ever-flowing fountain of inspiration. From there Wilson, Hogg and Galt draw all their patterns and ideas and they never lack new topics for their

[38] *Merchiston Castle. Merchiston was the home of John Napier (1550–1617), the inventor of logarithms. In 1961 the tower was absorbed into the buildings of what is now Napier University.* Grose

creations. Others before them did the same. In a country full of educated, virtuous and sensible people, topics for writing are easily found and the readers will not be missing. It is a most thankless task to write among barbarians, for barbarism does not stimulate delicate thoughts or feelings. This is why the Eskimo, the Greenlanders and other nations have no literature to speak of and cannot have one. I would not even attempt to quote all the beautiful works of art inspired by Scotland, especially romantic writings. Every part, every nook of that country has been touched and immortalised by some masterly pen. Edinburgh has been the happiest; the majesty of her natural surroundings and all the historical events attached to the place seem to destine this city to be an ideal source of imagination. Alone, or accompanied by my Scottish friends, I have visited Edinburgh and her neighbourhood, and I must say that I was full of admiration. The unending beauty and romanticism of the places visited awakened new thoughts in me.

On Sundays after service, if the weather is fine, the roads near the town are overcrowded with people going for walks. It is pleasant to watch these laborious and orderly people in their Sunday best taking a little respite. The fathers stalk along surrounded by their families and

[39] *Craigmillar Castle from the gardens. Built for the Prestons in the late fourteenth century, it passed to the Gilmours in the seventeenth century. Mary, Queen of Scots, was a guest at the castle when a group of her courtiers are believed to have plotted the murder of her husband Darnley.* Grose

their friends, keeping a careful eye on them that the sanctity of Sunday should not be profaned by a loud word or a light joke. Their attitudes are as modest as if they were still in church. They seem to go to nature for the confirmation of these great truths which they had heard a few moments ago from the lips of the minister. These Sunday walks are a triumph of education and perfection and they put the Scottish nation far above all others of the whole world.

Arthur's Seat and Calton Hill are the most frequented. Lovers of nature go there at night to watch the sun rise. As the [Calton] hill commands a wide view, beacon fires were lit on it in olden days, to give warning of the enemy's movements or to announce war. Nowadays the beacons are lit there only during festivals, as during the King's visit to Edinburgh. Arthur's Seat lies within the precincts of Holyrood Park and this park has a very curious privilege.[1] An escaped debtor, as long as he is within its precincts, is free and nobody can arrest him. He finds there cottages for hire and an inn with a billiard room. Many spent several years in that park, preferring to live there rather than go to prison. On Sundays they all leave the park and go safely to town to visit their friends, for on that day the secular authorities do not exercise their power. At the foot of the hill are the ruined remains of a hermit's cell, close to the ruins of St. Anthony's Chapel. The legend says that the hermit who lived here was a forsaken lover. He ate only dry bread, drank water from the spring and slept on the rock.

Following a path on the western side of the hill, one comes to a village, once frequented by Hume, called Duddingston. The park enclosing the splendid palace[2] of the Marquis of Abercorn touches this village. A little further is the half-ruined castle of Craigmillar[3] where Mary Stuart lived after her return from France. Her court, chiefly composed of Frenchmen, occupied the neighbouring village. This village is even now called Little France. Thus that unhappy Queen, transporting to Scotland the name of the country in which she had spent her happy youth, hoped to be able to bring back some of her past happiness.

The southern parts of Edinburgh are curiously lonely and quiet, in contrast to the others in which industry and trade enliven the streets. It is here that the wealthiest merchants have their houses and gardens, in which they live quietly with their families. It was there that Robertson the historian lived. It is there that Merchiston, the family seat of the Napiers, is situated. John Napier, the one who discovered logarithms, was born here in 1550. I have seen a small room in the attics in which he is said to have spent long hours over his mathematical problems. Though a man of genius, he was unable to rise above the superstitions of his age. He was firmly convinced that there was a bond between mathematics and the occult sciences (*doctrinae occultae*). He hoped to discover, by way of mathematics, the greatest mysteries. Allan Ramsay,[4] the writer of the Gentle Shepherd, also lived in this neighbourhood only a little higher up in the hills. The Scots know most of his poems by heart and visit in crowds the places he describes. A monument has been erected to him on the banks of the River Esk, with the inscription: 'Allano Ramsay et Genio Loci'. The writer of the novel *The Man of Feeling*, Mackenzie, has also got a monument on the banks of the same river. He has written many other things all imbued with tender feelings and exquisite taste. He has been honoured by this monument in his lifetime, for he is still alive.

All the above-mentioned places can easily be visited on foot. If one wants to visit others a little further away, this is made easy by stage-coaches. If the place is off the beaten track, then one has to hire a Tilbury or a gig or else go on horseback which, of course, is more expensive. To visit the places which I am going to describe we had to use all these means of communication in turn.

Dalkeith, where the palace and parks of the Duke of Buccleuch are, is several miles from Edinburgh. To Charles Buccleuch Sir Walter Scott has dedicated his *Lay of the Last Minstrel*. The castle has large collections of pictures which, however, I have not seen. The King, during his stay in Edinburgh, used to spend his nights here and it is also here that he held the military reviews. During the reign of James VI the castle was inhabited by the Regent, the Earl of Morton, and was then called 'The Lion's Den'.

On July 12th, the time when the inhabitants of Edinburgh go there to get strawberries, of which there are many different varieties, we also went to visit Roslin. It is a beautifully situated place but, except one hotel and a linen factory, there are no other houses. On a semi-island on the river Esk are the ruins of a castle and the Gothic chapel described by Walter Scott. The chapel is well preserved and adorned with sculptures. I remember one representing an angel playing the Scottish bagpipe. In different countries I have seen angels playing lutes, violins and harps, even horns, but up to now I have not been aware of the bagpipes forming part of the celestial orchestra. Evidently, just as the ancient Greeks and Romans transported to their imagined future life all their longings and desires, so now every nation wants to live, even in heaven, according to their own national ideas and traditions.

A fortnight before us, Walter Scott had been visiting the place accompanied by Miss Edgeworth,[5] the most famous living woman writer (in Britain). She was born in Ireland. I have been happy enough to meet her. She is small and swarthy, with clear-cut almost masculine features. If one is permitted to guess the age of a woman she must be nearly fifty. She travelled with two nieces, as small and witty as herself. The Edinburgh hostesses almost fought to have her but they were too shy to talk to her, because of her great fame, so they left the business of entertaining her to the men. She is intensely intelligent but very modest and has not even the slightest touch of exaggeration about her. She knew several Poles, amongst others the wojewoda Prince Czartoryski.[6] She left Edinburgh for the Highlands.

While making excursions along the wild and steep banks of the Esk, we came on a place with an inscription: 'Spring guns and man traps'. Carefully avoiding that place, which probably belongs to some selfish magnate, we soon found ourselves in Hawthornden. The present owner's house is situated high above the river. Once it belonged to Drummond,[7] a Scottish poet of the 17th century, who first began to write in English. His example was followed afterwards by Hume, Thomson[8] and others.

[40] *Roslin Chapel and Castle. Sir William Sinclair, 3rd earl of Orkney, built the Collegiate church in 1450. Probably the work of foreign craftsmen, only the nave of what would have been the largest and most elaborate chapel in Scotland was built.*

From later writers only Ramsay, Burns and Fergusson [9] wrote in the Doric or Scots. Walter Scott, Hogg and other gifted writers are fond of using the national dialect. The English have nothing against it; on the contrary they think that this scotticism enriches their language. It is not in the nature of the people of this country to quarrel about words or rules; they are more concerned with thought and real meaning.

Having left Hawthornden and walked over a hill, we were enchanted by the lovely sight of the village of Lasswade in a charming valley. We sat for a moment under lonely pines to admire the view. Lord Melville's castle; small cottages of the workmen employed in the industries; surrounding gay little gardens; all this like a chessboard stretched in front of us. Lasswade possesses two paper mills from which Edinburgh receives her best paper.[10] We visited both. Machines do most of the work. We were especially interested to see one, introduced only a year ago, which not only prepared the stuff for the paper but also threw it out into forms. Only three men are needed to collect the finished sheets of paper. The owner's young son has invented this machine. The Government has given him a patent for 13 years, during which time nobody else is allowed to use his invention. This is an excellent idea, for such patents not only reward the inventor and secure the profits for him, but they are also not contrary to the ideas of sound political economy. They forbid the uncontrolled buying up of patents and by granting them to the inventor only for a certain period they do not hinder the advance of the industry. It is always best and most natural if work is rewarded by its own profits.

The Earl of Rosebery's castle,[11] situated on the sea near Edinburgh and surrounded by a large park, is one of the most romantic places, nor has romance been lacking. An Englishman fell in love with the Countess and she returned his feelings. He came to Scotland dressed as a sailor, hired a cottage on the seashore and nobody except the lady in question knew anything about it. But such things cannot be kept a secret for long and the neighbours discovered everything. The noble Lord accused the Englishman and a lawsuit followed (called her 'Crim Con.'). The lover was made to pay £10,000 damages. The couple, as generally happened under such circumstances, married much later. Such fines and lawsuits are followed by divorce which, in other circumstances, only the House of Lords can grant to a noble pair. This is why divorce in Britain is not easy. I mention this event because such events happen only in Britain. In no other country would such legislation be tolerated. It must be considered as the remains of barbarism, of the ages when a woman was not considered as equal to man but rather as a chattel. According to Anglo-Saxon legislation, a husband under such circumstances was entitled to chase his wife out of the house with a whip, deprive her of everything or, with a rope around her neck, take her out to market and sell her to somebody else. This law, a disgrace to England, has not been used since more humane and enlightened ideas began to prevail but it cannot be stated that they have been entirely forgone. It persists as a form of divorce to be met nowadays only among the very lowest classes. Except for this, women are more respected in this country than in any other. This of course is the influence of the Middle Ages when, risking their lives, knights broke spears to receive a reward from the hands of the fairest lady (*La Reine de Beauté et des Amours*). But the true spirit of the nation is not completely reflected in the legislation. Most of the English laws based on the crude Anglo-Saxon ones deal with women in a manner completely alien to the chivalrous spirit of the Middle Ages. Punishing her mistakes by a fine as above-mentioned clearly shows that attitude to women. Adultery is treated in the same way as damage inflicted on an orchard and the fine is assessed in accordance with the

[41] *Edinburgh from the Fife coast. Lach-Szyrma's fishing expedition would have been in a boat similar to those in the foreground.* Grose

wealth, the walk of life and the birth of the co-respondents. It is difficult to imagine family life treated more grossly, as some material possession, the loss of which is compensated with money. The Courts also look to it that the accused should not be treated unfairly. If connivance or lack of opposition on the part of the husband is discovered, then it can be assumed that he did it for pecuniary profit and the whole responsibility falls on his own head. All these cases are from the beginning to end published in the newspapers in the minutest detail. The speeches of the advocates for and against and the dirtiest testimonies of the witnesses are printed without the slightest regard for decency. The newspapers at the time of the King's divorce were full of such disgusting, sordid and indecent details. Fathers of families had to hastily lock the newspapers in safe drawers so that they should escape the eyes of the whole family.

The neighbourhood of Edinburgh is very beautiful and highly culti-vated. The roads made according to the directions of Macadam[12] are simply excellent. The castles and churches are mostly Gothic but, though this style prevails, traces of Grecian architecture are found too, espe-cially in the colonnades. There are also beautiful places on the northern shore of the Firth. A regular steamship service facilitates the visiting of them. I have seen everything I could and once I even ventured out into

the open sea in a fishing boat. It was in August and we started at
nightfall. At sunrise, which happened to be very fine, we had reached
the place where the nets were left the evening before. It was low water
and very calm; this is the best time to take up the nets, for when the sea
is rough they can easily be torn. The buoy, which had been left floating
over the place, had been washed away by the sea. The fishermen
dropped an anchor and dragged it along the bottom and soon found their
nets, which I thought very clever of them. They took out eight lobsters
and 40 skate. Some weighed ten pounds. These fish look much more like
sea monsters than fish. They look like birds with open wings; their head
is small, their body too, their spine passes into a long smooth tail which
was at once cut off by the fishermen. Their mouths are in their stomachs.
They are so strong that one of them bit my stick in two. They do not
swim but lie on the bottom of the sea like oysters or crayfish. Their backs
are of the colour of an eel and their stomachs snow white, while the top
of their wing-like bodies is a delicate pink. They are very good to eat.

The fish market of Edinburgh is at its poorest in August. Only a few
fishermen stay at Newhaven and Fisherrow to provide fish for the city; all
the others go to Caithness to catch the herrings. At that time great shoals
of herring go from north to south and some of them go to the German
Ocean, whilst the others choose the Atlantic. Nobody quite knows what
happens to them later on. Some become the prey of more voracious fish,
some die out in warmer waters and some perhaps return north again.
The shoals are preceded by whales and sharks. The herrings caught on
the shores of Holland are the fattest and the best; near the shores of
France they are no longer any good. The statistics of the year 1618 say
that the Dutch employed 50,000 men to catch herrings and 500,000 to
hawk them round other countries. A monument has been credited to
Bukelst,[13] the Dutchman who discovered the best way of salting and
packing herrings. There is more than one road to fame. The real
discoverer of the art, however, was another man, Benkelson van
Bierfliet from Flanders. But so it is in this world. Monuments are not
always to those who merit them but to those who have luck. Poland buys
herrings from Holland; the English ones are consumed in the country
itself and a few are exported. The English do not know how to salt them
as the Dutch do and I have not eaten a really good salted herring here
but, fried fresh, they are delicious. The shoals of herring are so
numerous that the very water seems to be thick with them. Besides the
herrings, cod and mackerel and whiting are also caught in great
quantities off the coasts of Scotland.

XII

An Excursion to Dumfries. A Ball. The Races. Sociability of the Scots. Details about Dumfries. Gretna Green. The Tomb of Burns. The Polish Prisoners of War. Peebles. Penicuik

THE excursion to Dumfries was one of the most distant I made. I went there in November, which is not a propitious month for admiring nature, but even at another time of year I would not have had much to say. It is not everywhere that nature is at her best in winter. Having left the rich and fertile country of Edinburgh, we travelled along desolate hills infested with wild cats. On the almost bare, monotonous slopes sheep were grazing. The cottages of the shepherds in the valleys appeared miserable and lonely. There were hardly any cultivated fields as the soil is too poor. Here, more than anywhere else, I realised how much poorer Scotland is than England and how much less populated. Nearer to Dumfries the country looked less desolate; there were more fields and the houses of the tenants looked less poor. We also saw some ruins which made us think of the times of long ago.

We arrived at Dumfries about seven in the evening. Not knowing what to do with myself at so late an hour, I went to a ball which was given because of the races which were being held in Dumfries at the time. I met there all the first families of the district. The Maxwells and the Douglases played the leading role. The public entertainments of that country, as I have already stated, are neither gay nor enchanting, for the stiffness is far too great. Whoever enters the ballroom with people of his party has to keep to them anxiously all through the evening. The ball was thus formed of many different groups. Nobody tried to get near them and they also did not attempt any contact with the others. Nobody can be admitted to these groups who is not a well-known friend or at least introduced by one. New acquaintances are made with the greatest caution. People individually and the groups together are careful to behave

[42] *Dumfries Bridge. Devorgilla's bridge, built in 1250, was in use until 1789. In the foreground are women washing clothes in the river Nith.* Grose

respectably and to maintain the dignity of their circles. There is certainly no more polite and considerate society than the British. One can be certain that as long as one does not dishonour oneself, nobody else will try to, which is not at all a certainty in other countries. To be considered a gentleman, nothing more is needed than to keep to oneself. It is very diverting sometimes to see foreigners trying to do their best to be witty or to enliven company. This country is too sensible to care for such things and these endeavours, instead of bringing one credit, make one considered to be frivolous. To be a social success here one must not amuse and entertain but merely appear sensible. One must try to offend no one. This constant caution and diplomatic attitude to each other is certainly more meant for court balls than ordinary drawing rooms. As it is, people seem cold, distant and stiff, much too serious and too severe. No trace of friendly familiarity, of freedom or outspokenness. Without these attributes gay and intimate conversation is impossible, boredom inevitable. The hours seem to drag on hopelessly. This utter lack of charm or joy not only makes English social life very unpopular but it frightens from it all the young people. For instance, on that particular ball about which I am writing, there were almost twice as many women as men and the few men present did not want to dance. They all preferred to amuse themselves elsewhere, where etiquette and artificiality were not called for.

I attended the races the next day. These take place once a year in every county and aim at the improvement of horse breeding. It is chiefly to them that we owe the beautiful English horses which are so justly famous. The best-known races take place at Newmarket for the South of England, in Doncaster for the North. The races on Ascot Heath near London are also famous, but not so much for the quality of horses as for the amount of stealing and running over of people. These happen frequently owing to the great crowds of Londoners. These incidents are described in newspapers and greatly amuse the public. The prizes for the winning horses are great, from £50 to £2,000. The most famous horses in the races I witnessed were: Monreith, ABC and Fair Helen. At first they were not let out at full speed but, towards the end, the jockeys began to use the whip and spur and the horses raced like grim death. One should see then the fury and despair on the faces of the jockeys whose horses lag behind; hear the loud cries and shouts in honour of the winner! Often a horse which at first was kept behind won, only because it was not ridden too hard at the beginning. Much depends on the cleverness of the jockey who knows best how to ride his horse. A horse which has lost, even if the best bred, often meets a sad fate for it can happen that the owner shoots him dead on the spot. Rum is given to the horses when they reach the goal and they are given a good rest before they are allowed to run again. Both horses and jockeys have a special diet before the races, and the latter arrive at the race-course as white and livid as corpses. The day makes them so anxious beforehand that they neither eat nor sleep and scarcely keep sane; they feel like actors who suffer from stage fright.

Races are very popular in Britain and a foreigner is often astonished that so futile a pastime can awaken such passion and gather such crowds. But it is enough to be present at one to understand and share fully the enthusiasm races awaken. For there is something strangely exciting and beautiful in watching the emulation of animals as noble as horses are and their endeavours to do their best. Every time that I have participated at races I have not only enjoyed them but shared fully the feelings of the crowd. Besides this, lots of business is also connected with racing. The country gentlemen buy and sell, the young people amuse themselves and make friends, women have the opportunity of showing the beauty of their eyes, innkeepers and such like make large profits. Thieves steal, commoners have an exciting sight and the foreigner's curiosity is appeased. Ambition also has something to do there. Those who want to be popular give large dinner parties and dances and thus make friends who will vote for them at the next election. As to the foreigner, the very fact of watching the manifold activities of so varied a crowd is of great interest to him.

The evenings are spent in various social amusements. If not at balls, which as I have said possess little attraction in this country, a man either joins his friends or goes to a hotel. Though, like the English, the Scots are stiff and cold on first acquaintance, the habit of staying together in some hotel during the races makes them more friendly to each other and sometimes even affords the chance of bringing out social talents. Friendships are started mostly after dinner when the tablecloth is removed and the guests remain over their wine. This melts their icy disposition and makes them more generous in their contact with one another. Outspokenness and sincerity at last take the upper hand and everybody begins to relate, with greater frankness than he would have done otherwise, where he has been and what he has been doing. At last they get acquainted with each other, drink to each other's health and become friends. I myself thus made friends with an advocate and this friendship lasted all the way through my stay in Scotland and has been of great use to me. As a rule the character of the Scot is just as serious as that of an Englishman, only the latter is more open. It is better to make friends with him at once and with a Scotsman after a good trial. The cold stiffness of the Scots, which frightens so many away and at first does not give too good an impression of their hospitality, is caused by their caution in not making friends with someone they might not care to admit to intimacy. The Scots are more hospitable than the English. The only difficulty lies in the first steps, but if they once know and like one their devotion and true friendship can be for ever relied upon. They are extremely friendly to foreigners and as a rule less prejudiced against them. They willingly facilitate access to their homes and to their national institutions. The wealthy do this out of vanity, the poorer to satisfy their curiosity, the learned for educational purposes. But many do it also for very noble motives. The accusation of unsociability, which is always made against the English and the Scots, is not by any means caused by the attitude of the Government. This is freer than anywhere else and should only encourage friendliness and open manners. No, this is due partly to their education and old-fashioned habits. The English who spend more time abroad lose these characteristics, but they also lose, alas, the national virtues.

Dumfries is a small Scottish town as it has only 15,000 inhabitants.

These were once famous for their fierce devotion to Calvin's teaching[1] and, because of this, they were persecuted in the reign of James II who wanted to introduce the Church of England all over the country. Many of the richer citizens paid for their conviction with the loss of wealth and life. The cemetery of St. Michael is full of the graves of these martyrs of a misunderstood loyalty. Dumfries lies on the river Nith, which falls into the Solway. I went to see the estuary of that river. The ruins of the castle of Caerlaverock are on the shores. The sea flows so strongly into the Solway twice every twenty-four hours that a rider on the quickest of steeds could not escape from the advancing waves. A swamp called Locher Moss is nearby; old oak trees are dug out from it. Also toll collectors, in order not to delay the lovers, send after them to Gretna Green to collect the taxes.[2]

Scotland's greatest poet was a small farmer, Burns, who died and is buried in Dumfries. He wrote partly in English and partly in the Scottish dialect. His poems were extremely popular both with the poor and with the rich, who like to sing them during festivals. This great poet died as he had lived, in misery. Only after his death did he become famous.[3] Posthumous festivities are now made in his memory, his poor family is

[43] *St Andrew's, Peebles. Medieval churches were designed for Catholic worship. By the nineteenth century many had been replaced on new sites by churches more appropriate for Presbyterian services, in which the emphasis was on the pulpit rather than the altar.* Grose

being assisted by public subscriptions and memorials are being erected to him. I have seen one of them over his tomb. The poet is represented driving a plough his eyes lifted up to heaven. The genius of his poetry is floating above him.

In that same churchyard in which the poet is buried is a tombstone dear to the Polish hearts. Poles taken as prisoners in Spain were billeted to Dumfries for more than a year and a half. They were soldiers from the 2nd Vistula Regiment (Legia Nadwislanski).[4] Taken to Scotland and left free there on parole, they chose Dumfries as their abode. The names of these Poles, as far as I could make out from the extraordinary way in which they were pronounced were: Laszewski Ferdynand, Grabinski Seweryn, Sosnezki Jakob, Regulski Ignacy, Radiewicz Andzej, Straszynski, Dobrzynski, Radlowski and Stokowski. A daughter of a Dumfries merchant fell in love with one of them and he with her. The parents were not opposed to their marriage and the bride was already learning Polish and French. Peace put an end to the imprisonment of the Poles who were allowed to return to their country. The approaching moment of temporary separation was too much for the tender heart of the maiden. Delicate health added to her innate tenderness made her unable to survive the separation. She died of despair. The unhappy lover had the following words written on her grave:

> Anna Grieve, Daughter of James Grieve, Merchant in Dumfries, who died the 11th December 1823, aged 19 years.
>
> EPITAPH
>
> Ta main bienfaisante et cherie,
> D'un exile vint essuyer les pleurs,
> Tu me tint lieu de parent de Patrie,
> Et le même tombeau lorsque tu m'es ravie,
> Renferme nos deux coeurs.

Several persons told me this same identical story. The very tombstone, the only one in a foreign language, spoke for itself. Our countryman is said to be in mourning for her and often to be seen by her grave.

Years have already gone by since the Poles left Dumfries and yet their memory lived there. Having learned that some of them had lived in their houses and were considered almost as members of their own families, the presents the men had given them, though small and of little value, were kept with loving care. Most of these presents were made by the men themselves, for they tried to shorten the time of their exile by manual work. I saw one of these keepsakes, an unfinished but beautiful drawing

[44] *'Ossian Singing' by Alexander Runciman. In 1761 Sir James Clerk of Penicuik designed a Palladian house to replace the family home, Newbiggin. He commissioned Runciman to decorate the ceiling of the drawing room with scenes from the life of Ossian. 'Ossian Singing' was the centrepiece. Completed in 1772, the paintings were destroyed in the fire of 1899.*

of the Virgin, from which one could judge at once that the one who drew it knew what he was about. The inhabitants, seeing that I was interested in every detail concerning my countrymen, described them to me, their posture and looks, their hair and complexion, their manners and habits, as if they wanted me to go and track them down for them in Poland. They even repeated some of their jokes and could not emphasise enough the pleasure their manners and their charm gave them. They all said that these Poles had been perfect gentlemen. I was pleased to hear so much praise of my countrymen and to realise that not only happiness, but also misfortune, find faithful and devoted friends. For all these kind Scots had liked the Polish soldiers so much that they had accepted them to their family life and lent them money when in need. I made the acquaintance of one family who, at their own risk, helped one of them to escape from imprisonment.

We returned to Edinburgh through Peebles and Penicuik. Peebles is a tiny place on a plain by the river Tweed. There the Scottish Kings stayed sometimes to hunt and many of the Scottish nobles had their palaces which up to this day are called by their names. This town could never flourish because of the constant invasions of the English, who reduced it to ruins several times and looted and plundered it frequently. The ancient parish church is said to be one of the oldest in Scotland; it dates from 1190. The army of Cromwell, which did not respect ancient remains, turned it into stables and it has been left desolate ever since. Penicuik is a small place memorable only for the fact that the French prisoners-of-war among whom were many Poles were kept there. I have seen barracks erected for them by the Government, in which however they did not live, for peace came and they were set free. These barracks are called even now the 'Depot'. I have been told that the prisoners were looked after with great solicitude and had the best of everything. They were so numerous that their maintenance is said to have cost £1,000,000.

Close to Penicuik on the river Esk is the palace of the Clerk family. All lovers of antiquity and poetry visit this palace to see the hall which bears the name of: Ossian's Hall. The ceiling and the walls are covered with paintings, representing scenes from the Bard's ballads. They are the work of Runciman, who is considered to be one of the best Scottish painters. The paintings however are not good enough to speak for themselves. To understand them, one must bear Ossian's poems well in mind.[5]

XIII

*Country Life. A Stay in the Country. The Land Tax. Clubs
and Debates of Landowners. Body Snatching. Schools.
Roads. Visits to Country Neighbours. Serfdom. The Eolian
Harp. How Sunday is Spent*

IT is easier to become acquainted with the country life of the Scots than
with that of the English, for the latter are less hospitable. Nevertheless,
it is not easy for a foreigner to get to know them in their everyday home
life. The landowners are much more sociable when they are in town,
and it is easier to become friendly there. Their country houses are meant
for quiet family happiness and only a very few chosen friends are
admitted to participate in it. My friendship with two families whose
country homes were only a few miles away from Edinburgh allowed me
to have an inkling of that life and gave me the necessary opportunity.
With them and with their friends I did my best to learn as much as
possible about the ways of living, the spirit and the ways of thinking of
the Scottish gentry. They are a class between the merchants and the
aristocrats. These visits gave me such pleasure and taught me so much
that, in gratitude to those to whom I owe all this, I feel bound to mention
their names here. They certainly deserve to remain for ever in my
memory. Both my friends were Writers to the Signet; their names were
Young and Aytoun and they were both heads of families. I hope my
readers will forgive me for introducing my private affairs and my
personal friends, for this chapter, the most intimate, is going to deal with
them. But perhaps it is better so, as there are subjects impossible to be
written about and not even touched upon without a certain amount of
frankness and a personal touch in them. *Procul este Profani!*

The gentlemen Young and Aytoun were approximately of the same
age, well over fifty. I have always liked to do with people of that age.
They are bound to be experienced and their companionship an enlightened

[45] *Edinburgh from Corstorphine. Though roads in Scotland were improving by the late eighteenth century, many were still unmetalled. The Union Canal, which linked Edinburgh to the Forth–Clyde Canal in 1822, took passengers as well as goods off the roads.* Ewbank

one. The friendship of such men gains one's respect, for they have public esteem and public opinion behind them. Foreigners should always try to form such connections. They should be careful with the young and certainly have nothing to do with the striplings.

The country seat of my first friend was called Harburn and of the second Muiriston. Harburn was my frequent haunt. I often spent more than a week at a time there and had the possibility of becoming well acquainted with the peacefulness and freedom of Scottish country life. Country houses are arranged in exactly the same way as English ones. The same architecture, the same interior decoration, the same kinds of garden except that here, because of the hilly countryside, they are even more spacious.

The Harburn house was situated on the slope of a hill, the farms were some distance off and behind them lay the kitchen garden, divided by a pond and some trees. The park spread all around. It contained fields, pastures on which sheep grazed, sometimes even cattle could be met here and it all looked like some pleasant wood. An English park must always have some water in its precincts: Harburn was made more pleasant not only by a little river but also by some ponds formed out of its overflow. Near these ponds, where the banks were steep, several caverns and grottos had been arranged for those who liked solitude. They were artistically decorated with the bark of trees and moss. On the ponds we rowed and fished with rods and nets. Shooting or fishing, riding on horseback or walking in the fields were the pleasures offered to the guests in the Scottish houses. My host did not like going on horseback but he was indefatigable in walking. He often took me with him to have a look at the fields and I always enjoyed it thoroughly. He showed me everything, his steading and his park. He told me his adventures, everything he had done and was proposing to do on his estate, what his income was, and what gave him most profit. He made me think of our typical Polish landowner who will enlarge on: what his orchards bring him; what profit he has from his bees; what he gets for the wool of his sheep; how many lambs he has in spring; what his fields and meadows yield and how he gathers it all into his barns. I was not bored in the least. I fully understood that delight felt by every landowner at sight of the things he had created. Besides, I liked being introduced to the intricacies of farming in Scotland; I could observe the improvements and calculate the expenses. Farming with rich people, as far as I could make out, does not bring monetary profits; it only provides a luxurious life. Wide and fertile fields are turned without qualms into deer forests. No expense is spared to make them more beautiful, ponds are constructed and streams diverted so as to improve the view. Many, having reached a certain degree of wealth, think only of spending not of saving. Mr Young has a special passion for planting trees. Cicero considers this passion as part of old age. Mr Young had nurseries planted, replanted and grafted and he reminded me of a countryman of mine. Old age instinctively looks for means of outliving itself. When no other means of perpetuating the names and deeds of its life are possible, it takes to planting trees. In this way at least some sign of the past existence will remain in the world of the living. This is also why old people invariably live in the country. It gives them *sollicitae jucunda oblivia vitae* for which they would look in vain in the turmoil of the city. I also remarked another trait in the character of my friend; a wonderful trait, not often met in people of other countries, and sometimes I even think that perhaps only a few Britons possess it. Mr Young loved everything living. He flew into a temper if he saw anything damaging a tree or torturing an animal. Martin[1] would have greeted him as best of friends. He forbade all shooting in his park: woodcocks, wild duck and thrushes lived there in all security. Only nightingales did not sing over his well-

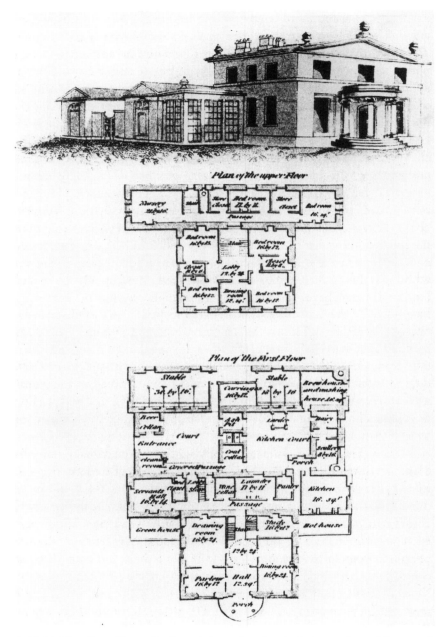

[46] 'A Plan for a House for Proprietors of moderate fortune who reside on and cultivate their own Estate.' Advertised in 1814, it would have cost about £3,000 to build and was designed for people like Lach-Szyrma's friends, Young of Harburn and Aytoun of Muiriston. They were both Writers to the Signet as well as landowners and would have had flats in Edinburgh.

shaded ponds, for there are none in Scotland. Even the fox which remorselessly strangled his hens had asylum in the park. I have witnessed once how Mr Young stopped a hunt and threatened them with legal proceedings if they dared disturb the quietude of his forests, spoil the green turf of his meadows and ruin his carefully kept paths. It made me feel a better man to be honoured by the friendship of such a man. What indeed can bring greater joy than the society of such people? Such wonderful feelings are by no means exclusive among the higher classes; they are also to be met among the poor. They are the result of philosophy applied to life, especially of Cumberland's teachings[2] about kindness and the unselfishness which causes that kindness. Hutcheson[3] again wrote about kindness deriving from moral motives, and Smith about feelings arising from a mysterious sympathy, which makes man put himself in the place of others and never do to them as he would not have done to himself. The popularisation of these great ideas combined with the religious ideals of this nation has made its people kind even to the humblest of living beings. This is the source of the philanthropic disposition of the British and of their laws forbidding the torturing of animals, to which in wilder and less cultured countries no attention is being paid. Often one sees a barbarous crowd laugh at the sight of a flogged horse or cow. The most sensitive will say perhaps 'Poor thing!' but in Britain the least tender of men will cry: 'For shame!' and will turn with fury on the tormentors. Thus one great human idea, if adopted by the hearts of other men, surrounds the forehead of humanity with a real wreath of glory.

In these parts of Scotland the soil is not fertile as a rule. Fields are covered with stones, rushes, heather and the poorest quality of grass. Most of the country is waste moorland. Mr Young has cultivated everything good that I saw at Harburn with infinite care and at great expense. Fields, which had lain fallow for centuries, now yield oats, barley and even wheat. At a small distance from the house are ancient Roman remains.[4] They form a quadrangle and in the praetorium many Roman coins have been found. It is difficult to understand what the Romans could have wanted to find in such an empty country. Their love of conquest must indeed have been immeasurable if they tried to subdue even such a country, out of which they really could have no profit whatever.

I was very much interested in the taxation system and wanted to find out all about it. Mr Young enlightened me by telling that one pays a twofold tax in Scotland, according to a twofold valuation of the estates, and that one must be sure to remember it and take this into consideration when buying. He did not think that taxation was high and indeed it was much lower than in England. He paid nothing from his estates for, during the last war when the Government needed money, he redeemed it in perpetuity. Thanks to this, Mr Young lives now on his seven square miles like an independent prince, having all the protection of the law and paying nothing, not even having to maintain a private militia as the German princes have to. Economists find redeeming in perpetuity to be the best means of getting rid of national debts; all other ways seem inefficient. Rich people like to buy land for it is taxed the least; capitalists and merchants lose in speculations, but land invariably brings the small income it is meant to give. The heaviest taxes apply to industry and to all luxuries. The first needs no encouragement in Britain and the second has no difficulty in paying.

I have accompanied Mr Young to four country meetings. The first was a parish meeting and matters concerning the church were discussed, the second was about the village school, the third about roads and the fourth a society assembly, a dinner party given once a month. Neighbours meet then for pleasure and to discuss affairs concerning them all. These dinners are very gay, toasts are drunk to the health of friends; if a foreigner is present, his health is drunk and that of his country. In doing so the Scots consider that they are being most civil, for in their conception a man cannot be separated from his country.

During the meeting concerning the parish, complaints were made against Edinburgh University for sending frequently for bodies to be exhumed in country churchyards for the use of medical students.[5] To protect the dead against such profanation, many people thought guards should be appointed for the cemeteries. But the plan was rejected, for one guardian would have to be controlled by another, and even then the arrangement might not prove satisfactory. Body snatching occurs frequently in Scotland and England. There are men who specialise in this sinister business and earn their living this way. They are called resurrection men. Those caught are sent like criminals to Botany Bay. But the severity of the punishment does not stop the procedure, for money is a great attraction. The Medical Faculty is in great need of bodies as it is allowed to take for anatomical purposes only the corpses of those who are hanged and very few are hanged nowadays, for civilisation destroys crime. There is no custom of selling one's body to the University during one's life.

Debates also went on about whether the ringing of bells every evening and every morning, as is the centuries-old custom, was really necessary. As no one was found who could explain what was the use of this, it was decided that the bells should be rung only on Sundays. The pay of the bellringer, who would have less to do there, was diminished. However, it was deemed necessary to awaken the inhabitants every morning by the beating of a drum.

At the next meeting the plan of building a second school was discussed. A parish school is attached to every church in Scotland. Reading, writing, arithmetic, Latin, geometry and elementary physics are taught. This would be considered a very good education indeed in our country; but not so in Scotland, where the poorest crofter craves for higher standards. Many become ministers later on, for the upper classes find it impossible to exist on the salary, which is much less than in England. To those who choose industry, the knowledge of geometry and physics is of great use. Others become bookkeepers in mercantile houses. In the parish schools the Bible is the foundation of the education. The young draw from it all the principles of future conduct in life; they imbibe moral ideals, which they generally hold sacred for their remaining

[47] *'Robert Knox demonstrating in Anatomy'. Knox was a gifted teacher whose extra mural classes in anatomy attracted large numbers. In 1829 he was implicated in the Burke and Hare body-snatching affair and had to leave Edinburgh. He continued his teaching career in London.*

years. A workman goes and returns from work, Bible in hand. The sacred book holds the place of honour in the cottages of crofters and is handed down from generation to generation. The most important events of family history, the births, the marriages and the burials, are recorded there. Through constant reading of the Bible the Scots so improve their minds that there is no subject on which the simplest man would not have sound judgement. It becomes for them the source of their virtues and of their happy family life. All crimes and misfortunes can be put down to the contempt of the Bible.

The third meeting dealt with the roads. There are three kinds of roads in Scotland: private, looked after by the owner of the land, parish roads, for which the whole parish is responsible, and county roads. Tolls are levied on these on all travellers, the proceeds of which are sufficient not only for the upkeep of the roads and bridges but also for their embellishment.

One of the most pleasant visits I made in the neighbourhood was to Lord Hermand. He was a hale old man of ninety, in full possession of his faculties. Having retired from the office of Lord Chief Justice in Edinburgh, he had devoted himself like a second Cincinnatus[6] to the cultivation of his land. In his house I met a certain Mr F. who had been to America in search of fortune, and having failed to find it there, had published on his return a book on his travels. He describes with enthusiasm the falls of Niagara which are said to be the largest in the world. But he certainly had more imagination than learning. He was in love with himself, as so often happens to those who are not sufficiently educated, and was most amazingly credulous. He talked awful rubbish. I remember him saying that one of his friends was about to publish a book in which he would prove that our planet is all empty inside, like a barrel, and is inhabited by living beings. The entrances to this subterranean world are to be found at both poles. On hearing that nonsense, Lord H. remarked: 'This should be both a warning to the Captains Franklin and Scoresby,[7] lest during their exploration to the pole they should fall into that cavern where the sun and the stars would be of no use and where lamps probably have not been invented'. I knew Captain Scoresby personally; he was then preparing for a second expedition to the polar regions and had just published an account of whaling on the coasts of Greenland.

From Harburn I went to Muiriston, the estate of Mr Aytoun. I spent four days there and enjoyed true Scottish hospitality. We talked in the evenings and spent the days walking or riding in the beautiful country-

[48] *The Last Sitting of the Old Court of Session, 1808. Lach-Szyrma's friend Lord Hermand is the bottom left figure in Kay's picture.*

side. It was the time of the sowing; all the agricultural work is done by hired labourers and serfdom is unknown. Mr Aytoun strongly condemned the system. 'It was once prevalent in Scotland,' he said; 'but was abolished to the great benefit of the country.' It still persists in many parts of Ireland,[8] which accounts for the extreme poverty there. A kind of serfdom similar to that existing in Poland was in the English mines. When a mine was sold, the miners were sold with it. Parliament, moved by compassion, abolished this, notwithstanding the resistance of the owners, who threatened that England would be left without fuel, for the toil of the miner is so arduous, that nobody would do it of their own free will. This however did not prove true; enough miners were found when good wages were offered to them. Formerly they used to be the most wretched class of people, but they are quite prosperous now, and fewer men are needed to produce the same amount of coal.

Once, when returning from a walk with Mr Aytoun and walking at dusk through a shaded valley, I heard some quaint music, which I took at first for some old ballad being played on the piano. But coming nearer, I became aware that this was the sound of an instrument unknown to me. The music was wild and wistful, soft and with a special rhythm; it had a curious effect on my nerves. Because of its monotony and constant repetitions it seemed not to be moved by human hand. And in fact so it was. It was the Eolian harp, which I had never heard and had said as much when the instrument was once discussed in my presence. Now this pleasant surprise had been prepared for me, while we went for a walk. Twilight had been chosen, for at that time people are most sensitive to music. What culture, what hospitality! Even the delights of the guest's imagination are taken care of! But this is usual for the Scots and nowhere in the world are the very thoughts of the guest divined as they are here. The Eolian harp is made of two parallel planks fastened together; one of them has a sort of cavity as the fiddle has, to increase the sound. Eight or ten sheep gut cords are stretched in a row between them, near to one another. The instrument is put outside when the wind blows. In Scotland, where the windows don't open as in Poland but are pushed up, the Eolian harp is put under the lower half of the window. The wind touching it awakes a variety of tunes. When the wind is light, all the chords resound in the lowest of notes but with the increasing of the wind the higher tunes call out. Kircheris is said to have discovered the Eolian harp, though Eustachius[9] had already mentioned that the wind passing through stretched strings plays beautifully.

The next day was a Sunday. In no other country, not even in England, is that day so strictly observed. We went on foot to the nearest church at Midcalder and had only to cross a field. I was happier than I had ever been for quite some time. I kept on thinking of the days when like today, surrounded by a happy family, I used to cross a Polish field to another church near the home of my parents. There is some special charm in going to church like this which is never felt when going to church in town. Sundays are extraordinarily quiet in Scotland; it almost seems that with man having stopped his activities, nature breathed more freely. Flowers seemed to smile brighter, grasshoppers chirp louder on the meadows, and one watches with pleasure groups of country people in their Sunday best walking towards the church. The feeling of solemnity reaches its highest when the clear voice of the bell is heard ringing through the pure air and the great silence of Sunday. The impressions awakened are so strong, that even an unbeliever would enter the church with other feelings than in town. This is probably the reason why one meets more real piety in the country and more ardent belief in the humble little country churches than in the proud cathedrals of this world. The church in Midcalder is memorable in history. It is here that

John Knox first preached Calvin's doctrine and was heard to pronounce the sacred words in the usual way: 'Take, eat, this is not my Body; take and drink, this is not my Blood, but do this in Remembrance of Me'.[10]

We returned as we went, on foot, and spent the rest of the day very quietly, making no noise and indulging in no kind of frivolity. In the evening the whole family gathered in the drawing room, where Mrs Aytoun said the family prayers. At first she read a sermon from a special book on the duty of observing the Sunday. Then she added a chapter from the Holy Bible. She finished with the usual evening prayers. This custom, which had been universal in Scotland, is still observed in many families, even the richest. No exceptions are made for guests. I was very happy indeed to have witnessed this; had I not stayed here during a Sunday, I might never have come across such a beautiful feature of the Scots. Seldom too do people begin or finish their meals without praying. I was present once when a boy of eight said his prayers aloud in front of a numerous company before breakfast; he did it with the seriousness and dignity of a grown-up person. It took place on board a ship in the open sea; everybody able to feel acknowledged that it was an incomparable and edifying sight. I thought that I would have liked to watch the expression of an Atheist just then.

When I was leaving Scotland, Mrs Aytoun deigned to augment my English library by giving me the very same book of prayers which she had used during my stay with them. Happy the country in which the fair sex want to be remembered by that lofty performance of their household duties. The book is called: *Sermons on the doctrines and duties of Christianity.* The fact that the copy I have is already the 34th edition proves best how popular it must be in Scotland.

XIV

*An Excursion to Hamilton. The Banks of the Clyde. The
Waterfalls. The River Mouse. Lanark. Hunting*

IN the pleasant company of Mr.Young, we visited the charming
neighbourhood of Harburn and the banks of the Clyde. Mr. Young acted
as guide, having brought me on purpose not to let me leave Scotland
without having seen what he called the 'Scottish Paradise'. And indeed,
nobody sensitive to beauty can omit seeing these places.

We started by visiting Hamilton, the seat of the dukes of Hamilton.
The little town of 7000 inhabitants lies on the Clyde and the Avon.
Travellers come to see the rich picture gallery of the Palace. I spent
nearly three hours there, only to feel what a superficial idea I had of the
treasures amassed by the present Duke, a great connoisseur, and his
ancestors, who spent fortunes on pictures. There is no bigger gallery in
Scotland and England possesses few that can equal it.

It is hopeless to try and describe here even the most outstanding of
these treasures. Many cannot be appreciated because of the lack of light.
The rooms are very dark and, though wide, they look much more like the
corridors of a gloomy convent than a picture gallery. The whole place is
not fit to be the seat of the first peer of Scotland and yet it is called 'the
palace'. The Duke himself comes here seldom (why should he!) and
spends most of his time abroad. The marshal who showed us round
bemoaned the fact and, when we suggested that the Duke certainly
needed a new home, he answered: 'The Duke would not build a new
home, for it would not be called a palace by the people'. The name of
'Palace' is in Scotland the privilege of only a very few places.[1]

In one of the rooms I saw a gigantic bust of the Empress Catherine of
Russia. This is in memory of the time when the Duke acted as envoy to
the Court of St. Petersburg. He visited the whole of Poland at that time
and made friends with many Polish families, became so intimate with

[49] *'The Falls of Clyde: Cora Linn', by Jacob More (1740-93). In 1784 David Dale and Richard Arkwright established their textile mills at what became New Lanark, half a mile down stream from the Falls. The Clyde remained the main source of power until the twentieth century.*

some of them that the friendship is being kept up even now. He is one of those nobles who invariably extend their hospitality and their protection to all Poles travelling in Scotland.

On leaving Hamilton we travelled a road as wide and as even as a table. To the left spread the park with its grazing cattle and sheep. Each acre yields £36 a year to the Duke. To the right lay the castle called Chatelherault,[2] in honour of the estates once possessed by the Hamiltons in France. Not far from there I was shown a cottage, the tenant of which had the misfortune of falling into disgrace with the Duke of Hamilton, the uncle of the present one. The angry Duke ordered summons to be taken out against the man. The summons began with the words: 'We, the Duke of Hamilton and Brandon, Marquis of Douglas etc hereby summon you to appear before our Court'. The tenant answered: 'I, XX, tenant of the farm XX, which belongs to the Duke, have paid my rent on time and owe you nothing, therefore I will not appear before your Court'. In Scotland, as well as in England, the master and the servant are equal in the eyes of the law. This principle was the most powerful factor in checking the uncontrolled passions of the powerful. We followed the most beautiful road to Lanark along the steep banks of the Clyde, which is seldom quiet and is mostly covered with foam. In some places it overflows and makes lakes of shining water. Woods, meadows and country houses with beautifully kept parks gave great charm to all the countryside. In a sudden transport of admiration for what he saw, Mr Young exclaimed: 'This is a true Scottish Switzerland'. 'Yes indeed,' I answered, 'but how much happier than the real Switzerland! Avalanches do not threaten the fertile fields, ugly goitres do not spoil the beauty of the women and half witted cretins do not surround the carriages, asking for alms.' The greatness of nature is often a stepmother to man, often he is happier in mediocrity. Everything here is pleasant to the eye and to the feelings. I think it is quite right to call these districts the Eden of Caledonia. The county of Lanark is the most populated part of Scotland.

Thus discussing, we entered a dense forest. We became aware suddenly of a dull noise which went on increasing. An inscription on a signboard informed us that this was the roar of the waterfall. We stopped and followed a slippery path down the Clyde. After about 200 steps we came in sight of that miracle of nature. The foaming water, like a huge white sheet of snow, fell into the river below, which seemed to boil all over. Some delighted traveller is said to have exclaimed; 'If I put my hand in, it would get scalded!' The effect cannot be expressed more accurately. I myself had the impression of watching boiling water. The eternally green vegetation puts into relief the white foam. The wind was blowing from the opposite direction and whipped the falling waters into a sort of mist, in which two rainbows were seen. These rainbows moved and changed their shape according to the direction in which the foam was blown.

Having looked at this waterfall, we went to see the two others. The Corra Linn is the most striking. The Clyde rushes down over an 84-feet drop, breaking as it falls on three ledges hidden in the rocks. We stopped in a place from which we had a most marvellous view of the whole gorge. Below, on the summit of a rock, were the ruins of Corra Castle. There is a curious little summerhouse over the waterfalls, with a mirror so arranged that when you look into it you have the impression of the whole waterfall coming and pouring right over you. The power of the falling water is so great that, putting one's hand against the rocks, one can feel them tremble with the shock.

The lowest fall is called Bonnington which is only 30 feet high but is considered to be the most beautiful. It reminded me of the falls of the Rhine in Schaffhausen, likewise divided into two by a tiny island. But the banks of the Clyde are infinitely more beautiful than those of the Rhine if, of course, one's idea of beauty is of cliffs, rocks, caverns, ruins and trees hanging down from cliffs with ivy and moss covering the whole. Such are the banks of the Clyde.

On our way back we saw another tiny waterfall only four feet high in Dundaff Linn. This waterfall is famous because of the curious habits of the trout that live in the Clyde in great quantities. These fish are said to jump up that waterfall. I only give here what has been related to me, for I have not witnessed these wonderful leaps myself.

Going to Lanark, we followed the new road made at great expense in the rocky Cartland Craigs. The route has been planned so that the travellers might have the most enchanting views and indeed they are marvellous. Culture and taste are necessary to do such things; a nation which was only rich would not have thought of such things. At that time a bridge was in building which was to unite the two hilltops and one of them was 410 feet high. The river Mouse flows in the valley below, so called because she hides and appears from among the rocks as if she were a real mouse. It flows deepest of all Scottish rivers and none, except perhaps some in the Alps, has steeper banks. Looking down from the bridge, one can scarcely perceive it and, though the roar of the water upon the boulders must be tremendous, nothing of it is heard. On the spot where it falls into the Clyde is a stone bridge of great age. Some say that the Picts, the primeval inhabitants of Scotland, built it and others that it was the Romans. In one of the numerous caverns seen in the cliffs Wallace, the ancient hero, is said to have sheltered.

Thence we proceeded to Lanark where we dined at an inn which owes its prosperity to the waterfalls. A thick volume in which the guests write their remarks attracted our attention. The following rhymes were found there which amused us greatly:

> What fools are mankind,
> And how strangely inclin'd,
> To come from all places
> With horses and chaises,
> By day and by dark
> To visit Lanark!
> For good folks, after all,

What is a waterfall?
It comes roaring and grumbling,
And leaping and tumbling,
And hopping and skipping,
And foaming and dripping,
And struggling and toiling,
And bubbling and boiling,
And beating and jumping
And bellowing and thumping,
I've much more to say
On both Linn and Binniton
But the trunks are tied on
And I must be gone.

The town of Lanark is said to have arisen on the site of a Roman settlement called Colonia. Many European towns have thus started from Roman encampments. Lanark has 6000 inhabitants and is divided into new Lanark and old. Cotton establishments are situated in the new and belong to the famous philanthropist Owen.[3] 1500 people were employed there at the time, mostly children, who are received there at the age of eight. Besides their wages they are educated according to

[50] *New Lanark c. 1817. By 1798, when Robert Owen became the manager of the cotton mills, New Lanark had become the largest industrial village in Scotland. In the foreground of the picture are members of the town band.*

Owen's plan. It was getting late and this prevented me visiting these most interesting factories. The owner is a real Scottish Fellenberg.[4] He was not at Lanark at the time, but later on I had the happiness of making his acquaintance in London, and I will relate all about this in due time.

(Extract from Volume III:) –
In the house of Mr Aytoun (in London) I had the occasion of meeting Robert Owen, about whose exemplary factories I have been speaking in Volume II. I have spent many happy moments discussing with him how to make humanity happier. His daring plans can apparently not be executed but he has represented them to the Emperor Alexander himself. Owen thinks that centuries of barbarism and the power of the rich have turned humanity from the roads it was meant to follow. He starts from the principle that all men are equal and advises that all should be given equal chances and opportunities. He thinks that governments should divide the population into communities composed of about 700 to 800 families, for greater communities are more liable to vices and bad habits. Any Government could arrange such communities and the form of Government does not really matter. Each community would have to live in special buildings, 'pallelograms' he called them. For easier communication they would be one alongside the other. They would possess their own land, factories, schools and church so as to be made entirely self-sufficient. Everything there would belong to everybody in common. Only like this can robbery, crime and misery be wiped out. As to the severe punishments for stealing which are applied in England, Owen, like Thomas More,[5] thinks that they are neither just nor fair, for robbery, even the greatest, is not such a crime as would merit the death penalty. The fear of punishments cannot stop those who have no other means of living. England, here, imitates the bad school-teachers who, instead of educating, flog their pupils. It is better not to punish but to find means of preventing crime. Owen is full of all sorts of plans: that work houses should be founded, where employment and pay could be always had; that food should be cheaper etc. As to education, he thinks that no rewards should be given in schools. The spirit of emulation fostered by the pedagogues only kills the purer motives. Scientists should not work to outdo each other, but only for the love of truth and learning. He advises the teachers to be kind and even friendly to their pupils, to have their trust and be asked as many questions as possible. He advises a lot of freedom to be given in teaching and learning. All his ideas about teaching and education are well thought of

[51] *Dancing class, New Lanark. Children employed in Dale's Mills were given an hour and a half's schooling at the end of their working day. When Robert Owen became manager and then partner in the firm, he was able to develop his ideas about education and, in 1817, opened the first day school for infants in Scotland. He employed music and dancing masters as well as teachers of the three Rs. In 1816 the Institution for the Formation of Character, where the dancing class is taking place, was founded to provide a dance hall, library, reading room and place of worship for the families working in the Mills. Between 1815 and 1825, 20,000 people visited New Lanark, and Owen's attempt to introduce humane industrialisation influenced employers throughout Europe.*

and he is certain that they would bring happiness to humanity. Once, talking about all this, he exclaimed with great ardour that if four or five thousand people agreed to help him wholeheartedly in working out his reforms of the world, such great changes would follow in Europe that even Napoleon, with all his power, could not have done so much. In a country like England, the existence of which is in many ways artificial and where there are such lots of ancient traditions and laws, Owen was bound to meet great and insurmountable obstacles. Nevertheless his ideas did a lot to ease the fate of the workmen and charitable societies and new schools were formed. Owen went to America where he was received by the President with the greatest enthusiasm. He funded there a community called Harmony, which was to be the first example of his ideas put into practice. At present (1828) he is in Mexico where he has also been received with the greatest enthusiasm. Owen is of middle

[52] *'The Knight of the Turf'. Lach-Szyrma met a large hunt on his return journey to Edinburgh. Kay's portrait is of Sir Archibald Hope of Pinkie who was President of the Caledonian Hunt at the end of the eighteenth century.*

height, swarthy, and now about 48. He is neither too lively nor too slow. He speaks with difficulty and with a strong Scottish accent being, of course, a Scotsman. He was a simple workman who made his fortune and increased it with marriage. He gives all his time at present to the good of humanity and no difficulty can stop him. He only lives with the hope that his ideas may one day be realised. He is anxious to tell everybody about his plans and is very glad when these are criticised, for only in answering criticism is he able to refute it and explain at full length what he means. He bases everything on principles.

On our return to Edinburgh we met a big hunt. Hunting begins in autumn when harvest is finished and lasts all through the winter. As nothing in this country can exist without a club, so hunting also has a special club, the Caledonian Hunt. The first families of the country belong there, mostly young people though the elderly hunt too and even with great enthusiasm. Hounds, servants and a few horses for common use are maintained by subscriptions. Horses used for hunting are of a special breed; bigger and stronger than the usual riding horses, they have long necks and dilated nostrils which prevent them from getting winded. The hunting men wear a special attire, pink coat, white breeches, top hats, a coloured kerchief, and a hunting crop with a long lash to whip the hounds. Whoever is first in at the death, is awarded the fox's brush. This he hangs on his horse's head and thus returns to town in triumph. The fox itself is thrown to the hounds to break up. The huntsman employed by the hunt throws the fox, already dead; up into the air and the hounds then tear it to pieces. The hounds are trained to follow only the scent of the fox. Should one chase a hare, he is then shot on the spot. Hare hunting also has its rules but the principal quarry is the fox. The hunt we met consisted of about 50 pink coats, not counting the servants. Under the circumstances, these are considered as nobodies. Though there are laws for its preservation, game is very scarce. There are too many people and too few forests. If five foxes are killed, this is considered a good day, but often nothing is found. Even so, the chase itself is amusing and many leave home for three weeks to spend them hunting. Compensation for lack of success in the field is found in the inn over good wine. If the day had been a blank one, stories of other hunts provide ample topics. Who broke his neck and when, who jumped over a ditch, hedge or wall, who hurt his leg, all is carefully recorded and remembered in the annals of the hunts. Many might be surprised that so serious a nation should occupy itself with such trifles. Nevertheless so it is, and he who today blows his horn to the hounds, tomorrow will be speaking in the Courts of Law, or decide the fate of Britain and other nations in Parliament. It is a great art to be able to combine business and pleasure, duty and amusement. This is necessary in order to be better able to accomplish everything required from a good citizen.

XV

Excursions to the Highlands. The Canals. Glasgow Green.
The Monuments of Nelson and Moore. The Handicrafts.
The University. Hunter's Museum. The Observatory.
Anderson's Institute. The Lunatic Asylum. The Dairy

A traveller through Scotland who would not trouble to see the Highlands would be devoid of all sentiment or curiosity. I visited them in my
last year in Scotland, when I was already well acquainted with the
population, the history and the literature of the country. Beauty of
nature though in itself enough to affect us is greatly intensified if we
know the history and the legends attached to the places we see. I visited
the Highlands with a book of history in my hand, or perhaps rather in
my memory. For books would be too heavy to carry about in the country
where one must perform most of the excursions on foot. Those who start
on this expedition generally begin in Glasgow. I have been there twice
before but I have no more to say about the country I have been passing
through except that it seemed fertile and that Midlothian is certainly a
well-cultivated shire. This time I went through the Union Canal and the
Great Canal,[1] which certainly deserves this name as it unites two seas,
the Atlantic and the German Ocean. The Union Canal from Edinburgh
to Falkirk had been recently finished and curiosity made people want to
travel by it. This way of navigation is not a hasty one. Steam not being
used for small boats as yet, they are towed by horses and the sails of
course can only be made use of when the wind is propitious. But the
beautiful sights and sometimes gay company do not leave time for
boredom. The very meditation on what an extraordinary thing such as a
canal is should be enough to occupy an intelligent traveller, for in the
building of this canal nothing could daunt the human brain. Hills have
been flattened and plains made into hills. Near Edinburgh the canal
passed from hill to hill over arches fifty feet high. A stream flowed far

[53] *Port Hopetoun. The Forth–Clyde Canal, completed in 1790, terminated at Bo'ness, nearly twenty miles west of Edinburgh. The Union Canal brought it to Port Hopetoun, at Fountainbridge. The planned extension to Leith, which would have taken it through Princes Street Gardens, was never made.* Ewbank

below, a high road ran beside it and farther off a village lay. It really is an astounding thing for the people driving on the high road to watch ships passing overhead, or a river in the air crossing a river on land. But in this country no marvels are impossible and one can observe extraordinary things at every step. The Great Canal has more wonderful sights consisting of several such rivers in the air which are called aqueducts. The biggest is two miles from Glasgow and is called the Kelvin. It is held up by four arches and passes through a valley 400 feet wide; in some places it is elevated to as much as 80 feet. A downpour, to my great dismay, prevented me from having a look at these wonderful achievements and only from time to time was one able to peep out of the boat. The mechanism of the locks and the drawbridges is very noteworthy. There are 20 locks on the eastern side of the canal and 19 in the western. The water from six lakes supplies them. The greatest height of the canal is 156 feet above sea level. This huge and tremendous enterprise did not cost the government a penny; it has been entirely carried out by citizens who thought it of use to trade and have paid its cost, divided into shares.

[54] *The Lady Chapel, Glasgow Cathedral. Little has survived of the church consecrated in 1197 but the magnificent crypt of the Cathedral dates back to 1238. The Lady Chapel was added c. 1500. When it was threatened by a mob during the Reformation, the people of Glasgow protected the fabric of the Cathedral.* G. M. Kemp

The Union canal cost £24,500 and the Great Canal £421,525. When the canal was finished in 1790, the Glasgow Town Council caused a barrel of water to be brought from the Forth and poured into the Clyde, thus uniting the German Ocean to the Atlantic. This canal is 35 miles long. It is a wonderful thing to be able to tow ships from sea to sea through land and yet posterity will regard it as something quite usual. The income from toll and tax is quite sufficient to cover all the expenses of repairs, which amount to £1500, and the shareholders enjoy quite a large income.

There was a time when the duty on corn from Poland was an important source of income but nowadays only hemp and timber are imported; the latter is considered much better than the American or the Norwegian. Polish timber is harder, so wherever buildings are meant to last ours is used. Masts for ships are the most paying. Specialists are sent out to Poland and they know so much about wood that they are able to say at once which tree will be healthy and ready for felling and, marking the trunks, they buy the timber which still grows in the forests. Wood is so expensive here that it is not sold in blocks but measured and sold by feet. It is not used as fuel, for coal is sufficient, but only for building. Mahogany is much in vogue for furniture.

Glasgow is the most populous city in Scotland: it has more than 160,000 inhabitants, and in the year 1740 it had only 17,000.[2] It competes through trade and handicraft with Manchester and Liverpool. The Clyde passing through the middle of town facilitates trade with all parts of the world but, though navigation on the river is a source of wealth, the floods it causes often destroy the lower parts of the city. The misery and poverty thus inflicted become at times very distressing. In 1817 poverty was much increased because of the introduction of many machines into the handicraft establishments: this deprived more than 6,000 families of their livelihood. The Government, anxious to heal the evil, employed many hands in mending roads and in making walks in parks. Those who remained unemployed were taken care of by the charitable societies and by voluntary contributions.

Though Glasgow has not such a splendid exterior as Edinburgh, it possesses numerous impressive streets and remarkable buildings. The Catholic Chapel is one of them and also the ancient Cathedral, which towers over the city with its tall spire. It is a curious specimen of mixed Saxon[3] and Gothic architecture. The theatre and the prison are among the new beautiful buildings. The latter is erected on the hill overlooking the Clyde, commanding a magnificent view; this really brings credit to the humane feelings of Glasgow Town Council. The heavy and solid columns, on which the front of the building leans, bring to mind the heavy weight of crime and punishment and cry for pity. All houses are made of hewn stone. Carlton Place, overlooking the Clyde, is most pleasant to the eye.

The Green is meant for walking; it is a considerable space of lawn and trees belonging to the whole city. Schoolchildren play there; the sick enjoy fresh air after long suffering and the army is drilled there. One part of the Green was hired for £600 a year by a public laundry for drying linen. On Sundays after service craftsmen and artisans walk there with their families but on weekdays the place is almost deserted, for the city is far too busy to have time for walks.

Nelson's monument is in the middle of the Green; there is also a Nelson Street and the respect for the great Admiral is such that it is forbidden to go through that street on horseback or in a carriage. I have also seen another monument, which glorifies great deeds; it is the statue of John Moore, the valiant leader of the English in Spain. He was killed in 1809 by a cannon ball. He was born in Glasgow and fought in America, Corsica, Holland and Egypt. I have seen his second monument in London at St. Paul's Cathedral. While the hand of death pushes the hero into his open grave, fame deposits a laurel wreath on his brow.

Glasgow owes its wealth both to trade and industry. The cotton industry is its speciality and it equals Manchester in the quality, cheapness and beauty of its products. I had letters of introduction from Edinburgh to several tradesmen in Glasgow and I had no difficulty in visiting all the establishments I wanted to. Foreigners are not readily shown things if it is suspected that they are tradesmen who want to find out or to learn some secrets. The owners of industrial establishments are very jealous and a foreigner unable to conceal his aims will certainly not be admitted anywhere. They are even prepared to send letters of forewarning wherever he would go, as they did in my time to several Russians sent by their Government to study the secrets of the trade. I have heard endless complaints that they had been making drawings of machines, and wherever I went I was asked anxiously whether I had ever been an artisan. Only when they were sure that I had never been one and that I was merely visiting these places out of curiosity was I admitted and a guide appointed to me. The trading establishments are so spacious that one would get lost, as in a labyrinth, without a guide.

I never saw anything like the cotton spinning factory, nor is it possible to see such an establishment anywhere else. A steam engine of 45-horse power worked all the machines on the four floors of this building.

Machines did everything, cleaned the cotton, prepared it for spinning, spun it and wound it onto thousands of reels. Seven hundred workmen supervise this complicated mechanism. Work is not measured here by measures or weights; I was shown a special clock on the wall, which is connected with the machines and measures the work done as well as the time. On leaving the factory, I expressed the wish to visit another belonging to the same owner, which I discovered on the opposite side of the street. I was told however that I had already been there and my guide asked me whether or not I had observed a long gas-lit corridor as we passed along? It was a subterranean passage uniting both buildings. The owner was himself a simple workman once. Even now he looks like one, has the same manners and wears the same clothes as the workmen. He is also said to live just as simply. Nobody would have guessed on seeing him that he was a millionaire. Rothschild was once a small trade apprentice in Manchester.

The establishments I have been speaking about only spun cotton. I have seen others in which calicoes and muslins were being woven. Here too machines did the work; people only have to supervise it. I saw a girl of eleven working there for the equivalent of 20 Polish zloty a week. The introduction of machines has greatly reduced the price of muslin; it used to cost 25/- and now it is 5/- instead; this is a small price as the tax is high. But it is not the price but the export trade and the amount of produce needed that keep the industry going and really count. The underwear of the Britons and all their household linen is chiefly made of different kinds of cotton products. Real linen is far too expensive. The best comes from Ireland. Silk is a luxury here too as it is everywhere else. The silken stuffs which are made in this country are inferior in quality and high duties are imposed on the French ones; only the very richest can afford them. I have not seen, alas, these great establishments working at night. The brilliant gaslight bestows on them a new charm; the secret powers of the engines working evenly and monotonously, the few human beings supervising them who slip by, silent and mysterious like ghosts, change these places into enchanted realms about which one might read in the Arabian nights.

Glasgow is also famous as a seat of learning. Glasgow University is the second in Scotland as regards age. It was founded in 1450. The oldest is St. Andrews which dates from 1412. The later ones are those of Aberdeen and Edinburgh but the latter is by far the most famous. The University of Glasgow differs in its internal arrangements from the other universities of Great Britain.[4] It has a Chancellor, who is generally

[55] *The Saltmarket, Glasgow, 1844. Until the eighteenth century houses in Scotland were often built of wood. The risk of fire was so high that town councils offered financial incentives to encourage building in stone.* W. L. Leitch

one of the best-known Scottish magnates. In my time it was the Duke of Montrose. The Chancellor presides over all the University meetings and degrees. He is not appointed by the Government but chosen by the professors and the Rector. The Rector is chosen every year and has the title of Lord during his officiate. The undergraduates vote as well as the professors to choose the Rector. There are no other examples of this prerogative in the story of universities. A majority of votes is necessary and if there is no clear majority, then the voice of the former Rector has the casting vote.

Owing to such arrangements the rectorship passes to the most eminent men. In the time of my stay in Scotland the famous Jeffery was the Rector. After him came Mr Hume,[5] a member of Parliament, and in the present year (1828) the poet Campbell, a member of the London University Council. Glasgow University has the reputation of being the most liberal. The Rector and his Council (nominated by him) sit in judgement on all the cases arising between the undergraduates and other citizens; he also convokes the meeting for the election of his successor and for the yearly church meeting of Edinburgh. It is he too who presides when petitions to the King or Parliament are being composed. In one word he is the leading personality in all political or other important matters which have to do with learning.

The second in importance and also chosen every year is the Dean of Faculty. It is his duty to arrange the programme of studies and the examinations. But as in other Scottish universities, degrees granted to pupils are mostly honorary and an examination is generally not required except in Medicine, for which one must pass two private 'rigorosa' and one public examination. Every undergraduate who has attended medical studies for three years is entitled to try and win the degree. The University has large revenues at the disposal of the professors. They decide themselves the amount of their salary, but that salary is so insignificant that they could not exist on it, were it not for the fees paid by the undergraduates.

[56] *Glasgow University. The College received its papal bull in 1450. The buildings of 1632 were destroyed in the mid-nineteenth century when the University moved from the High Street to its present site on Gilmorehill.* T. Fairbairn

The Medical and the Philosophical Faculties have the most outstanding lecturers. The first sends forth excellent doctors famous all over Europe and the second educates the undergraduates in all moral respects. It is to this system of the universities that Scotland owes so many thinkers, writers and excellent officials, as well as the moral values in which the Scottish nation surpasses all others. Moral Philosophy was then taught by Mylne, and logic by Jardine. This teacher died last year full of honours. His *Outlines of Philosophical Education* may well serve as the model of how to develop and to educate the young.

One of the professors to whom I had a letter of introduction took me round to the more interesting parts of the university. I visited the Library which is full of ancient manuscripts and rare editions. In the Assembly Hall were some good pictures and portraits of those who had been benefactors of the University, or had brought credit to it. I was impressed to see the portrait of Napier,[6] the discoverer of Logarithms; Buchanan, the Latin poet of the Middle Ages; Smollett,[7] the author of the *History of England* and of so many charming novels. Also the portraits of Watt,[8] the discoverer who, after Fulton,[9] perfected the working of steam ships, of Reid,[10] Adam Smith and Hutcheson, who taught Philosophy and left behind immortal works. In the Theological Hall hang pictures of Luther and John Knox.

Thence we proceeded to the Hunterian Museum, which belongs to the University and lies within its precincts. It is a rich collection of animals, plants, minerals, medals and manuscripts left by the famous doctor Hunter[11] who had studied at this University. The collection is valued at £120,000. The Anatomical Hall is the most interesting of all. I have seen there all the parts of the human body preserved in alcohol, healthy ones and sick ones too. I have also seen a child with two heads and other monsters in the human form. Here also have I heard that the earliest movements of the unborn child are observed first by the physiologists, first in the heart and then in the brain. The seats of feeling and of thought are thus the places where life begins! The development of the unborn child is here better represented than anywhere else, for other waxwork anatomical collections cannot be compared with this real one. They are only adequate imitations of nature but here we face the real thing.

We then visited the Observatory which consists of three parts. The first is purely scientific and all the observations of the skies are written down here. The second is for public use; anyone can enter it on paying. There amusement is combined with study. A great camera obscura represents the surrounding objects in such splendid colours as no painter could have ever done, for nature always surpasses art. Telescopes show the endless world of the stars and microscopes reveal the tiniest secrets of the tiniest creation. The microscope of Dolland,[12] which had arrived lately, attracted general attention. It is the biggest that has ever left the laboratory of the famous optician. The first experiments made with it have led to the discovery of extraordinary phenomena. Several hundred worms have been seen on the body of one gnat and about three score feeding on the leg of one moth. There, tiny beings unseen by the eye seem quite big through the microscope. The minerals, their crystallisation and the splendour of their colours gave new delight, surpassing everything imaginable.

The third part of the Observatory is only accessible to those who have participated in the founding of it. A collection of maps of the earth and the heavens is kept there, several big globes, and many writings concerning Astronomy, navigation and trade. The big telescope of Herschel[13] is to be seen there. The erection of the establishment cost £3,000.

Anderson's Institute[14] is the second important establishment. Anderson was teaching physics at Glasgow University. Burning to spread science and adapt it to the needs of life and, seeing that this was impossible for lack of a suitable establishment, he gave his own fortune to found one such institution. He bequeathed a large building, his own physics laboratory and his library to that end. This Institute has done much to unite theory and practice and to popularise knowledge in a manner which is necessary to the exigencies of modern life. Science taught there descends from her pedestal and becomes accessible to all sorts of people. Garnett[15] and Birkbeck[16] taught the elementary precepts of science. It is here that all the polytechnics, technical and handicraft schools which now exist in all the industrial towns of Britain have their origins. In adapted forms similar schools can be found throughout the whole of Europe. How much can a single sensible Institution achieve for the advancement of Humanity! And many other such institutions could be mentioned which have been founded either by one or several Glasgow citizens. This could be cited as proof that the mercantile spirit (for Glasgow is a city of tradesmen), though so often spoken of with contempt, is by no means alien to great and noble impulses and sacrifices. On the contrary, establishments founded by merchants have such a characteristic that there is nothing showy or vain about them; they aim straight at a useful, practical object.

The Lunatic Asylum is one of such useful institutions founded by a noble impulse. It is the best arranged, perhaps, not only in Great Britain but also in the whole of Europe.[17] The arrangements are simple and well adapted to their aims. The building has the arrangement of a cross, surmounted in the middle by a dome. It has four two-storied wings which contain 135 rooms. Between the wings there are lovely gardens surrounded by the walls where the patients can walk. There are special rooms for the rich and others for the poor. Relatives pay for the former and the parishes pay for the latter. More than a hundred patients were there at the time, and more women than men. I have been astonished by such great numbers of lunatics, for there are lunatic asylums in Aberdeen, Perth and Edinburgh as well as many private ones. When I asked for the reason for this, the Warden told me that the lunatics from England and Ireland are sent here and that the Government sees to it that lunatics should not be left uncared for, whereas the Continental Governments are less scrupulous as to this. I left it at that, although the answer did not seem to be a sufficient one. There are plenty of lunatic asylums all over England and Ireland as well, and the Scottish ones are not able to take in all their lunatics. When I was in Oban on the western coast of Scotland, I saw one of those unfortunates wandering through the street. He was throwing stones at a passer-by as he was said to have been doing for more than a year for lack of any care given to him. I also knew a family whose father was mad and they looked after him for more than three years until he died. This makes me think that some other reason must be found for lunacy being so frequently met. It cannot be ascribed to heredity, for the same could then affect the whole world. Perhaps it is due to sudden changes from one extremity to the other by losing money, which often happens in so rich and industrial a country. Also perhaps the high standards of living, the high culture, the comforts and exalted feelings predispose people for lunacy. These seem to be more natural and creditable reasons for this affliction than those given by Shakespeare, with whom I do not agree on this point. The great dramatist simply considers his country to be the home of madmen. He says in the scene with the gravedigger that the Danish Prince should be sent to England to be cured of his madness, for if he is not cured, his madness will at least be not apparent in a country full of madmen (Hamlet, Act V, Scene I).

It must be said to the credit of the Asylum that human feelings are respected there. The patients whom the illness has brought into a humiliating state are not turned into exhibitions for public curiosity. Nobody is allowed to see or talk to them except when they walk. But even in most of the cases one has to observe them from a hiding place so as not to be seen by them. The Asylum has a peculiar way of finding out whether the brain is really affected. It is a chair on which the patient is made to sit and which then begins to turn with a dizzying rapidity. He that is sane will be sick, he that is mad will not mind. It really is giving too much power to machines to expect them to decide who is a lunatic and who is not! I asked the doctor whether it really proved true in every case but he seemed to have some doubts. Somebody trying to define Man called him 'the discoverer of tools'. This definition is nowhere as true as in this country.

The inhabitants of Glasgow though very thrifty are extremely orderly and care for the comforts of life, a general characteristic of merchants. They possess such household arrangements as are seen nowhere else. I have already spoken of the public laundry in which linen is washed well and at low prices. But a public dairy is one of the most striking establishments. It provides the milk and the cream which are, as a rule, badly lacking in towns. It has been established by a wealthy citizen of the town who now has 200 cows. These cows are so beautifully kept and in such cleanliness that many people go on purpose to see them. There is a special balcony built over the byres so that the public can watch the cows at leisure. Seeing such lovely cattle as the English have, especially those carefully bred, is bound to make the taste for milk increase. This establishment is a new one but being very useful as well as lucrative, it has already found many imitators in all other industrial cities. How useful it would have been in Warsaw, where milk is so dear when compared with the provinces and, in most cases, it is diluted as well! But if somebody wanted to start such an establishment they would of course have to do it on a large scale.[18]

XVI

Dumbarton. The River Leven. Loch Lomond. The Cavern of Rob Roy. Tarbet. Arrochar. Glencroe. Cairndow. Inverary

HAVING seen everything worth seeing in Glasgow, we started on a further journey towards the Highlands. The highroads followed the right bank of the Clyde. Prosperous villages, splendid country houses, the castles of the Scottish lairds – some in ruins - and forests and glens diverted the eye. To the right was a chain of hills, covered from head to foot with heather. Having passed one of the hills called Dunbuc, we suddenly saw the rock of Dumbarton, bathed in the Clyde and resplendent at the moment with the setting sun. A fortress was on the summit. Ossian speaks of this castle and tells us that it belonged to the brave warrior chief Carthon, the son of Klessamore and the blue-eyed Moira. Ossian calls the castle 'Balkluth'. The Romans had a garrison there which kept the inhabitants in order; they called the place 'Theodosia'. Even now the castle is a fortress and soldiers are still stationed here. It is here that Napoleon was to be kept prisoner until fear of his escape caused a more distant and lonely island to be chosen. The cliff is 560 feet above sea level, which is a considerable height for a lonely rock springing out of the vast plains. Experiments and research by physicists prove that some parts of the rock are magnetic. Whichever way one looks the view is marvellous. The Clyde and the Leven wind through fertile plains; to the north is a chain of hills with the peak of Ben Lomond veiled by clouds. Life is given to the view by the sight of the ships moving to and fro in the harbours of Glasgow and Greenock.

We spent the night at the foot of the rock in the little town of Dumbarton and the next morning we crossed the Leven, called by Ossian 'the Kluthe'. Modern poets call it 'the transparent stream'. The neighbourhood is classical. Smollett, the true interpreter of the human heart, was born there and also Roderick, the hero of his first novel

[57] *George Buchanan (1506–82). A great Latinist, Buchanan was born at Killearn, near the Clyde. Educated in France, he held chairs at Bordeaux, Paris and Coimbra before returning to Scotland. Although a Protestant, he became classical tutor to Queen Mary and then tutor to her son James VI. In his* De Jure Regni *he asserted the supremacy of law over the crown.*

Roderick Random. He is called by Walter Scott 'the Rubens of the writers'. A tall stone column, erected in his honour, stands at the roadside and bears an inscription in Latin, several yards long. This terrific length frightened me from reading it. Buchanan, the tutor of James, son of Mary Stewart, was also born near here. He is the Horace of Scotland and writer of *De Jure Regni*. The cottage in which he saw the light of this world is preserved. It is very humble and thatched but travellers visit it for they respect Buchanan's memory. An Irishman used to come and spend the night there. He slept on the bare floor under the central beam, for the middle beam has a great significance in the superstitions of the people, and the Irishman wanted to become imbued with the genius of Buchanan. An obelisk, 100 feet high, proclaims Buchanan's fame from the top of a hill.

Not far from these places we saw Dun Fion, the hill of Fingal, the place where this Caledonian ruler is said to have hunted. We also passed Glen Fruin, or the valley of plaints, so called because of the slaughter which took place there when the clans of Colquhoun and MacGregor were fighting. The former were beaten and their chief, who took refuge in an underground cavern, was seized and mercilessly murdered. James V then proclaimed clan MacGregor to be a robber clan. Its name was not to be mentioned in official acts, nobody was to be christened by that name and followers of the clan were hunted in the Highlands like wild animals. It all happened at the beginning of the sixteenth century, when Scotland was still wild and unruly.

We reached at last Loch Lomond. We came at a time when a passenger ship was about to weigh anchor. Some ten years ago the place was only known to those living around the loch, and a small boat was then sufficient means of transport. Now that the enchanted pen of Sir Walter Scott has revealed to the world the beauty of the place, and the romantic legends attached to it, ships moved by steam had to be brought to the lake. We embarked on the loch near the village of Luss, which is a sort of gateway between the Lowlands and the Highlands. We heard Gaelic spoken for the first time. This language is incomprehensible to the English and is not like any other language in the world.[1] It is spoken all over the Highlands, on the neighbouring islands and in Ireland. It is called Erse and was the language of Ossian.

The signal to leave the shore was given to us by music. A Highlander was our Orpheus and, instead of a lyre, he played bagpipes adorned with ribbons, with which the wind played gaily. He wore the national dress and gave a finishing touch of beauty to the place. He did not stop playing throughout our sail across the Loch and he intermixed mournful ballads and gay reels. In this enchanted country, amid such great beauty, each of us kept looking at the constantly new pictures revealed to our eyes at every turning of the ship; while we looked in wonder and admiration, we each of us thought about some special thing dear to our hearts. I was immersed in the reality I saw and in the history and legends attached to it. The dark green of the shores is a colour only to be found in a wet country and it was reflected strangely in the black waters of the loch. For the Scottish lochs remain up to now what Ossian has called them, 'His dark watered lakes'. It is an enormous loch, 30 miles long with its end lost in the mists of the glen. To the right rose the heather-covered slopes of Loch Lomond, its peak hidden in the clouds. We kept on passing tiny islands which form quite an archipelago; there are more than thirty. Some are bare rocks, others, called by poets 'emerald green', serve as hiding places for frightened does. As they are not inhabited they exhale that special quietude and serenity which is to be felt only in the vicinity of islands. These are ideal places for meditation and happiness. This is why temples have been built on islands, why monks choose them for their contemplative lives of silent meditation on the futility of things, why they are offered as places of rest for the bodies of the dead and, even more, why they are destined by legend as places of appeasement and happy wandering grounds for their shades. What in other countries seems invented here becomes real. The Druids held their religious ceremonies here and the scholars find numerous proofs of this. The family graves of the famous MacGregors are on the island called Inch Caillach.

The credulous population related three wonderful things about this lake: that it has finless fish, waves without wind and floating islands. Though nobody believes this now, it is nevertheless invariably told. The fish without fins are real, a kind of water snake, *coluber natrix*; they swim from one island to another and have the misfortune of falling into the fishermen's nets. The miraculous floating islands must of course come from the realms of poetry, but the waves without wind can be explained. The surface of the waters here remain uneasy for a long time after the wind has quietened down. It happens the more frequently because stillness comes here very seldom and the lake has little chance to become immobile. The wind here is often scarcely felt as it passes over the loch between the mountains from which so many streams and rivulets fall. It is said about this lake that during the earthquake in Lisbon in 1755 its waters rose considerably. If this be true, it would mean that there is some secret subterranean communication between Scotland and Portugal. Nobody however seems to have tried to verify this.[2] Extraordinary things always appeal to us and we seldom like to dispel pleasant illusions and straighten out agreeable errors.

Rob Roy's[3] cavern was the last stage of our journey. He was the last chief of the MacGregors. He hid here from his persecutors with his clan and troubled the South of Scotland by his expeditions. On the shores of Loch Katrine a woman was still living who descended from Rob Roy. His six-foot-long musket was in her possession. Curiosity attracts numbers of Scotsmen who are most of them lovers of the past and

[58] *Dumbarton Castle. The rock, a volcanic plug, had been the site of a fortress since at least the fourth century. It became the capital of the Celtic kingdom of Strathclyde and, after 1018, an important centre of power for the kings of the Scots. It guarded the lowest crossing over the river Clyde which, until nineteenth-century dredging, was still fordable at Dumbuck.* Grose

nobody passes nearby without visiting the old Manna and her musket. The cavern has nothing interesting in itself. It is accessible only from the lake and it possesses two entrances. The middle cavern is the largest and there is a stone table in its centre. We found there a man who was ninety years old and claimed to have been Rob Roy's companion. He was dressed in Highland dress and lived there out of devotion for his chief, existing on the generosity of the visitors. We returned from thence to Tarbet, a small village on the very shores of the lake, where the travellers find, what is not common in the Highlands, a comfortable hotel supplied with everything necessary. Thence according to plan the travellers generally make an excursion to Ben Lomond and then return to Edinburgh through Loch Katrine, Callendar and Stirling. Some go west and we had chosen that route. We proceeded to Inverary, and the isle of Staffa, on the Atlantic Ocean, was to be the furthest limit of our travels.

The best and almost the only way of making that journey without unpleasant experience, is on foot. A carriage is impossible because of the bad roads, hilly country and constant crossing of lakes. The travellers generally hire a guide with a horse who carries their luggage and this is what we did. If ever we attempted to hire saddle horses we invariably got into trouble, for few horses are reared in the hills and the ones we got were always weak, thin and old and stopped out of exhaustion in the middle of our route.

The road to Arrochar leads through a gloomy forest in a deep valley to Loch Long, a sea gulf 20 miles long penetrating into the land. Loch Long means in Gaelic the lake of the ships. It is here that the King of Norway, Haco,[4] landed in 1263 and filled the country with terror, destroying churches and villages. If the ancient chroniclers say the truth, this country must have been richer then, for today the invader would not gain much and there would be very little to destroy. An inn and a few poor fishermen's cottages contain the whole population and all the wealth of the country. Having passed to the other side of the sea loch by a road, which winds along its shores, we found ourselves in a dark, gloomy and savage-looking glen. This was the Glencroe so famous for its beauty. On both our sides were mountains cloaked purple with heather or in places entirely bare and rocky. The peaks were cloud-capped. Heavy rocks menaced the passers-by, ready to fall into the valley at any time; they have been carried there by many torrents which unite and then divide into two streams which fall into the loch. Their noise is like some tremendous humming of innumerable bees. We exclaimed: 'Ossian had been here!' and indeed he must have been, if he was able to describe as faithfully as he did the wild gorge shut out from the world by moss-covered and darkened and aged rocks. The heavy clouds chased by the wind clung to the mountains as shadows of Ossian's spirit flitted by. Some of the huge rocks standing among smaller ones made one think of the Morvern Knights [of Ossian] who after a battle had fallen asleep for eternity among the people they defended. The darkened and gloomy rocks seemed to bend down and cover them with mourning cloths, as the soul of the passed ages would have done. A foaming stream leaping from stone to stone made one think of the loving son who carried his dying father from the battle field, and having reached the stream, laid him down and waited for the Bard to come, so that his father should not die without being sung for. As he pined for him, lo! there appeared the Bard descending from the mountaintop over the heather, holding a golden harp. Oh world of imagination and feeling, what infinite charm thou hast for man!

Having reached the top of the glen, we discovered a seat made of grass and beside it a stone with the inscription: 'Rest and be thankful'.

[59] *James Macpherson (1736–96). Lach-Szyrma had read Macpherson's translations of Ossian's poems while still in Poland. Although expressing doubts about their authenticity, his picture of Scotland was deeply influenced by Macpherson.*

We accepted the invitation, for having walked up the hill we were tired. For this kind thought the traveller must be thankful to the 24th English Regiment which, having finished the road in 1746, wanted to leave a memory not only of its labour but also of its kindness. A lake lay close to that stone and its waters though pure were as black as coal, which was caused by the reflections of the flowering heather and the dark crags. Looking back we saw Loch Long stretched like a mirror between the rocks; looking to the road which still lay in front of us we saw tall mountains and shadowy glens veiled by mist. To the right we had a mountain with a curiously curved peak, which is called the 'Cobbler' because of that attitude. Human imagination likes vivifying inanimate nature. Sailing later across Loch Fyne, we asked a sailor whether a 'cobbler at work' could be seen from there. He answered that we certainly would see it if the cloud did not 'cover the man's face'. This was the highest mountain belonging to the clan Campbell.[5] After the Chief's

169

death the successor was obliged to climb to the very summit, which alone entitled him to the leadership of the clan. If one did not succeed, the next of kin were to attempt it in succession. But those times are already gone in which physical fitness was the most important quality.

Walking through Glencroe we saw only a few miserable cottages scattered far apart. Not the slightest trace of cultivation, only heather, flocks of sheep from time to time and tiny Scottish ponies. These parts seem too great and too lofty to be able to bear humanity at close quarters. Men, if encountered, seemed tiny dwarf-like creatures against the mountains, their cottages like birds' nests clinging to the walls, or like dolls' houses built by children for fun. Only eagles and hawks are in keeping here.

We reached Loch Fyne, another long sea loch penetrating deep into the mountains, passed Ardkinglas, the seat of the Campbells, the oldest part of which lies in ruins, and arrived at Cairndow. Here we spent the night. The next day we started for Inverary and we chose the road across Loch Fyne. We started at noon in a fishing boat though the wind was not favourable. It grew in strength and stopped our boat and, though the fishermen did their utmost, we were unable to move forward. Everybody in turn had to take to the oars and at last we managed to reach open water where the wind was less strenuous than in the narrow mountain gorge and we were able to unfurl the sails.

The sun was setting when we landed at Inverary. Before we had time to unpack and have a meal, night came and prevented us from seeing on that very day the castle of the Duke of Argyle. We only watched through the hotel window, in the falling dusk, the mighty quadrangle of the castle surmounted by its dome. The light grey walls were distinctly seen against the dark background of the park, which is said to be the largest in the whole of Great Britain, for it is 30 miles in circumference. Beyond the dark forest we saw a rock, the Dunicoich, 700 feet high, on which a watchtower was built. In the centuries of internal trouble a watchman used to warn from the summit if an enemy was approaching. The silence of the night, the murmur of the forest and the monotonous beating of the waves against the rocks, plunged the soul into deep meditation. The immobility of things at night gave a curious solemnity to everything. It seemed as if nature called to the sea, the trees and the rivers to say in common a whispered prayer. Tranquillity invaded the soul and full of ecstasy I went to bed and fell asleep at once, a peaceful and happy sleep.

The next morning we went to the castle. It was surrounded by a moat; in ancient times, according to Walter Scott, five gallows stood in front of it with five corpses dangling, but nowadays all traces of terror have disappeared; lawns and gay paths surround the castle which invite rather than frighten away. The roaring river Aray flows across the park; the drawbridge is gone and one enters the castle through a stone bridge. Taste and culture have made the interior a delightful abode of light air, art and refinement. There are quantities of valuable pictures, a large library, arms and rich material on the walls and daylight streaming down from the dome. A gallery runs around it and an organ is placed there, the tones of which must fill the castle with divine music. When we were leaving, a large book was presented to us wherein to write our names. This is also the time for tipping one's guide, for nothing works in this country without expense, even in ducal castles. The tip is called 'compliments' here and certainly means something more than a mere bow. On our way back we saw in the town a monument of stone and read that it had been erected in memory of seventeen Campbells who in defence of the Reformation[6] paid for their beliefs with their lives. The Duke of Argyle himself was among them. It happened in 1685. How much trouble religious beliefs caused in Scotland is best illustrated in Sir Walter Scott's book, *Old Mortality*. The stern defenders of Calvinism were called at that time Puritans or Covenanters and their graves are shown in the churchyard. A saner outlook on things has with time succeeded in killing the spirit of madness which seemed to possess the nation and has brought more toleration. On that very monument erected in 1754, we read the words: 'Prospera lux oritur, linguis animisque farete'.

Inverary is a small place of 1200 inhabitants. Of the houses scattered along the bay, all except one belong to the Duke of Argyle. The people busy themselves with catching herring for which Loch Fyne has a great reputation. They are most plentiful from June to December. The saying goes that Loch Fyne is two parts herring and only one part water. The town's emblem is a hanging herring, with the motto: 'Semper tibi pendent halec'. Sometimes as many as 500 to 600 smacks go out fishing and the fishermen remain for a whole week in the bay. They fish at night and prepare fish during the day. The little free time left they spend sleeping or playing the bagpipes and singing their favourite songs in Gaelic. Most herring are caught during storms and bad weather.

XVII

Loch Awe. Cruachan. The Legend of Loch Awe.
Dunstaffnage. Oban. Dunollie. The Quarrel of the Sailors.
The Lady's Isle. The Views. The Singing of the Sailors.
Morvern. Aros. Character of the Macdonalds

HAVING made preparations for our further journey, we left Inverary the next morning. We followed a road or rather a path, for a horse with a tiny cart could scarcely follow it, to the north. We took to the valley of Glenaray, down which a stormy torrent tears. We had to stop at an inn at Loch Awe to wait for the ferry which was on the other side of the lake. It was the first time I saw in Britain that means of transport so common in Poland. The prosperity of Great Britain, which enables shores to be united by subterranean passages as well as by bridges overhead, renders unnecessary such means of communication. The roads in these parts are very bad because of the bad soil and bitter climate; it will probably be long before they improve. The Highlanders are very few in number, not more than 300,000. Their means of livelihood are limited to sheep and fishing. Our next stop was at Cruachan, a hill so high that for a long time we seemed unable to leave it; wherever we went it towered over us and we could not seem to lose sight of its sharp outline. Not being competent to study the flora of the mountain or the formation of her soil, as some scientists might have done, I fell instead into conversation with our guide. I asked him a rather silly question: 'What is your opinion of such a high mountain?' – 'Cruachan is a bad omen,' he answered, 'he is girded with clouds, the spirit of the hills may begin moaning at any time.' Rather astonished by such unexpected and poetic an answer, I asked again: 'And what would happen if the spirit of the mountain began to moan?' – 'The spirit of the mountains means a storm is coming,' answered the Highlander. I have already stated many times the fact that mountaineers have an extremely vivid imagination and they believe in different prognostications to the point of credulity. There is also no spot on their hills about which they would not remember something. Their legends remind one of the Greek mythology and also go far back into the dim past. Our guide related to us a legend, which I later discovered came from a song about Cruachan, which is supposed to have been composed by Ossian. The story of the Scottish Homer goes as follows:

> Bera, an old lady bent by age, lived in a cavern of the Cruachan. She was the last of her family. A rich and fertile country at the foot of the mountain belonged to her as well as the numerous flocks of sheep grazing on the neighbouring slopes. But she herself was perpetually engaged in guarding a well which, it had been predicted, was to bring misfortune to her family and to the land of her forefathers. Every evening before sunset she used to close that well with a stone covered by some mysterious writings. But one evening, having returned exhausted from hunting, she fell asleep before sunset and did not cover up the well. The unguarded waters burst forth from the bosom of the mountain and inundated the whole space where Loch Awe now is. The unhappy Bera woke only on the third day and ran at once to cover up the well, but the mysterious stone had disappeared. She looked there at the land of her fathers and cried out in horror. Her cry shook the mountain and the spirit of Bera fled away to the land where the shadows of her ancestors lived.

Having passed Cruachan, we found ourselves in a less hilly and more fertile country; it was also more densely populated. The weather too became lovely and a delicate western breeze was blowing. I will never forget the impression of extreme beauty when, in the rays of the setting sun, we perceived Loch Etive and on a rocky isthmus Dunstaffnage, an old half-deserted castle. Nearby were the ruins of a Gothic chapel with the graves of the owners of that place. The setting sun showed through all the windows and the dilapidated walls until they seemed to be transparent. As it was getting late we did not visit the castle though our road passed quite near. We were told that some cannons, which came from the Spanish Armada, were preserved there and old Scottish armour and an ivory statue representing one of the ancient kings. For Dunstaffnage had been Scotland's most ancient capital and the Kings of the Picts resided there.[1] It is from here that the famous 'Liafail' seat came, which is called 'the Stone of Destiny'.[2] It is on that seat that the kings of Scotland were crowned and, as legend goes, the fate of the dynasty was to be attached to it, for where it would be, there would be the capital. It left Dunstaffanage for Scone and Scone for London; the power and the Government followed. A prediction has never been more fully accomplished. I saw that seat in Westminster Abbey, and this important treasure is nothing more than a grey stone, roughly hewn. In ancient times it was believed that the stone uttered a voice when the lawful heir sat on it. But nowadays it certainly keeps silence. Though nobody considers it any longer as a miraculous one, this stone is as indispensable to coronation as all the other insignia, for the British love tradition. George IV, as well as a long line of all his predecessors, received the emblems of royalty sitting on that stone. The custom of crowning kings seated is not only observed in England and Scotland. The chair on which Charlemagne[3] was crowned is still to be seen in France. The Slavonic nations also set their kings on stones; chairs came into fashion later. I have seen a seal of one of the Polish mediaeval kings of the Piast dynasty;[4] the seal did not bear the white Eagle, but a Gothic stool.

[60] *Dunstaffnage Castle. One of the few thirteenth-century castles to have survived almost intact, Dunstaffnage was held directly from the crown by the MacDougalls of Lorne and then by the Campbells. It guarded the route from central Scotland to the western seaboard. The house inside the walls was built in 1725.* Grose

Leaving this capital, so ancient that some meaningless details about it are all that can be found about it in the legendary history of the country, I started thinking about the destinies of countries and nations, but my thoughts were constantly disturbed. Night was falling; the narrow and difficult road led over precipitous places and common sense advised caution. At last at ten in the evening we reached Oban. It is a small village from which every week a ship leaves for Iona and Staffa but, as the ship had just left the day before we arrived, we were obliged to hire a special one. Thanks to this we were able to choose our route and passed through the bay of Linnhe, the Sound of Mull and along the shores of Morvern, the land of the Knights of Ossian. We saw on a rocky cliff the ruins of Dunollie Castle, which had once been the seat of the powerful Macdougals. The family became poor later on and the last heir of these ruins had been killed lately in Spain. He died the death worthy of a descendant of worthy men. Not far from the castle is a lonely cliff called the plum pudding stone, for it is composed of multicoloured little pebbles. Fingal is said to have tied his faithful dog Bran to the rock while he was hunting.

We passed the island of Lismore, made of limestone. Formerly it had been the seat of a Catholic Bishop whose diocese spread over all the Western Isles. Violent sea currents and winds no less violent, which come tearing from between the mountains, make navigation very difficult. Our sailors had often to take to the oars, and in the moments of respite, when sails did their work, they gave themselves courage and strength by drinking whisky. It is a good drink indeed for a country so cold and wet. When coming to terms with us, they claimed a certain amount of that drink and, in order to convince us the more easily of its necessity, they several times quoted the saying that a Highlander feels sick if he does not feel the taste of whisky in his mouth. Whenever they drank, they civilly handed the cup to us first. When the glasses went round I asked where they got such excellent whisky? 'From the hills,' they answered, 'it can be obtained only in the Highlands, and it has to be smuggled to other parts of Scotland'.[5] At last we came to discuss this point, whether one should indulge in smuggling. For a Scotsman will discuss even while he drinks, and it is one of his characteristics that everything he does has to be carefully thought over and reasoned about. One of the sailors, delicate and pale-looking, whose wan face betrayed subtlety, maintained that smuggling is a kind of stealing and is forbidden by the Bible, as well as by the country's legislation. He looked at things from the point of view of a priest and he reasoned like a magistrate. I don't remember what the reasoning of the second sailor was; I only know that he did not agree with the view of the first one. The third, a sturdy, hefty fellow, red-haired and looking like a real companion of Rob Roy, did not indulge in discussions; he asked simply: 'Why then do you drink the whisky?' This was not in the tone of a question but rather an exclamation, followed by such a gloomy and threatening look in his eyes that he alone would fain destroy and annihilate the clever conclusions of the others about the Bible and legislation. Though unimportant, this small episode throws some light on the Scottish character. The first sailor, who obviously had been in touch with civilisation, might well represent the common people of the South of Scotland. The South is much wealthier, the towns more frequent and industry well developed, all of which is favourable to culture and education and fosters an easier and softer life. The second, who had only the innate common sense of the Scots but no education, might represent the Highlanders. For though in parts education has reached the Highlands, people there as a rule still live in quite a wild state, believe in their superstitions and keep to their ancient habits. The lairds do not live in their Highland homes. They have tenants and, spending most of their time in Edinburgh, London or in their other domains in the South of Scotland, are unable to bring culture to the people. Besides, population is so scarce that people can hardly gather together to talk, discuss, and exchange thoughts and opinions. The population is decreasing steadily, for the Highlanders migrate south to the industries and to England, or they join the army where they distinguish themselves by their gallantry. While the South of Scotland has attained high standards of culture and wealth, the North still dwells in the shepherding, fishing stage. The Highlander still acts on impulse, prompted by his natural instincts, which gives his acts beauty and a special poetic charm. The Scotsman from the Lowlands, on the other hand, has cooled down his feelings and they have become blunted by bad manners. Too much education often makes him sophisticated. The Highlander makes one think of Ossian. The poet's songs appeal to him and he repeats them with emotion, while his brother from the South is lost in doubts about whether Ossian really existed and accuses Macpherson, the publisher of these songs, of extorting money from credulous people. The Highlander, in one word, is a child of nature and the Lowlander of civilisation. The former is moved by fresh, unspoilt instincts in all their strength, the second is full of artificial forms acquired by reason.

We passed a number of islands full of different kinds of birds. The

[61] *Oban Bay. From Oban, Lach-Szyrma hired a boat to take him round the north coast of Mull to Staffa. The ruins of Dunollie Castle, the fifteenth-century seat of the clan Macdougall, are in the distance.*

sailors called our attention to the Island of the Lady, a bare rock rising so little out of the sea that the waves cover it twice a day. Once an old Scottish chief left his wife there and they showed us the ruins of his castle, Duart, on the opposite shore. This event, as I discovered later on, is not a popular legend but an historical happening.[6] Two clan chieftains lived in constant feud in the fifteenth century. Their clans, the MacLeans and the Campbells, shared their hatred. The former were at last beaten and their chief had to beg for mercy. Later on the chief of the MacLeans asked the chief of the Campbells, the Duke of Argyle, for the hand of his daughter. The Duke agreed willingly, hoping to put an end, at last, to this eternal strife. Immediately after the wedding MacLean returned to his native Mull and a year afterwards his wife bore him a son. But the members of the clan, dissatisfied with the union of their chief with the hated family, were unable to keep quiet any longer now that they realised that they would have a chief of Campbell blood. They all went to MacLean and demanded that, unless he freed them from his wife and son, they would have to disown him. MacLean resisted but at last gave way when they promised not to shed the blood of his wife and child. During a dark night the Lady was taken to the island where, notwithstanding her tears and threats, she was left for the waves to

[62] *Dunyvaig Castle. In the thirteenth century Islay became the centre of power of the Lords of the Isles. The castle was built by Donald I to guard the southern shores of the island and to protect his fleet. On an islet on Loch Finlaggan, in the north of Islay, the chiefs of the fourteen principal clans of the Hebrides met in council to debate problems and administer justice. The destruction of the Lordship by James IV, at the end of the fifteenth century, created a power vacuum and a period of lawlessness.* Grose

drown her. The sea was already flowing in and she was scarcely able to stand any longer when some fishermen who belonged to her father's clan saved her. They recognised the daughter of their chief and took her back to him. The Duke rewarded them generously and asked them not to repeat the story while he waited for news from his son-in-law. The news came soon; the Duke was told that his daughter had died suddenly. Soon the son-in-law arrived in person, accompanied by his most powerful vassals, to console his father-in-law. All the MacLeans wore deep mourning and pretended great grief. Burials were always occasions of banquets so a banquet was prepared. Soon everybody had taken his or her seat but one to the right of the Duke remained empty. Suddenly the door opened and his daughter, splendidly attired, entered and took her seat. The guests were horrified, MacLean was thunderstruck for one moment and then tried to save himself by fleeing, but the first lover of the lady, whom the father had rejected, caught him and killed him. His friends and companions were all kept as hostages to safeguard the baby son. The son had been saved by his faithful nurse and the mother later married the man who had undertaken her defence. This event is well known in Scotland and Gaelic songs are sung about it; Campbell composed on that topic his beautiful ballad 'Glenara'.

Having passed the Lady Island, we took to the West, and though the wind was still unpropitious, the sailors were so good at manoeuvring the sails that we overtook vessels which were far ahead of us. The build of our boat, which was light and oblong, was of great help. The views were perfectly glorious and our emotion and admiration reached its highest pitch when our sailors took to the oars and began to sing. There are places which seem to be made for song and where the power of music is most strongly felt. So it was here; the very Gaelic of Ossian appealed strangely to the imagination. Their way of singing was very strange and peculiar;[7] we were simply torn out of the present and transported into the legendary past. The 'Song of the Oar' impressed us most. One of the sailors was singing alone and then the others fell in, in a chorus. I remember this song even today and I can quote the words though I do not understand their meaning:

> Tha tighin fodham! Fodham tha titdghin fodham!
> Fodham, fodham, tha tidghin fodham!
> Fodham eirigh!

The tune of the song fell into the movement of the oars and the rhythm was given when they were plunged into the water. The waves beating against the sides of the boat, the roar of the sea, the humming of the wind overhead; all played a marvellous accompaniment. Such songs to the oars are called 'Jorrams' and are sung by the clansmen when the Chief is being rowed in his galley. We also heard some love ballads, all in Gaelic, and only one of the sailors spoke enough English to be able to tell us a little of what they meant. All these songs applied to a Macdonald who lived on one of these northern islands. I wondered whether she composed them herself but was unable to learn anything about her later on. So this Gaelic Sappho, whoever she was, remains unknown. They have so many sources of inspiration in this country that they themselves do not know what they possess.

We observed the shores of Morvern as we passed them; Ossian describes them as wooded but now there are no woods, only bare rocks and castles here and there. We landed at Aros, a miserable little place consisting of several poor cottages and a rather decent inn. The tiny harbour lies at the foot of the rock on which are the ruins of the castle of the Macdonalds,[8] to whom this island as well as several others had belonged. The very ruins of the great building, beneath which the sea tosses restlessly, spoke of the power of its ancient owners. The view from the ruins of Ben More and the Loaf is marvellous. The hill, alas, has nothing in common with the loaf except its shape, for it is a most unfertile barren rock. The whole island indeed is nothing else and, of course, the population is very poor.

Ruins always make one feel sad and I felt so now, though the former inhabitants of this castle would certainly not have indulged in anything as weak as sorrow. They were proud and relentless both in prosperity and misfortune. Two historical facts will best illustrate their character. Soon after the Union of England and Scotland in 1603, when James VI sat on the English throne, one of the Macdonalds from Aros travelled through Ireland and was invited to dinner by the Lord Lieutenant. Macdonald was late and, having entered the banqueting hall, took the first chair he had found empty which was one of the last ones near the door. The Lord Lieutenant asked him to come and sit in the place intended for him next to himself. Macdonald, who did not understand English, asked what he meant. When it was explained to him that he was expected to go and sit in the first place he answered, 'Tell that kerne that where Macdonald sits is the first place'.

The unconquerable pride of that family seemed to speak even from their graves. One of them buried on the island of Iona has this inscription on his tombstone: 'Macdonald fato hic', by which he made it understood that fate alone can conquer a Macdonald. They lived splendidly, almost in the manner of Kings. They rewarded even small merit by grant of land. They had a special formula to be used on such occasions: 'We Macdonald, the chief of the Macdonalds, here in our castle of Aros, give to N.N. the right from tomorrow for always etc.' But notwithstanding their generosity, they were not successful in populating this barren rock.

A Scottish chieftain considers himself the father of the whole clan and, in bestowing the soil. he also gives his name to the inhabitants of the land. This is the cause of such numbers in Scotland bearing the same name, although they are not related to each other. Some say that the common names are due to the ancient habit of having common wives, which of course would cause a great intermixing of blood. This would be the reason why so many Scotsmen are related to each other; in fact one is sometimes inclined to think that every Scotsman is some kind of cousin to every other Scotsman. But all this is not historical and the

Spartan habit of having common wives is unknown here. The need for family ties is found among all primitive nations; as long as a State does not give sufficient protection to its citizens, that protection must be found in family bonds and clans.

XVIII

The Isle of Mull. The Night. Poverty of the Population.
The Isle of Staffa. Fingal's Cave. The Cavern of Clamshell.
Cairn. The Isle of Iona. The Atlantic. The Hospitality of
a Scottish Chief

HAVING left our boat at Aros, we hastily proceeded to the western part of the island of Mull, where we wished to spend the night. We went all the way on foot, which really is the pleasantest way of travelling through hills and not as tiring as in the plains. Almost at every step something new attracts the attention and shortens the way. If one feels like it one can stop and look and admire, or even leave the beaten track; nothing really prevents one and there is plenty of time. Those walking through a country see and observe much more, for the movement of one's body is in some curious connection with the flow of one's thoughts, which are much freer and more active when walking. In Switzerland most people who really wish to profit by their travels perform them on foot. For painters and those who wish to study nature, such means of travelling are of course essential. Horses, mules and carriages are *male necessarium* but if possible it is best to engage a guide, talking with whom, while walking, might prove to be of the greatest interest.

We reached the bay at Keal after sunset; a lonely little hut was to shelter us for the night. More occupied with our plans for the next day than with anything else, we at once asked the host whether we could find a boat that would take us to the isle of Staffa on the morrow. He did not possess one himself but promised willingly to try and find something for us. But things became much more complicated when it came to our needs of the day. There was no food in his hut, nothing except potatoes; even the usual oatcakes were lacking! We had not eaten since the morning and felt an imperative need of some adequate supper.[1] To our delight, however, the country house at about a quarter of a mile distance

[63] *Gribune Head, Mull. The smoke in William Daniell's drawing comes from burning seaweed. Kelping, in which kelp and other seaweeds were cut, dried and incinerated to produce a low-grade alkali used in the manufacture of soap, alum and glass, provided an important source of income for Highland landowners.* Daniell

supplied us with everything that we needed and in fact gave us much more than the *lignum et sal*. Servants brought us tea, sugar, rum, fowls and lamb, which is exquisite in the Highlands, and all this with real Scottish hospitality, not dreaming to let us pay, except a tip for the servant. We lived on these provisions even in the latter days of our travels, not so much out of need, as because we wanted to remember the warm hospitality of those who sent us all this. The person who behaved so charmingly to us was the sister of Colonel Campbell, whose estate she managed during his absence. Our minds were so busy with this extreme kindness, that we no longer minded the great discomforts we had to endure during the night in the hut. We slept on wet hay without blankets or sheets; the hay had been cut ten days before but it had rained so incessantly that it had had no chance to dry.

The Highlanders as a rule are extremely poor. An acre of potatoes and an acre of oats or barley, from which they have to pay rent, is everything they own. They have practically no cattle; sometimes a cow, several sheep and a few goats constitute their whole possessions. The soil is so full of stones that they cannot plough it and have to dig with a spade. Their oatcakes are dry and sweetish, unpleasant to eat, and to be able to swallow them at all one must drink water after every mouthful. The few rich ones eat them with butter but, though excellent then, very few can afford such a luxury. In the houses of the rich lairds oatcakes are served too and played about with butter but, of course, more for national tradition than for food. The huts of the Highlanders are exceedingly miserable, built of different kinds of stone plastered together with clay and covered with earth. The windows are made of tiny little bits of glass put together and scarcely let any light in at all. The roofs are thatched with reeds or straw and sometimes covered with heather. Inside the huts are almost unbelievably sad. In a narrow space, divided only by a few thin boards, human beings lie down on the floor beside the animals. Their only bed is dirty straw or sometimes heather covered by a rough sheet. The floor is earth and clay; there are no chimneys and the fire burns on the floor. In some huts there are no windows at all and the only light comes through a hole in the roof. There are no barns; corn is left in stacks and, though it rains far more here than in our country, they are such experts at making these stacks that the corn never gets spoilt. If at

[64] *Cottage on Islay. Black houses, in which peat smoke filtered through a thatched roof and animals and families were separated only by a low partition, were still in use in the twentieth century. Lach-Szyrma was horrified by the poverty of the Highlanders.*

least these miserable farms were their own the poor people would be happier, but they have to pay rent. What a comparison with our peasants who have wide fields of fertile soil for all kinds of crops, orchards and vegetable gardens. They have spacious houses for their whole families, separate outhouses for their animals and large barns! Nevertheless, notwithstanding this great misery, the Highlanders are far better educated than one could have expected. Their talk is full of common sense and very serious, and each hut possesses a Bible, prayer books, and sometimes national songs or histories. These provide the only amusement they have in their lonely lives, especially in winter, when the snow and frost isolate them from everybody else. A German lady, Mrs Schopenhauer,[2] travelling in Scotland, asked a young girl in the Highlands: 'And what, my young lady, do you do in winter?' 'We spin and we pray,' answered the girl. There is a certain difference between misery and poverty. Poverty does not deprive one of human respect or even happiness but lack of morals plunges one into unspeakable dire misery. When poor, a human being is merely a pauper, when immoral, a miserable wretch.

The next morning when the sky was beginning to lighten, heralding the dawn, we started in a galley with three sailors. Dawn comes late in the glens; in some particular seasons of the year the sun only appears at noon. The wind was favourable this time and we made rapid progress to the isle of Staffa and straight into the cavern called 'Fingal's Cave'. Seeing that glorious cathedral made by nature's hand, exalted by its greatness, I threw myself into the sea, wanting to reach the doors of that temple by my own efforts and, if unsuccessful, to be buried in this proud cemetery. The sailors, trusting my courage more than my skill at swimming, which apparently is insufficient by Atlantic standards, kept at some distance with their boat. But when I swam under the basalt columns the water became much colder and the waves more violent and the sailors began to fear that I might get smashed against the rocks. I perceived the danger myself and returned to the ship. We then got into the cave and sailed to its very end, which is impossible if the sea happens to be rough. The cave is filled with water and is very deep too. At its entrance it is 53 feet wide, 250 feet long and 117 feet wide. The walls are formed of regular and slim basalt columns on which a vaulted roof of two uneven parts rests. This vaulting really resembles a Gothic work of some great master. The whole reminds one strongly of Gothic cathedrals, but the gloomy shade of the basalt, the darkness and the spaciousness impress one far more strongly and are not to be compared with what one feels in the achievements of a human hand. We were especially impressed by the sound of the waves beating against the columns and the roar of the sea tearing into and being pushed out of the neighbouring cave, called 'the Melodious Cave'. It seemed to us that we were listening to some mysterious service, Vespers said by nature herself. I felt very much the same as the famous Joseph Banks[3] did when he visited these spots and wrote:

> And what are the works of the human hand when compared to this? Cathedrals and palaces are mere toys. Human achievements are nothing but a feeble imitation of the great works of nature.

Faujas de St. Fond,[4] another traveller, also enlarges upon this cavern in his writings.. Along the right wall, well above the water, there is a long line of columns, as regularly cut as if sawn by hand. One can walk over them far into the cave. These columns are called by common people the chairs of Ossian's Knights. They were to sit on them during council or when they came to ask Fingal's advice. Having left the cave, we climbed up the basalt columns which were lying over one another like felled tree trunks. Some were so bent as to suggest that there must have been a time when they were in a liquid primeval stage: most were hexagonal. Following these natural stairs, we came to the surface of the island. Nobody lives there; only about fifteen cows grazed in the poor fields. They are brought here for the summer and are taken back for winter when the island is completely deserted. We were told that one winter a poor family tried to live here but had to leave, for the island went on shaking and trembling which the people here explain as the artifice of the devil. But even without the spirit of darkness the phenomenon can be easily explained. During storms the sea enters the caverns with such violence that the air, suddenly pushed out, gives reports as loud as those of heavy shooting guns.

We were on the island during a calm sea but we could easily imagine how very unpleasant it must be here when it is rough. Nobody goes there at such a time, for even to approach would be impossible. The landing place is in a cavern called Clamshell, for its shape reminds one of a sea creature *phala crocorax*. Here is the harbour of the island. We dined there thinking of the banquets of Ossian's knights, who drank wine out of seashells. The echo of this cavern is famous and the sailors, wanting to give us proof of it, again sang the same song of the oars. The entire island is only one mile long and half a mile wide. It belongs to one of the Macdonalds who calls himself Macdonald of Staffa. On the

[65] *Iona. Only the earthworks of the monastery, founded by St Columba in 563, have survived but one of the great crosses of the early Celtic church is visible in Grose's engraving. The monastic buildings of the thirteenth-century Benedictine monastery were in ruins by the 1820s. They were restored in the twentieth century to create an ecumenical centre.*

highest point of the island, over Fingal's Cave, there is a pile of stones, as is often seen in Scotland, which is said to date from the time of the Druids; they are called cairns.[5] Some served for the religious ceremonies of the Celts; others as tombstones for their heroes. Some are 140 feet long. Under one, according to Pennant,[6] 70 graves have been found, only he does not know where. These artificial hills of stones were not made all at once but little by little. Those whose people were buried there used to add stones in their honour. This custom seems to have survived up to now in the speech of the common folk who, when asking the powerful for something add 'Curri mi cloch er do charme' (I will add a stone to your tomb).

Having reached the summit of the cairn, we had a wide view over the ocean; Iona lay in front of us. The ruins of the monastery and the chapel of St. Columba are very noteworthy as they are the most ancient Christian remains, the monastery having been founded by the Saint in 565. Forty-eight Scottish kings, five Irish kings, eight Norwegian as well as one French king are said to be buried there. A little beyond the graves of the monarchs are those of the Lord of the Isles. There are many inscriptions on the tombstones but, alas, they are no longer decipherable. Many of those buried there probably thought that humanity would not forget them soon, if at all, and now their very names are forgotten. The reason for choosing this island as a safe burial place was an ancient prophecy telling that the sea would swallow up Ireland and Scotland seven years before the end of the world but the blessed Iona would be spared. Looking at Iona, about which Johnson[7] says that it is from her that civilisation came to Caledonia,[8] I recalled all his words about the island which now came to my memory with great accuracy.

Before leaving Staffa, we gave a last look at the sea, beyond which Ireland and America lie. The Atlantic is more beautiful than the German Ocean, its waters are more transparent and there are more seaweeds and shells to be seen and the shores are steep and wild. The western coast of Scotland is far gayer to look at than the eastern; even the vegetation here is two months advanced. On our way back we saw the two islands of Colonsay and Ulva. On the former, a few years ago, an impoverished Scottish chief was living. I forget his name. Though poor, he was so hospitable that he felt seriously offended if a visitor to Staffa failed to stop at his shores; he offered them the 'Mountain Dew' as he called whisky. Though old, he liked to have some himself. Knowing that he was already dead and would not send after us to ask us to his home, we passed his lonely shores thinking that perhaps his hospitality had died too. Perhaps, as on the deserted Staffa, here too only cattle were grazing. But our ideas of Scottish hospitality had been revived in the beautiful home of the Campbells, which can be seen from the Bay of Keal. In the home of the dead chief we would have been entertained with ancient Scottish hospitality but there we met hospitality which was modified by culture and education. The pity is that such hospitable and friendly countries are separated from other nations by the unsociable sea. Here, where even inns are lacking, country houses receive travellers instead. Man must help man and hospitality is the need of his heart.

XIX

The Roads in the Mountains. Inverness. Culloden. Glencoe.
Loch Tay. Dunkeld. The Braan Waterfall. Ossian's Cave.
Scone. Perth. Loch Leven. The North of Scotland. Return to
Arrochar. The Students. Return to Tarbet. Ben Lomond

FOR those returning from Mull there is a choice of two roads. One is through Fort William and Fort Augustus to Inverness, crossing the great plain of Scotland at the foot of its highest mountains. The second road leads through Glencoe, Tyndrum and Killin, along Loch Tay to Dunkeld and Perth. We did not follow either of these roads but I will describe them and their most interesting parts as far as I can, having gleaned information from the reports of those who have used them.

The Fort William road can be taken either by land or by Loch Linnhe. It leads along the lochs whose waters are increased by numerous streams from neighbouring hills. The Caledonian Canal[1] provides good sailing facilities and a link with the German Sea. Of all Scottish lochs Loch Ness is the longest and, because of its great depth and the height of the surrounding mountains, it never freezes. On the Loch's banks lies the castle of Fort Augustus and from there one can reach Inverness, the most significant township in the district. With a population of only 5,000, Inverness prides itself on having an academy. It is not a university but a kind of high school, similar to our county schools. In Inverness people speak the purest English. It was introduced here by Cromwell's troops during their long stay in the area.[2] Shakespeare made this part of Scotland famous by his play *Macbeth*, which can stimulate the imagination. You can still see the ruins of the castle where Duncan was slain by the treacherous hand of Macbeth's wife. There was so much blood that even the sea could not wash it away. You can also see the moor where, during the violent thunderstorm, Macbeth met the three witches. In Cawdor Castle you can see Duncan's bed, which was brought there when Macbeth's castle in Inverness was ruined.

On the way to Nairn lies Culloden where the Stewarts were finally defeated in 1745.[3] You can still see the site of the battle where, amongst the heather and grass, are the graves of those who were killed. It was the Camerons, devoted supporters of the Stewart cause, who particularly distinguished themselves in the battle in which their chief was killed. Campbell,[4] the poet, immortalised Culloden in his work *Lochiel* and Burns, in *The Lovely Maid of Inverness*, tells the story of the girl who mourns her father and brother, both killed in the battle.

The second more widely known road from Mull leads through Glencoe. This is a valley or rather a narrow gorge amongst very high, bare and rocky mountains which almost reach to the sky. The highest is Ben Nevis,[5] its peak always covered with snow. During the reign of Scottish kings the amount of tax paid to the court was measured by the amount of snow on Ben Nevis. In these wild surroundings there was

[66] *Ben Lomond from Cameron Wood. The Fort William–Loch Lomond road in the foreground was one of several built after the 'Forty-five as part of the government's attempt to pacify the Highlands. By 1800, 750 miles of road had been added to the 250 miles built earlier by General Wade. P. Sandby*

ample opportunity for violent human behaviour, of which the most famous was the massacre of the Macdonalds. The aggressors were the Campbells who killed a large number of Macdonalds, irrespective of age or sex, so that only a handful escaped.[6] At the bottom of this gruesome gorge runs the river Coe (Kona Ossiana). Apparently this is where the bard was born. On one side of the gorge is Con Fion, also known as the mountain of Fingal, on the other is Malmar. This is what Ossian has written about them:

> I looked at Kona – and I do not see Kona; I looked at the rocky mountains, divided by the river, and they are leaning towards each other like aged oak trees with the branches almost touching one another.

Much has changed since Ossian's time. The oak trees and the woods where Ossian used to hunt are no longer there; only the steep bare rocks remain. They are bold and grim. There is mist in the valley while the mountain peaks are shrouded in cloud. A thousand little streams descend as from the Ides of Homer. Glencoe brings you the most sober and gloomy thoughts. This place would not have pleased the bard who, as we are told, first saw the light of day there. However, he did draw inspiration from it later.

From Glencoe the travellers proceed by little-used roads to Tyndrum. There is nothing remarkable about that village. – it is only a lonely stopping place, like many others in the mountains. In a similar category is the village of Killin, which has extensive grazing ground for the sheep. Then we have Loch Tay. There is a road along the Loch and to the right the traveller can see huge mountains covered with woodland and, above them, Ben Lawers, 4015 feet high.[7] Now and again there is a small cottage with a bit of arable land and sheep grazing freely but, apart from that, the area is quite bare. Numerous cairns indicate the presence of graves while the shadowy clouds, racing across the mountains and valleys, remind you of centuries gone by and departed generations.

You can admire the beauty of all these places but only an artist could do them full justice. Those interested in man and his pursuits make their way to Dunkeld, a seat of the Duke of Atholl. The mountain ranges come close to a charming fertile valley and the beauty of the place is enhanced by the splendid castle of this rich nobleman. It has a very large courtyard and is close to the ruins of the old abbey [cathedral]. Prior to the Reformation this must have been a most imposing building; the tall columns, stonework and sculptures bear witness to the past glory of its

Saxon–Gothic architectural style. Within the walls there is a cemetery where the ashes of former foes now rest together in peace. Thus the hand of death has overcome the hate and strife. New graves are placed beside the old ones as if to show that the victors and the defeated have been reconciled.

Near Dunkeld the traveller can admire the waterfall of Braan and the bridge over the gorge and the river, 50 feet below. However, the greatest attraction is the house of Ossian, which can be reached by a lovely footpath. This is the second home of the bard, a true hermitage. Inside there is a picture of the singer Selma with a spear, a bow and his beloved dog. In his hand he is holding a harp while the Maidens of Morvern are listening to the songs of bygone days. But, while the traveller is somewhat surprised by the appearance of the old bard and imagines himself joining the maidens listening to the music, suddenly, as though moved by secret springs, everything disappears. He finds himself standing in a most wonderful summerhouse, surrounded by mirrors. From there he can see the fast-flowing stream and hear its deafening roar. All this is reflected in the mirrors and leaves the traveller totally bewitched.

On the banks of Braan is a cave partly man-made, partly natural, called Ossian's Cave. According to legend, the bard had occasionally taken refuge there. On the closely marked wall you can see an inscription. In her sleep Malvina speaks drowsily to Ossian:

> Behold the figure like misty shadow!
> It is Oskar! He is rushing here to console me
> Och, it is him departing, shadowy like mist
> Wait Oskar, let your shadow sweeten my dream!
> Wake up my harp, let my sorrow move you.
> Sing the fame of Oskar the song will soften my sorrow
> Come to life, Fingal's son, famous Ossian
> And join me in my tears and suffering.
> From the day of defeat by the hand of Kerbar
> The cup of the feast has not appeared in Ossian's homes.
> The deer are running through the valley of Morvern
> And Ossian's dogs are not chasing them.
> When the hunter encounters four stones in the valley
> He will say 'Peace be with you' and pass the grave.

From Dunkeld the road turns south to Perth. After crossing the river Almond you may turn left to visit Scone, a former capital of Scotland. The recently renovated palace is a sanctuary for many memorabilia, like

Mary Stewart's embroideries. A large collection of paintings occupies the area where Scottish parliaments used to meet. Scone's proprietor is the Earl of Mansfield, whose ancestors received the palace as a gift from James II. Some time ago the sacred Stone of Destiny was kept at Scone, a much cherished symbol of Scottish pride. However, in 1296, Edward I took it to London where it still is.[8] The last Scottish king crowned in Scone was the famous Robert the Bruce, in 1306. His bravery and leadership secured Scotland's freedom from attacks and domination by the English. Records indicate that national debates were held in Scone as far back as 906.

A few miles from Scone lies the town of Perth, a short distance away by a very attractive route. Perth is one of the oldest towns in Scotland. The Latin name was Bertha. Having conquered Scotland in 70 AD, Agricola had his headquarters there.[9] Fragments of Roman roads and stones with inscribed names of stations bear witness to those times. Perth is situated on the banks of the river Tay, whose beauty had so enchanted the Romans that they exclaimed *Ecce Tiberim, ecce Campus Martium* (Here is the Tiber, here is the Martian Camp.') Throughout centuries Perth acquired various rights and privileges which have contributed to the prosperity of its inhabitants. Now it is a most attractive town with a population of 20,000. It is well known for sheet metal works and for cotton and linen mills.

From Perth the road leads to Abernethy, the former seat of Pictish rulers and the centre of Christianity and learning. Now it is only a very modest village. From Abernethy the traveller follows the road to Kinross with the ruins of the old castle, which was the place of Mary Stewart's detention, and the lonely little island in the middle of Loch Leven, with the ruins of the Chaldean priory whose monks were the first to bring Christianity to this part of Scotland.

After seeing all the above mentioned places, the visit to the Scottish Highlands comes to an end. People who want to visit Scotland generally go to all these places, but the northern parts of Scotland, as well as the Western Isles and the Orkneys, are seldom visited. Historical remains are always what attract people most and the North does not possess any.[10] The population, owing to the severity of the climate and the barrenness of the soil, is more than scarce and the few people who live there are almost as wild as the mountains themselves. The beneficial light of education, so well diffused over other parts of Scotland, has not penetrated there. The inhabitants differ from the rest of Scotland in their customs, language and religion which, as in Ireland and many of

[67] *Abernethy Round Tower. The tower at Abernethy was probably built by Pictish monks in the ninth century as a refuge from Viking raiders. There is a similar tower at Brechin and several in Ireland.* Grose

[68] *Loch Leven Castle. Built c. 1300 as a royal castle of major importance, the castle changed hands several times during the Wars of Independence. In 1390 it was granted to the Douglas family. Sir William Douglas, 5th earl of Morton, acted as jailer when Queen Mary was imprisoned there after her defeat at Carberry Hill in 1567. It was a younger William Douglas, Keeper of the Boats, who helped her to escape.* Grose

the islands, is Roman Catholic.[11] This is the reason why the Catholic house of the Stewarts found more devotion among the Highlanders than among the Protestant Lowlanders. It is only to their devotion that the last descendant of that unfortunate family, Charles Edward, owed his first successes and, after the defeat of Culloden, his escape to France.

We decided not to visit that part of the country which the Scotsmen themselves do not know and instead we returned through places which every inhabitant of Scotland, if not entirely devoid of good taste, tries to visit if only once in a lifetime. Thus we travelled by Ben Lomond, Loch Katrine, the Trossachs and the road to Stirling. A foreigner, travelling for amusement and instruction, feels he must see them.

We reached Tarbet by our former route. In Arrochar we were caught by such a violent downpour that we were obliged to spend three days at the inn. Such torrents of rain occur often in the mountains and sometimes last for several weeks. No wonder a Frenchman, on meeting a friend back from Scotland, asked him first of all whether it still rained there. In the inn we found the same Cambridge undergraduates whom we had met on our way up. They had already been staying there for two months and they planned to spend the rest of their vacation in that rainy spot. They shared their time, as advised by sensible people, between work and play but the latter seemed to occupy the greater part. Their views as to what play meant were very different. One went with a shotgun to shoot and the other with a rod to fish. When back at the inn they used to play chess. Blackstone[12] and Horace were their 'vade-mecum' in studies but they certainly did not open them too often, for they both lay on a table covered with dust.

On the fourth day the barometer promised better things and we started on the road to Tarbet. But at Tarbet there was little hope of good weather and, when I asked the innkeeper whether it rained here the whole year, he answered very seriously: 'No, Sir, sometimes it snows'. Unable to wait any longer, we decided to climb Ben Lomond even in the heaviest of rains. So we started all our preparations that very evening and engaged a guide and a boat. The guide, anxious for our wellbeing and also for his own, told us to take a good bottle of whisky and drew our attention to the lines which were written on the pane of our bedroom window:

> With measured pace and slow ascend the steep,
> Oft stay thy pace, oft taste the cordial drop,
> And rest, oh, rest, long, long upon the top.

The ascent of Ben Lomond is six miles long and the expedition takes the whole day.

The next morning at dawn, though it was very cloudy, we got into the boat. We crossed Loch Lomond in a place where it is said to be 600 feet deep. and probably because of this the water there seems to be entirely black. The lower slopes of Ben Lomond are covered with rushes, which were of great help to us in our climb. The upper part is nothing but tall heather which was in bloom just then. Ben Lomond, called by the Highlanders 'The King of the Hills'. was truly cloaked in a splendid robe of purple and scarlet. The summit itself is bare rock and at the northern side there is a sheer drop of 300 feet. The precipice below is said to be the crater of an extinguished volcano.[13] One must have strong nerves to dare to look down into it. I crept on my knees to the very verge and told my companions to hold me by the legs. It was the only safe way of looking down, especially as the wind blew so violently that one had difficulty in standing up. But this wind, though unpleasant, chased the clouds away and then the view was magnificent. The speeding clouds threw deep-moving shadows over the countryside, clung to the mountains, leaving us at times cut away from the world below, alone in the sunshine, or again we too were enveloped by clouds and for some time saw nothing. Though the cold, increased by the altitude, the wet mist and the bitter wind, was so intense that we all shivered, yet nothing could cool our warm enthusiasm for such extraordinary and incomparable beauty. I remembered what a well-known French writer[14] said about this place, that there would be nothing to hope for from a man who, were he transported to Ben Lomond, would not become aware of having a human soul when standing over the precipice. The pure air of the hills is too noble for low creatures: vipers are unable to exist on the tops of mountains. The view is so wide that on clear days Edinburgh and Stirling can be seen to the east, the highest peak of Ben Nevis to the north, and the hills of Mull and even of Ireland to the west.

Thoroughly wet and entirely stiff with cold, we tried in vain to warm ourselves by drinking whisky. In this damp country it has no apparent effect, though in other places much smaller quantities of it would have been dangerous. Having poured part of the whisky on the ground as an offering to the 'genio montis', we began our descent by entering a cloud which poured with rain which luckily fell below us. Our wet shoes slipped on the steep slopes, and in places where we found no heather to hold to, our road was not easy. About halfway down, we found ourselves in such a morass that we had to wade up to our knees in mud. Our guide told us that there are some places over which it would have been impossible to pass. Such swamps exist where the waters find no way out until they form rivers: *laeta susurrantes fugiunt per gramina rivi.*

We returned to Tarbet carrying a few pebbles from the summit and several bunches of the heather which grows so tall there that it reaches up to one's shoulders. Our excursion had lasted twelve hours. We spent the evening reading Hogg's *Wake of the Queen,* in which he describes these places with real art. Only then, when we had seen reality and compared it with the description, did we realise how great the difference is between life and art. They are separated by a sort of gulf which increases or diminishes according to the genius of the poet. An artist in his inspiration will forever see things in a different light than would a cold critic. They see the world from entirely different angles, so no wonder that understanding between them is almost impossible. When people do not agree on essential points, discussions are sheer waste of breath they will never come to any decisive conclusions and the dispute will go on forever.

XX

*The Douglas Torrent. Inversnaid. Loch Katrine. Benvenue
and Benledi. The Trossachs. Loch Achray. The Brig of Turk.
The Road to Stirling. The Castle Hill. Historical Events.
Linlithgow. The Highland Chief*

THE next day the ship with other passengers arrived at the usual hour
and took us over to the other side of the loch, whence we were to start
on a most romantic journey to Loch Katrine. We landed near the Douglas
stream; it rises on Ben Lomond, and its turbulent waters are not transparent and clear as of other mountain torrents, but a curious dark grey,
which has given it the name of 'Douglas' which means grey in Gaelic.

Many an artist's brush has immortalised the course of that stream,
which is beautiful enough to have been peopled by muses and other
supernatural creatures, were it flowing in Greece not Scotland. We satis-
fied ourselves by a look in its foamy waters falling into Loch Lomond,
and then followed a twisting narrow path between the rocks and a
tangle of bushes to Inversnaid. Having ascended the hill dividing Loch
Lomond and Loch Katrine, we saw the ancient fortress which had been
built to subdue the Highlanders, but now it has been converted into an
inn, where the tired traveller can get a meal, good beer and oat cakes.

Having rested there we proceeded to Loch Katrine or Katturine,
which means in Gaelic: 'cold lake of black rocks'. A good name indeed,
for the loch is surrounded by steep rocks which scarcely allow a sun-
beam to reach it. The loch is long and narrow and the Highlanders compare it to an eel; Walter Scott describes it thus in his *Lady of the Lake*:

> One burnish'd sheet of living gold,
> Loch Katrine lay beneath him rolled,
> In all her length far winding lay,
> With promontory creek and bay,
> And islands that empurpled bright

The Douglas Torrent

Floated amid the livelier light,
And mountains that like giants stand
To sentinel enchanted land.

We parted with our guide in a low little hut that stood on the shore of the lake and having hired a boat with two oarsmen we started to row across the loch. The rain poured down and the waves rose so high that we thought that during a good storm crossing the loch must be dangerous. Our boat had no sails and our oarsmen, wanting to make their toil easier, cut quantities of birch branches and stuck them at the sides of the boat and the blowing wind helped them. One of the sailors was then occupied with the steering, while the other sat idle reciting the above-quoted passages from Walter Scott. Listening to him we observed as we passed it the Goblin's cave and then the black rock arising from the lake. This is called 'the foaming black dog of Roderig Dhu' For, as the sailors explained, it 'bites' the passing boats, damages or even wrecks them. We also saw the shady island of the Lady of the Lake, and the ancient oak tree from which twigs are taken by travellers

[69] *Loch Lubnaig by J. M. W. Turner (1775–1851). Turner toured Scotland in 1818 in order to make sketches for Walter Scott's* Provincial Antiquities. *Some of the engravings, which were of exceptional quality, were used by Lockhart to illustrate his* Readings from Scott. *Ben Ledi rises from the southern end of Loch Lubnaig.*

[70] *Church of the Holy Rood. The twelfth-century parish church of Stirling
was replaced in the mid-fifteenth century by a building which reflected its
importance as the church of the royal court. 'Mar's Wark' in the foreground
was never completed. It was to have been the lodging of the earl of Mar who
became Regent for the infant James VI in 1571 but died the following year.* Grose

as remembrances. We followed their example. The genius of Walter
Scott has taken these places out of oblivion; deserted and unknown
beforehand, they are now swarming with people who come from many
distant parts, anxious to see their beauty.

The steep heather and forest-covered shores add much to the charm
of the scenery. Two great mountains are seen on both sides, Benvane
and Ben Ledi. The former is considered to be the most beautiful mountain in Scotland. It is all granite and there are no large trees on its slopes.
The sailors told us that the Duke of Montrose, to whom it belongs, had all
the trees cut down which has greatly damaged the appearance of the
mountain. Eagles used to live on Benvane, but the population did their
best to exterminate them and now we only saw hawks. There is a cave at
the foot of the hill where a kind of goblin called the 'Urisks' used to live;
they were apparently easily tamed and then could be induced to serve
their masters. The Highlanders believed that every family in order to
have good luck should at least have one Urisk living with them.

Ben Ledi is situated on the opposite shore of the loch and means: 'the
stone of the Gods'. It was a Celtic sacred mountain. To this day there is

a path leading to the summit, covered with soft grass, which must have been made by human feet. People used to assemble on the top of the mountain on the first of May and light a huge bonfire in honour of the sun, which was called 'Belis' in Gaelic.

We disembarked in the narrow part of the lake where, as the Bard says, the water is so shallow that the geese can scarcely bathe in it. There, having dismissed our rowers, we proceeded with a guide into a most lovely glen called 'The Trossachs'. Walter Scott has sacrificed a whole chapter to the description of hunting here. Looking at all these glorious places, I felt sorry that our Carpathians are so little explored and known. Instead of exploiting the scenery of other countries, we should know how to kindle our own fires. It is a pity that our Polish mountains are not more fashionable.

We spent the night at an inn, the name of which I no longer remember. Anyhow the traveller found there all the comforts he needed. The next day we left the splendid country of the mountains and proceeded along the shores of Loch Achray. This lake, certainly one of the most beautiful, is serene and quiet. The surrounding cottages and the fertile-looking fields give it a look of happiness and of peace. When we reached the western end of the loch our road crossed over the Turk by a bridge. We then followed the shores of Loch Vennachar to Callander where the River Teith, joined by both her tributaries, becomes quite wide. There is a splendid view of Ben Ledi from there. Afterwards, although the hills were left behind, the countryside remained very picturesque. We passed the ruins of Doune Castle, where Mary Stewart lived for some time, then Blair Drummond, an industrial place full of cotton industries. Some time ago Lord Kames used to live here; he was well known both for his virtues and for his writings (*Sketches of the History of Man*).[1]

We drove to Stirling across a plain which, judging by the stubbles, must be fertile. Stirling Castle was visible from afar on its steep and rocky hill. This hill had some likeness because of its solitude with the castle hills at Edinburgh and Dumbarton. I remembered Walter Scott's description of this place in *Waverley*. The tall Gothic towers of the church remain in which the knights of old would have made their sacred vows. The fortress and the palace stand too; from there the generous hand of the King rewarded the deserving, and in the evenings, after the tournaments, the knights and the fair ladies danced, sang and banqueted. Stirling Castle is one of the best known in the country; the kings often stay here when they visit Scotland.[2] Some, especially those of the Stewart dynasty, lived there. Within its walls James IV was born, and

James V and Mary were crowned. This noble and popular King is represented in the *Lady of the Lake* under the name of Fitz James. The buildings have now been converted into army barracks. There are perhaps few places in the world around which so many memories survive. Invaders attacked this fortress, Highlanders fought with Lowlanders and Wallace, in 1297, defeated the English here. There is no spot of ground which has not been drenched with human blood. From the castle one can see fifteen famous battlefields. These indeed are places over which humanity weeps. Looking on the fertile fields of the present day, one feels like exclaiming with the French poet:

> 'Le sang humain dont vous futes couverts
> Vous engraissa pour plus de cent hivers.

St Ninian, Banockburn, Falkirk and Linlithgow[3] through which we returned to Edinburgh had nothing of interest. We reached the capital just after the departure of the King. On our way we met numbers of mail coaches crowded with people who had been to pay their homage to the King. A chief in his ancient beautiful dress was also returning home. He was no longer surrounded by his clansmen running around his carriage, their muskets on their shoulders, as I saw him that time when he was presented to the King. Now, deprived of all his glory, he was sitting with craftsmen and merchants on top of the mail coach as if he belonged to their set. I have never seen anything as incongruous as the feudal chieftain, with an eagle's feather in his hat and a sword at his side, sitting quietly among common people in their frock coats and hats. Somebody seeing him for the first time would certainly think that some wild man had lost his way and by mistake found himself in the civilised world. Such is the difference between Scotland of the past and of the present. The Chief was Glengarry.

XXI

*History of Scotland. The Clans. The Choice of the
Successors. The Castles of the Chiefs. Manner of Fighting.
The Swordsman and the Bard. Hospitality. The Harp.
About Bards. Popular Poetry. The Inflexibility of the Chiefs.
The Faithfulness of the People. The Lack of Morals. The
Results of the Union*

I would like to give some time to the History of Scotland,[1] before leaving
that country altogether. The Scottish nation, as historians generally accept,
is a fusion of the ancient Caledonians and the Britons, two branches of
the Celtic tribe, and to these were later joined the Picts, the country's
aboriginal inhabitants. The modern name of Scot is taken from Scuti,
which in the language of the ancients means 'wanderer', doubtless because
they migrated to these parts. Whatever the case, Kenneth II, who was
their king or leader, having defeated the quarrelling Picts and Caledonians, gave to the conquered country, from that victorious generation
onwards, the name of Scotland. This occurred about the year 840 AD.

This year, however, is not the oldest date in the history of Scotland,
which reaches back into the most distant of times. Her first king, and
indeed the founder of her dynasty, was Fergus I who ruled about the
year 330. Acceptance of Christianity took place in the year 201,[2] that is to
say eight centuries earlier than in Poland. Of Fergus' successors history
relates nothing memorable, except that they fought valiantly against the
Romans. Vanquish them they could not however until, finally, their state
fell apart. After 27 years without a king Fergus II ascended the throne of
Scotland. He waged several unfortunate wars against the Romans
which often resulted in his defeat. In the last, together with the King of
the Picts, he was slain. Nevertheless, Fergus is held in high esteem as
having brought about the renaissance of his state. His descendants ruled
from 404 until 1370 and through this period of 960 years gave Scotland

[71] *'Grant's Piper' by Richard Waitt. The portrait of William Cummine, Piper to the Laird of Grant and wearing a tartan unlike any now known, was painted in 1714. The castle in the distance had recently been classicised.*

60 kings. After the line died out the Stewarts ascended the throne and, reigning for 230 years until the year 1603, produced nine kings of whom the last, James VI, son of Mary Queen of Scots, ascended the throne of England following the death of Queen Elizabeth. Though Scotland and England were at last united under James VI, who became James I of England, the two nations still remained apart. The more real union of the two Kingdoms came in 1707.[3] Ireland joined the union only in 1801. The three united Kingdoms took the name of Great Britain.

This union, joining the arms and the powers of three countries, has greatly benefited each of them and increased respect for them in Europe. But it was unable to wipe out the old differences and dislikes, which went on smouldering and bursting into flame at every occasion that the national pride was touched. At this time each of the three nations feels like becoming independent again. The reason for this state of affairs is their differences in character which, being the growth of centuries, need centuries to change. The forming of these different characters was influenced by different feudal systems, peculiar to each nation, different governments and, most of all, a different religion. These causes still exercise their influence, especially in Scotland which, having united with England of her own free will and not like a conquered country as was the case in Ireland, was able to safeguard her ancient rights and liberties. This is the reason why Scotland is far wealthier and less unhappy than Ireland. Scotland is also much more willing to collaborate with the government. Scotland has her own legislation based on Roman Law. From the Anglo-Saxon institutions she has accepted only the Courts of Law with juries, but these are also different in Scotland. As things are, the Scottish nation, free and unoppressed, develops as it did beforehand, only under less severe forms. This of course is due to the advance of civilisation. All offices are held by Scotsmen and barred to Englishmen and anyone who is not of the Presbyterian established religion.[4] Other religions, the Church of England included, are only tolerated. Their churches are called 'chapels' and are not allowed to have bells of their own. Only Presbyterian churches have the right of ringing for their services. England pays Scotland back by calling the Scots 'dissenters' and their churches in England 'chapels'. It does seem strange that besides such great freedom of thought, such narrow-minded pettiness could exist.

From time immemorial the whole nation has been divided into clans, the equivalent of which is found in our Slavonic 'generations'. Each clan was led by a chief, not elected as in some countries but hereditary.[5] His attitude to the people of his clan was entirely patriarchal. It was he who kept them at peace among themselves, protected them from outside enemies, had the first place in Council, leadership in war and the power of life and death. Nobody disputed his judgements either from trust in his justice or fear of his vengeance. Everybody belonging to his clan bore his name and inter-married; each clan had its own tartan by which the clansmen could recognise each other.

The Highlands were the habitation of the clans. The people in the Lowlands, quieter by nature, were more obedient to the king and were more often the victims of aggression than aggressors.[6] The warlike disposition of the Scots can be solely attributed to the Highlanders who, living in their hills and around their lochs, quarrelled, fought and filled the whole country with unceasing disturbances and terror. Their quarrels were often hereditary, handed down from their forefathers to later generations; their vengeance – quick and terrible, depending solely on the will or passion of the chieftain. A chief who meditated vengeance set fire to a piece of wood shaped like a cross, then dipped it in the blood of a freshly killed kid and handed it over to one of his clan, who handed it over to the next one, mentioning the place where they were to meet. This 'Fiery Cross' or the 'Cross of Shame' circulated around the clan in no time, and it was the greatest shame not to answer the call. War was not declared; such a proceeding would have been thought very rash: a sudden attack on the enemy's household, the seizing of his cattle, his only wealth, was the beginning of war. Fires and slaughter ended it. The vanquished clan either had to pay a ransom or passed under the rule of the conqueror. This however seldom happened, as everybody preferred death to the rule of the enemy. Smaller clans joined larger ones for help in case of attack. The most famous of these were the Campbells, Gordons, Macleods, Macdonalds, MacKenzies, Macfarlanes, Macgregors and Macphersons.

After the death of the chief, his successor obtained power only after having accomplished some deed of fame, courage and wisdom. To achieve this, he generally made a foray into the country of an enemy clan where, if he was successful, he stole the cattle and destroyed everything. The flower of the youth of the clan accompanied him to win renown. When on enemy soil, they killed the first animal they met and sprinkled its blood on their banners. Then the druid, later on the bard and last the chief himself made a speech emphasising the honour of victory and the shame of defeat. The deeds of the past generations were also cited. A young chief was generally the victor, for he would have preferred to die

[72] *Dunvegan Castle. The MacLeods of Dunvegan are descended from a son of Olaf the Black, the last Norse king of the Isle of Man. The fourteenth-century Fairy Tower was in ruins by the eighteenth century. It was restored in the nineteenth and a bridge was built to link the castle with the land. In the foreground is a black house.* Grose

rather than to appear unworthy in the eyes of his people. After the return from the expedition he became head of the clan. The ceremony of his election was accompanied by numerous rites dating from ancient times. He was made to stand on a pyramid of stones, surrounded by his clansmen etc. The most faithful of his friends handed him his father's sword, somebody else a white staff as a sign of his power. Then the bards proclaimed in song the deeds of his family. A banquet followed during which the young chief had to give proofs of his manhood in drinking. Johnson saw at Dunvegan on the Isle of Skye a huge ox horn containing two full quarts, which had to be quaffed in one draught by every MacLeod who had reached manhood.[7]

The houses of the chiefs were places of gathering for the whole clan. Important matters were settled there, banquets held and rewards given to the most valiant warriors. In times of danger, they served as shelter to the clan, for they were well defended fortresses, built on inaccessible rocks or on islands. We saw many such castles which had once belonged to the Lord of the Isles on the western shores of Scotland. They occupy much space and are built of huge boulders; they are sure to last for centuries to come. Some are so huge that, reading about them, one can still scarcely believe it. The Tara Palace in Ireland, where the people assembled every third year, occupied 900 square feet; it had 150 halls, as many dormitories, in each of which 60 people could sleep. The ceilings were 27 feet high; dinner was served daily for a hundred people in the times of Cormac.[8]

The chiefs often made alliances, the wording of which paints to perfection the spirit of the times. Parchment was not considered long lasting enough so they carved them in stone instead. One such stone is walled in over the entrance to the gate of the MacLeods: 'Whoever from the clan Maclonish will come to stand in front of this gate, be it at midnight and he be holding a human head in his hands, can be sure of finding in this castle shelter and protection against everything and everybody, except the King'.

Their ways of fighting had nothing in common with ours; they rather belonged to the age of Homer. Like the Greek poet, Ossian represents his heroes fighting from chariots. For a long time the weapons of the Caledonians were a bow, a dirk and a claymore. Muskets and pistols came later on. Spears, so often mentioned by Ossian, have not been used for a long time; they only appear in the battle near Prestonpans as a weapon against the English cavalry. An oaken targe served as protection from blows; it was covered with leather, or else made of interwoven twigs and surrounded by an iron ring. Armour was seldom used; a man's breast was generally defended only by his courage. To fight better, upper clothes were generally discarded, as in 1546 in the time of the Battle of the Shirts. The enemy was attacked with wild cries; in regular battle, the clans fought in groups. Families kept together so that everybody should fight better, surrounded by those of his own blood. They started at a run and then stopped at some distance from the enemy for a short respite. They shot from their muskets only once and then threw them down; darting a little nearer, they shot from their pistols next and then flung them at their enemies and themselves took to swords. Having done all that could be done, they finished off with daggers. They owed many a victory over the English to such unexpected methods until these tactics became well-known. They feared cavalry most, for Scots are not accustomed to horses and they maintained that the English steeds were taught to bite and to stamp. A chief always addressed his clan before the battle.

To the person of the chief a bard [9] and an armour bearer were attached, and these two never left his side. The armour bearer carried his weapons in war and preceded him for etiquette's sake at councils; a strong and unflinching man was always chosen for that office and at banquets it was his right to receive double portions. The bard was the poet of the chief and his clan; he recited the deeds of the past generations and stirred hearts to fight during battle and to gaiety during banquets. No important event could be celebrated without song, which meant without a bard. He was called in Gaelic: 'Senachi' and his office was hereditary which, before printing had been invented, was perhaps the surest and the only way of preserving historical events in the memory of the coming generations. But on the other hand what could be expected from a poet who has to be one by the laws of heredity, not because of his talent? The tradition of bards survives in what are the 'Laureates', court poets, whose sole duty consists in making an ode on the King's birthday and on New Year's Day. Southey[10] is the present Laureate.

The chiefs not only helped their own people in need; they also gave hospitality to strangers. This custom has survived until the last days of the existence of the clans. Martin[11] says in his book of his travels that at a banquet given by one of the chiefs a majordomo went around filling the glasses. In wealthy houses these banquets lasted until dawn and did not always end without excesses. Music and song were greatly appreciated, and those who left the table even for a moment had to make excuses in rhyme on their return.

I would not have liked to have been accused of credulity in what I say about bards. There is no doubt that they existed but their fame faded away in the first centuries of Christianity. The popularity their songs had among the Celts was also diminished. The songs of Ossian might have been considered as an important echo of past ages, but their authenticity is uncertain and, were that riddle solved, perhaps it would have weakened not strengthened the reputation the bards still preserve. All that I have said about the bards, Ossian, or ancient songs should be taken not as an article of faith, but as the average opinion of intelligent people. Let us leave it for the Scots themselves to decide what is a legend and what a historical truth.

Nowadays people believe nothing which is not written down and solidly documented by various proofs. This attitude destroys of course many lovely illusions. A veil therefore must be drawn over those centuries of which the living voice and the memory of the nations are the only remains, and traditions the only historical source. To those who do not wish to believe, nothing is sufficient proof that the bards had existed. What is it to them that, no longer ago than the middle of the last century,

Clanranald had a bard, or that other clans numbered many descendants of bards among them? These descendants of the bards, though no longer appearing with harp and song, for they could hardly have withstood competition with the modern virtuosi, possessed valuable knowledge about the genealogy of the clans and historical events. The unbelievers pay no heed to the fact that the ancient Scottish castles have special places for the bards to sit down and sing, that there is a Bard's Window in Duntulm Castle in the Isle of Skye and, in Castle Lachlan in Argyle, a special Minstrel's Gallery. The writers who gather and spread such news are accused of gross credulity, though for those who search, many things can be discovered about ancient days. But nowadays proofs are needed. To a true lover of the history of mankind, where documents are no longer to be found, a legend is welcome. When no legend is available, even a tale will be a treasure, for tales have foundations which remain for the thinker to ponder upon.

Scots, anyhow, love legends and few nations possess a richer collection of these. Percy,[12] Ritsom,[13] Pinkerton,[14] Jamieson,[15] Finlay,[16] Evans, Herd,[17] and Walter Scott gathered them. Fergusson, Burns and Hogg owe the development of their talents to the spirit of the popular ballads. Most of the ancient songs are extremely sad, as if the tragedies of old times are also imbued with deep sorrow. Books speaking of human suffering have more right to survive in the human hearts than gaiety. Most of our own mournful Slavonic songs survive longer than the gay ones, for jokes are born of the moment and die with the moment, not appealing to feelings which are eternal.

The chiefs of the clans had unlimited power which they exercised not only over their own people but also over strangers.[18] A historical fact is a good illustration of this. After Queen Anne's accession to the throne, George, a Danish Prince and her husband, then Chief Admiral, heard that one of the Scottish chiefs had marvellous forests. Needing wood to build ships, he sent his men with special letters of introduction to that chief. The messengers departed and on arriving showed to the Chief the Prince's letters. Having read them, the Chief said that he did not know any Prince of that name. The messengers tried to convince him that the Prince was the husband of Queen Anne. 'I do not know Queen Anne, either,' The Chief replied 'I only know that tramps from Ireland come here pretty often to make fun of us. I give you an hour's time limit; either prove who you are or you will be hanged on that tree'. And, pointing to the oak tree in front of the house, he departed. The unfortunate messengers left in such an unpleasant situation began to lose all hope of getting out of the business, when they suddenly remembered that when they were passing through Edinburgh somebody gave them a note to the Chief. In the unexpected danger they had entirely forgotten it. Using that note as the last means of salvation they went with it to the Chief after the hour had passed. The Chief took it, looking very fierce, but while he was reading his face softened. 'Why on earth did you not deliver it at once? It is a note from one of my neighbours; I assure you that were it not for this note, I would have done what I had told you I would.' Whereupon he received them with great hospitality and allowed them to see his forests.

Faithfulness and devotion to the Chief was the most appreciated virtue of the clans. History provides us numerous examples of this. During the battle of Inverkeithing, fought against the armies of Cromwell, Hector MacLean and his clan were fighting. Three hundred of his people had already fallen, when seven remaining brothers decided to save the life of their Chief, who was surrounded by the enemy. They fought beside him and when one was killed the second took his place, sheltering the chief and crying: 'Another for Hector!' Their courage won

[73] *Detail from* The Airs and Melodies peculiar to the Highlands of Scotland and the Isles (1816). *Many of the tunes were collected by Capt. Simon Fraser from MacKay of Bighouse, an officer in the Black Watch. Although proscribed after the 'Forty-five, Highland dress and pipe music were permitted in the Highland regiments. On the left of the Muse is Niel Gow, the great violinist and composer, with an idealised picture of Highland life in the background, and, on the right, a Bard. Behind him, tourists are being rowed out to Staffa to admire Fingal's Cave.*

general admiration and their cry served the Highlanders in years to come, when in imminent danger. The Pretender experienced no less devotion and faithfulness when he was hunted by the King's soldiers after the defeat of Culloden. One of the Mackenzies who stood by him to the last strongly resembled the Pretender. The soldiers who did not know the Prince and were unable to catch him alive, decided to kill everybody. Mackenzie got shot in the breast and he fell crying: 'Miserable men, you have killed your own king!' The delighted soldiers let the true king escape, cut off the head of Mackenzie and brought it back to town, hoping to get the £30,000 reward. Only then did they learn how they had been taken in. This unhappy descendant of the Stewarts experienced even more devotion when later on, during his wanderings in the Highlands, he was taken care of by the three brothers Kennedy, simple robbers. They knew of the huge reward given by the Government for the head of the Pretender and yet they did not betray him and sheltered him for a long time in their hiding place. Having nothing to live on, they used to go and steal at night and then in disguise went to Inverness to buy food. At least one of them who did not yield to the temptation of gaining £30,000 reward was hanged for stealing a cow worth 30/-.

The morals of the Scots of those days were very peculiar. The noblest sentiments and deeds were combined with the lowest. The greatest sacrifices were considered as nothing when for one of themselves but they had the deepest hatred and vengeance for their enemies. Apparently everything was permitted to satisfy these feelings; they plundered, killed and were cruel. War was their element and they saw no wrong in looting, for often this was their only means of livelihood. In constant fights with England, they did not care for agriculture, for in most cases their enemies would reap what they had sown. Cattle was the only wealth worth having for it could be hidden in the Highlands and even if seized by the enemy could not be taken back. The difference between 'mine' and 'thine' was entirely forgotten in such ways of existence. All ideas of property were very vague. Plunder was considered as quite legal, and far from being a matter for remorse, they prided themselves on it. Some family coats of arms throw vivid light on the morals of the times. The Hardens had: 'Reparabit cornua Phoebe'; the Cranstouns: 'You shall want ere I want'. The Haliburtons: 'Watch well'.[19]

These moral standards prevailed amongst both sexes almost up to our times. As recently as the year 1745, a poor woman who was begging for bread was asked how many husbands she had had? 'Three,' she answered. When asked whether they had been good men, she said that the first two ones were very good men indeed and had died for the law, for they had been hanged for theft. Only the third one was no good at all and rotted at home, like a handful of dirty straw.

If moral ideas were all wrong, so was justice faulty and most unfair. There was a law, for instance, that if the actual evildoer could not be found, then the punishment he deserved could be inflicted on any one of his clan. Once a Campbell got into trouble with the Macdonalds and was hiding from them with men of his own clan. The Macdonalds discovered him and when the Campbells refused to give him up, they made a fire in front of the entrance to the cave and suffocated them all. Johnson relates some terrible stories too about the cruelties of the Macdonalds.

The union of Scotland and England put a limit on the power of the chiefs and their rights of jurisdiction were taken from them, though not without resistance and even bloodshed.[20] After the unhappy experience of the Pretender in 1746, Parliament forbade the carrying of arms, without which no Scotsman was seen beforehand, and even the national dress was forbidden so as not to awaken ancient feuds. Today when old troubles are past and clan tartans no longer frighten but are a historical tradition, this order has been repealed. The kilt is now worn by the Scottish militia and by the Celtic club and society, but now it is only a kind of national dress by which Scots can be distinguished from other nationalities. The King himself wore it and the people were mad with joy to see their King in the scarlet tartan of the Stewarts. His guards, all of them young men of the first families, also wore their kilts and their tartans and went on duty to the sound of the national bagpipes.

Better order and education began from the union with England. Cromwell started the first newspapers by the leaflets he edited to his soldiers.[21] He also taught the Scots how to mend their shoes and how to plant cabbages,[22] for these two elemental needs of everyday life were unknown before his time. Even today one sees many people walking barefoot in Scotland, which would be considered almost indecent in England. The Scots are ashamed of it and I would not advise any foreigner to start a conversation about it unless he wants to offend them. It is difficult to understand how a nation which lacks not only luxuries but also the most elemental necessities of life can have such an appreciation of art and literature. This problem would be enough to make many an economist less conceited and less confident in his theories. Scotland's ruins, cathedrals and literature bear witness that though a poor country she can still produce great things. The fifteenth and sixteenth centuries in Scotland were as glorious as far as literature goes as at the present times. The collective Latin works of the *Deliciae Poetarum Scottorum* would bring credit to any country. Their philosophers were known all over Europe: (Boethius[23] and Buchanan). And yet, at a time when these men were so enlightened for their century, they had no encouragement from industry or trade, which are now considered to be the chief sources of a nation's wealth and her inspirations both for art and science. There is some hidden reason which makes intellectual perfection and nobility of sentiment entirely independent of wealth. And it would have been fatal for humanity were it otherwise.

XXII

The Present State of Scotland. Character of the Population.
The Love of the Highlanders for their Country.
Superstitions. Present Condition of the Highlanders.
Education. Language. Bagpipes. Crofters. Learning.
Religion. Popular Music. Dances. The Influence of Song on
Customs. Family Devotion

THE character of the Lowlanders has been formed under English influences; the same education and industry have been adopted and by now little difference is left between them and other nations who busy themselves with industry and agriculture. The people of the Lowlands can be considered entirely modern, laborious, temperate, orderly and quiet, loving a comfortable and peaceful home life. The Highlanders are so different that they seem to be another nation. They are more perspicacious, more hospitable and more civil. The first quality is developed by the greatness of nature in which they live: the second by their loneliness, because of which they come to appreciate human companionship: the third remains from their feudal existence in obedience to their chiefs who exercised kingly power over them. Civility is certainly one of the attributes of a monarchy in a country. The good manners of the Polish peasants are also chiefly due to this. We have been a Kingdom, and the polished habits of our gentry influenced the villagers. The difference of manners is striking between remote villages and those which are in the neighbourhood of a country house inhabited by a kind and cultured owner.

The Highlanders who had lived under their chiefs in incessant fights and disputes preserve all their virtues of courage and daring. They make excellent soldiers and join the army willingly. They are lively by nature, both physically and morally, for they often have stormy dispositions, Their life in the mountains not only teaches them agility, it also gives them a great love of freedom. It develops their imagination and inclines them to poetry to such an extent that all memories of their country are invariably united to the memory of all the poems which have been created there. They love music, song and dance but there is a strange sadness in their faces which travellers ascribe to the lonely lives they lead in a rainy and cloudy country. They spend the whole winter entirely shut away from the world and visit the towns only in the summer. For days and weeks, sometimes wandering in the hills after their flock, they meet nobody or, if they meet anyone at all, it is another shepherd like themselves. Their talk does not last a long time. They tell each other the news of their respective villages, their prophetic dreams and signs predicting weather, which are often more accurate than the meteorological tools.

Living alone with nature, the Highlander becomes as devoted to his country as the Swiss are to their mountains. Wherever fate will take him, he will never forget his hills and he speaks of them with an emotion almost incomprehensible to the Lowlander, for the Lowlander, spending all his time over his machines and concentrating on profit, forgets all about the place of his birth and finds a home wherever he earns most. Highlanders leave their homes only when forced by dire misery. One sees them standing on board the ships which are to transport them across the Atlantic to America. They look wistfully towards the Highlands and sing:

> Ha till, ha till, mi tuillidh!
> (We shall not return, we shall see thee no more.)

This tune and these words can never be heard by a Highlander without bringing a tear into his eyes, so great is his longing for his native land. The Irishman is like the Highlander. Whether unloading ships on the Thames and carrying on his powerful shoulders the wealth of others, while he himself possess nothing, or fighting someone else's battles, persecuted as he is by his own Government, he invariably sings:

> Erin mavourneen, Erin go-bragh!
> (Erin, my darling, my country for ever.)

I could if I wanted quote many popular superstitions but it is scarcely worth while as the belief in them is quickly dying out, owing to improved education. But one still meets in forests the so called 'Fairy Circles',[1] made of stones, and babies are carefully guarded before they are christened so as not to be snatched by the fairies and changed into

[74] *Scotch plough and* cas-chrom *The old Scotch wooden plough could only scratch the surface. By the mid-eighteenth century it was being replaced on arable land by Small's iron swing plough. This could turn over a clean furrow and deepen the soil in cultivation. The* cas-chrom *was used in the Hebrides on land too rough for horse-drawn implements.*

something else. Some stones which are said to have belonged to the ancient Celts were thought miraculous. He that possessed such a stone was considered to be lucky. A young man of pure habits looking into its polished surface would see there his whole future life. The famous magician, Dr. Dee,[2] whom Wojciech Laski[3] brought over to Poland, possessed such a stone and called it sacred; from it he predicted the future of his credulous protector, or perhaps he only made fun of his foolishness. It is also a custom of the Highlanders to extinguish all fires in a house where somebody is dead and to put on the chest of the body a little salt and earth. The earth means the destructibility of our human bodies and the salt the immortality of the soul. Up to now many people believe in second sight. People who possess that gift predict the future and also describe present events happening in some distant place. This gift is extremely rare and only to be met among Highlanders. There are diverse opinions as to the possibility of the existence of such a thing. It certainly is difficult to explain except perhaps on the same grounds as magnetism to us.

The Highlanders still live in their primitive way. They fish and rear sheep and are not given to agriculture for their soil is too barren. At home they are lazy and inactive, but transported elsewhere they become the first in everything. Many of them have gone to the industrial towns and are beginning to lose their prejudice against trade and industry. The Highlands become more and more deserted, for they no longer serve as shelter to those in hiding or as a place from which to ambush an enemy. Their hard life has taught the Scots endurance in bearing cold, hunger, bad weather and all sorts of difficulties. For a long time the Highlanders looked down on the Lowlanders, calling them an effeminate nation and giving them the name of 'Sassenachs'. For they despised all comfort and once, when at war, a young man rolled himself a lump of snow and put it under his head instead of a pillow, his grey-haired grandfather kicked it away, scolding him for such unpardonable effeminacy. In the extreme north and on some of the islands, the Highlanders still resist Presbyterianism and remain Roman Catholics. Though uneducated, nobody would call them barbarians, for life with the splendours of nature develops their innate intelligence.

But their education is also well thought of by now.[4] During the time of my stay in Scotland, I witnessed how schools in the Highlands are promoted with great zeal. The chief obstacles were the differences in language, the lack of books in Gaelic and also the scattered population and the difficulties of communication. The respective glens are too distant from each other for the children to be able to assemble in a common school and too sparsely populated to have each a school of their own. There are very few churches for the same reason and the remote parishes can do practically nothing to raise the standards of learning. The better-off have to give their children some kind of elementary home education and then send them to school in Edinburgh. The simplicity of these children of nature before they become children of civilisation is sometimes very diverting. I knew a girl called Fanley, who had come from the Orkney Islands. She was about sixteen and lived with a family in Edinburgh and went to school there. The school was not far off; nevertheless, poor Fanley invariably lost her way, for in the Orkneys there was only one path. She also complained that the trees hampered all views for there were no trees on her island. From anywhere one could see the open space of the Atlantic, with sometimes a boat or a whale in the distance, and at night the glow of the aurora borealis.

The Scots speak in fact three languages: one English, two Gaelic and three Scottish. This is a dialect of English.[5] It has fewer of the French words which have been brought by the Normans and more of the Saxon ones. In pronunciation and syntax it is more like platt-deutsch, a German dialect. It is not unpleasant to the ear and, on the contrary, it has more softness and the special simplicity of expression that is called naïve which lends such charm to the dialects of the Slavonic peasants. The best Scottish dictionary has been published by Dr. Jamieson; his work is as important as that of Johnson who, by his dictionary, brought such profit to the English language.

The Scottish dialect was formerly the common language of Scotland; books were written in it as well as laws and both lairds and crofters used it. It began to die out in the reign of James VI who, by some curious freak, though himself unable to speak decent English, was very exacting and ordered that those who asked for an audience should address him in English or in Latin. The removal of the capital to London and the introduction of English into legislation and government did not of course encourage the development of the Scottish dialect. It remained the language of the middle and lower classes and would have probably disappeared had it not been that modern writers introduced it into literature. This has done much to add to the dignity of the language of the Scots and they are no longer as careful as they had been to avoid Scottish words and expressions. Though many are still very particular and even start their children at English schools to give them proper intonation, for Scottish curiously interferes with English and those who have been brought up in Scotland never can speak English with the 'English' accent. But this anxiety about the right way of pronouncing is only met among those who are just as anxious that their frock coats should be cut in exactly the same manner and their hats in exactly the same shape as those of men of fashion. They must look and behave in the same way as everyone else, for otherwise they would be afraid of appearing ridiculous. But scientists and those who care for real things are not superficial; they are entirely indifferent to pronunciation and one hears, in fact, the broadest Scotch in Law Courts, at the university lectures and from preachers.

Having finished with the popular Scottish brogue, I will now deal in turn with the popular music. Besides the romantic harp there are of course the much talked-of bagpipes. They also are of very ancient origin. A bas-relief was found in Rome on which a man in Scottish garb, playing the bagpipes, was represented. Bagpipes are also known in Poland, but they have never been perfected and have never gained popularity. All the music of Scotland was either played on the harp or on the bagpipes. The former was the instrument used in peace, the latter in war. Its loud and shrill tones were of great use when the dispersed clansmen were to be called together in the mountains. The playing of the bagpipes is in keeping with the rattle of the swords and armour; it prepares the spirit for the slaughter and deafens the moans of the wounded and dying. Nobody, perhaps, has better described how that music can sound during battle than a Scotsman writing about the battle of Waterloo and the impression it made when the Scottish regiments fought against the French cavalry: 'Like a thousand tinkers at work mending pots and kettles,' he said. The Scots-born warriors love this instrument. During the Anglo-French war at Quebec in 1760, the Scots suddenly began to retreat. Infuriated, the English commander accused them of being cowards, but the Scottish officer took up their defence. 'It is your own fault,' he cried 'why did you not allow the bagpipes?' – 'Then have these blasted bagpipes, by all means!' cried the commander. The moment the tunes of the 'Pibroch' were heard, all the Scotsmen returned and fought like lions. After the Union of Scotland and England, the Earl of Moira became the Commander-in-Chief of the Scottish Army. He was so hated that he could not live in the capital and had to hide in villages, for it took a long time for the Scots to get used to English leadership. He succeeded, however, in gaining popularity later on by having pipers always in attendance and by offering snuff to all the Scotsmen who came to see him; a big hornful of snuff was always lying near-to-hand. Nevertheless, he never allowed more than five glasses of wine at meals, for he was anxious not to overheat their turbulent brains.

Doctor Johnson, that extraordinary man of genius who gave culture to others, though himself uncultured, loved the pipes so much that he stood with his ear pressed to the instrument. Even today there are such lovers of bagpipes who will attend concerts and reward lavishly the best players. In ancient times every Scottish chief had at least one piper and there were special schools on the Isles of Mull and Skye where they were taught by the famous teachers, the MacCrimmons and the Rankins. Nevertheless, there will always be people speaking irrelevantly of the bagpipes, as for instance Butler does in his *Hudibras*:[6]

> Then bagpipes of the loudest prones
> With snuffling broken-winded tones
> Whose blasts of air in pockets shut,
> Shout filthier than from the gut,
> And made a viler noise than swine
> In windy weather when they whine.

So great are the differences of human opinion! I have tried to give at least a glimpse of every side of Scottish life, but the picture would remain very incomplete if I omitted mentioning the crofters,[7] who form the truest backbone of the Scottish character and, one can state the fact with assurance, bring great credit to their country.

I propose to at least mention all those in Scotland who busy themselves with the tilling of the land. The lowest class among them is that of the hired farm hands, honest, trustworthy and industrious; then the gardeners, the tenants and the gentleman farmers. These are often as important and as wealthy as the lairds themselves. There are no such peasants as in our country and there is also no serfdom. The crofters are the middle class; their ways of living, their education and importance, everything puts them in this category or, perhaps, to explain it more clearly, their ideas and conceptions of life are by far loftier and nobler than those of the craftsmen, artisans or workmen in industry or trade. From these come the discoverers in the fields of mechanics and science, or again people who make great fortunes, but the crofters are the pride of the church and from their homes come clergymen and great scholars. This does seem incredible, for the artisans have by far the better education and greater possibilities, but so it is. It is enough to read the literature of the country and become acquainted with the lives of those who have become famous in these fields. Ramsay[8] and Burns were crofters, and though they are already dead, the memory of their poems is still green. Macpherson, the editor of Ossian's poems, was no more than a country schoolmaster. Among the living is Hogg, who was a shepherd and could not read till he was twenty, and the famous Leslie of similar origins. In England there are Bloomfield[9] and Cunningham[10] the poets and Chantry[11] the sculptor. England's population is chiefly industrial and because of this popular poetry is not as frequent there as it is in Scotland. Thomson, whose Seasons were so admired, was a Scotsman. Here we must come to the conclusion that the most complicated and wonderful mechanisms are unable to give to man even the tiniest part of those treasures which nature bestows on those who dwell with her.

Nevertheless, it is not incomparable nature alone which has educated Scotland. As early as 1645 the necessity of education was realised and the parish schools introduced.[12] In 1696 the educational system was improved, and ever since education throve besides industry and trade. Peace was a safeguard of security and prosperity, and that high offices in the country were attainable only by those who had adequate education, was a great stimulus. Now it would be difficult to find illiterate people in Scotland, even in the poorest of huts, and many can write and reckon as well.[13] They always choose serious and instructive things for reading.

Once when I was walking through a field I saw a shepherd engrossed in a book; I came nearer and asked what it was. It was, to my astonishment, Pope's *Essay on Man*. Reading has become such a necessity in Scotland that even the men who carry the sedan chairs in Edinburgh, while they stand and wait at the corners of streets, read newspapers. The shepherds in Scotland buy newspapers second- or even fifth-hand. When one has read them he puts them under a stone on some chosen spot for the next one to take, and so the newspaper circulates in the hills and the fields until all have read it. In England reading is not as popular and there are still illiterates; but they enjoy being read to so much that, in industries where eight are working, the eighth is chosen for reading. He does it while the others work, and between themselves they pay his wages.

Where the desire for education is so keen in Scotland there is no need for compulsion, as in other countries. Here everybody understands the blessings of learning. There are more and more schools and they cost nothing to the government for they are either kept by private subscription or by contributions in a parish. A country schoolteacher receives a cottage, an acre of garden and £22 a year. This is not however his total income for he gets fees from his pupils. They pay him according to the difficulty of the subject he teaches. The lowest price is for reading and writing, only half a crown in three months, and six shillings if arithmetic is taught too. Latin is 5/- and book-keeping 5/- to 7/-. The prices are higher in towns and elementary physics and mathematics are taught there as well. Those applying to be schoolteachers must have a very good education indeed. The knowledge of Greek is required, though Greek is not taught in elementary schools. Parishes announce that a post is vacant and sometimes as many as ten candidates appear. The best is chosen and good care is taken that his morals should be exemplary, for without moral principles teaching is no use. The old system of teaching is still used in parish schools; but in schools arranged on common subscription grounds, the teaching is mostly reciprocal. Many parents think that the methods of Bell[14] and Lancaster[15] are no good, for they are too mechanical, and they consider them even immoral for they seem to awaken in the pupils a sort of hatred of the teacher. But if there is no more criticism to be given, this is scarcely worth mentioning, for in other ways these schools have very many good points.

The minister of every parish supervises the schools and helps the children and the teacher. Schoolmasters are very often future clergymen themselves and they teach meanwhile, either for practice or to be useful to mankind. They have to pass through a long period of waiting before they are allowed to become ministers, this period being a kind of test of their morals. No wonder that schools which possess such eminent teachers soon teach Latin classics. Many a poor father will refuse himself food to be able to send his son to such a good school. Expense of tuition does not amount to much, but maintenance of the children sent out of their homes is rather costly.

These schools need no advocates; their influence over the population speaks for itself. The high moral and educational standards of the country are striking. The high education however awakens a spirit of enterprise which makes many people migrate later on to England or to America. Bacon[16] has called knowledge power; others perhaps less appropriately have called it a virtue and happiness. I consider knowledge as an impulse and a means. For the wider the horizons, the greater the longings and the easier the possibilities of gratifying them. Desire and ambition if awakened will last and will be increased by imagination. Distant objects will become near at hand, uncertain ones will gain security, and hopes of attainment will be changed by imagination into real possessions.

Such a spirit reigned in Scotland when the two long-divided countries united and the frontiers became merged. It was then that education and poverty drove the daring Scotsmen to the fertile and wealthy plains of England or to some of the English colonies all over the world. Those Scots wandered everywhere and sought their fortunes; many settled in Pennsylvania and to this day that country is called Nova Scotia.[17] This stream of people flowed from north to south as long as the reasons which caused it existed. The reasons will cease to exist when England's population becomes as educated as the Scots, and the Scots as rich as the English. Only then will equilibrium be attained. England has benefited greatly by receiving a people educated, clever and industrious and hardened by poverty and a life of labour.

The established religion of Scotland is that of Calvin. Stern by itself, it has become even more so in Scotland where it had to fight first with the Catholic church and then with the Church of England. A nation which has spilt her blood in the defence of her creed is much attached to that creed. Alas, a certain relentlessness of character seems to go with it, a severity and a dislike of all who have other convictions. The puritan spirit is still alive and appears in public, syllogising and disturbing private lives with its narrow-mindedness. The furious dialectics of the clergy are taken up by the people who are brought up on the Bible.

Children are taught to read on the Westminster Catechism, and finish their studies on the Bible. The church services and sermons teach not only the foundations of religion but also how to defend it against the infidels. The Scots look eagerly for religious discussions and they do not give in easily. It is difficult to praise this, and yet there are certainly good sides to such a profound knowledge of religion which then is never superficial. Religion has given character to this nation, has founded her morals and has become the real source of the people's welfare and happiness in their family life.

Puritanism, though it has stopped the development of art, was unable to kill music. This was so dear to the nation that it existed in Scotland's most ancient traditions and has been handed down from generation to generation. The tunes and the measures of this music are so original as to appear almost faulty; this alone is the best documentation of the music's origin. Popular songs deal in other countries with love, war and banquets. The love ballads are the most numerous, for the realm of love is, was and will be the most powerful of all, and the agonies of unreciprocated love the most difficult to bear. Though not created by some tremendous imagination, the songs betray a thorough knowledge of the human heart and a great simplicity which constitutes their chief charm.

Dance is connected with song and music. The Presbyterian church does not approve of it either but, disregarding Calvin's opinions, the young do not forsake this pleasure. They do not dance in inns, for this would be improper, but they assemble in empty barns. Of course dances can only take place on weekdays, never on Sundays. Reels, strathspeys, country dances and hornpipes are the most popular dances. The jig, popular among English peasants, is considered too slow here and not accepted.

Though it is difficult to find the origins of the love songs in Scotland, the influence they have is very great. The young are imbued with romantic imaginings and ideas and are ready for the most touching actions and sacrifices. A Scottish crofter when in love is prepared for anything, there are no difficulties; the Spanish knights, so famous for their romantic love, would no more than equal his display of amorous ardour. Having finished work, he goes to the home of his beloved; no distance or impassable road will put him off; he knocks lightly at her window and she comes out, unseen by her parents. These are the favourite topics of love poems in all the languages of the world.

The distinguished upper classes have of course different ways under such circumstances. Common folk are everywhere the same but the

[75] *'The Highland Wedding' by David Allan (1744—96). This was painted after the proscription of Highland dress was lifted. The figure in the foreground is probably the laird who, had he ridden to the wedding, would have worn trews.*

more educated, the purer their habits and the more delicate their feelings and customs. Music and song are undeniably very strong factors in adding beauty and poetical charm to love. They influence the heart and all virtue springs from the heart. And thus the Laplander runs across the snow and the inhabitant of Angola across the burning sands to see the love of his heart; both try to shorten their way by song. Music uplifts their feelings, cleanses them from selfishness and awakens impulses for even more poetical ideas. This is why the barbarians of North America, who have no devotion for their women, have neither music nor poetry. They can have no pure habits, nor can they know any family happiness, which can only exist where there is mutual devotion. If only we could be quite sure that Fingal had lived and Ossian had sung, finding so much about mutual love in his songs we could have been sure that for long centuries Caledonia had been a country where happy family life had flourished.

Marriage is greatly respected in Scotland and all the young people think of it as their natural life later on. This respect is one of the reasons for the greater freedom given to women, and this freedom has seldom reason to be deplored. Young people who were immoral used to be most severely punished. They were made to sit on a chair of repentance in church, their names were proclaimed for three Sundays and, in front of all the parishioners, they were fastened by the feet in the village stocks. But as such severity often led to despair and crime it has been abolished and so has branding. But the dishonouring irons and the punitive chairs still remain in churches. It is quite fair that the government should have taken over the administration of justice, whereas consolation is left to the church. There are many laws in Scotland which facilitate marriage, as for instance the Gretna Green law, also that children born before marriage become legitimate when the marriage is at last concluded.

The manners and the appearance of the Scots do not strike one at first as those of a wealthy nation. The English country folk are superior to them in this way. The clothes of the Scots are clean but less smart; the houses, the food and all their possessions seem rather second-rate. But innovations and improvements are seen everywhere and the advancement is already great. These differences apply only to farmers. For the workmen and the hirelings are everywhere the same, especially as in both countries the wages and the cost of living are equal. I have already spoken of the love of the Scots for their native land. I must still speak of their devotion to their families for this is one of their most charming features. Family love begins with the parents, who though poor, refuse themselves a lot in order to give a good education to their children. They consider learning to be the greatest treasury of man. Their healthy outlook on things is generously rewarded for learning awakens the heart as well as the brain. If the children live and have luck in life, the parents do not remain onlookers, but participate in the children's happiness. Even among workmen, where the children win their bread by hard toil, to share it with their parents is not considered charity but simple duty. There is perhaps no country in the world where such a large part of money earned by the children goes to those whose days of earning have already gone by. Such devotion is to be met in all walks of life, even among the upper classes. The eldest brother who inherits the title and the estate looks after his younger brothers and provides for his sisters. This once again reminds us of the ancient, patriarchal days and of the chieftains of old. It is pleasant to trace the good right to its very sources, and generally it is the best life which has foundations rooted deep down in the past centuries.

XXIII

Conclusion

HAVING spent a week at Dover waiting for propitious weather for the crossing, for during that time only the mailboat risked crossing the Channel, we saw at last a day on which we could sail. We crossed in a steamer; on the two former occasions we did not risk it because nobody trusted those steamers much.[1] When we were at some distance from the coast we looked at Albion whose shores seemed lower and lower until, quite suddenly, they disappeared from sight as if they had been drowned in the sea. With them the real Britain vanished from our sight but not from our memory. Imagination paints a picture of these islands between two obedient oceans, of the islands whose fertile fields are more like gardens, whose Arcadian valleys, shady woods and grazing flocks have been described by great poets. These are the islands where industry and trade have brought wealth, the islands of rich cities, luxurious life and art. The islands are small and yet they rule over the seas and over nations all over the world. And she rules solely by the justice and kindness of her laws and by her intellectual superiority which make all these nations look up to her and obey her. Her scientists, philosophers, artists and politicians are incomparable and the deep wisdom of the Government and of the various institutions make Great Britain the wonder and the envy of the whole world.

Here end my remarks about England and Scotland but not the remembrances of everything I have seen and witnessed. Many subjects have not even been touched upon, and yet they are important. They apply to the government, literature, religion and national spirit. The picture of these is difficult to draw as it must contain a number of different items, dependent on innumerable coincidences, reasons, climate, form of government etc. As it would be difficult to put all this within these volumes about my journey, it is very likely that I will one day publish another work on these countries, or at least publish the materials given here in a more adequate form.

[76] *Frances Grose (1731–1791). It was of the English antiquarian Francis Grose that Burns wrote:*
A chiel's among ye takin' notes
An' faith, he'll prent it.
This might well have been written of Lach-Szyrma. Grose's Antiquities of England and Wales *was followed by two volumes of engravings of sketches made during his tour of Scotland in 1790. Many of these have been used to illustrate Lach-Szyrma's journey.*

228

Notes

1. Aristarchus of Samothrace (c 215–143 B.C.), Alexandrian reviser of Homer's epics.

1. The quality of the roads built for Turnpike Trusts by John Metcalfe (1717–1810), Thomas Telford (1757–1834) and John Macadam (1756 1836) reduced travelling time from London to Edinburgh from ten days in the 1750s to two in the 1820s.
2. Sir Isaac Newton (1642–1727), English scientist and mathematician.
3. Angelica Catalani (1779–1849), Italian singer of international renown whom Lach-Szyrma may have heard in Poland in 1819.
4. Sir William Wallace (1274–1309), Scottish patriot and, with the Earl of Moray, leader of the Scots against the English in the early years of the Wars of Independence, was a supporter of John Balliol. Robert the Bruce opposed the Balliol cause and paid homage to Edward I in 1296, '97 and '99. There is no evidence that he was ever imprisoned in Durham Castle.
5. Jozef Borulawski (1739–1837) had been King Stanislaw August's court dwarf. He came to Britain in 1782 and was not a count.
6. Captain James Cook (1728–79), the British navigator and explorer who charted the coasts of New Zealand and eastern Australia and claimed Australia for Britain. The Dutch had sighted it a century earlier.
7. Hadrian's Wall became a northern frontier of the Roman Empire and protected it from Picts and Scots until 383 AD.
8. The Wars of Independence had been intermittent since 1296. When Henry VIII attacked Scotland's ally France, James IV invaded England and was killed at the battle of Flodden Field.
9. Tantallon Castle fell to General Monk in 1652.
10. In 1760 James Macpherson (1736–96), an Inverness schoolteacher, published *Fragments of Ancient Verse collected in the Highlands*. These were accepted as genuine translations from ancient Gaelic poetry by Edinburgh's literati, some of whom financed Macpherson's search for further ballads. *Fingal, an epic poem in Six Books* was followed by *Temora, an epic poem in Eight Books*. The validity of his sources was questioned by some of his contemporaries and it is now generally believed that his 'translations' were largely his own composition, though based on scraps of ancient Gaelic poetry. As a Romantic, deeply interested in folklore, Lach-Szyrma had studied these while a student at Vilnius University.
11. Lach-Szyrma's route took him near Siccar Point where observation of the configuration of the rocks led James Hutton (1726–97) to develop the ideas

about the age of the earth's crust which became the foundation of the science of geology. His *A Theory of the Earth* was published in 1785.

12. John Knox (1513–73) was the most influential figure in the development of the Protestant reformation in Scotland.

13. Canongate churchyard is the burial ground of many of the leading figures of the Scottish Enlightenment. These include the economist Adam Smith (1723–90) and Dr. John Gregory, one of the third generation of distinguished doctors and mathematicians connected with Edinburgh University.

14. The first New Town had been planned by James Craig in 1767. Access to the Calton Hill had been made possible by the completion of the Regent Bridge in 1818. By 1820 the New Town embraced Princes Street in the south, the Water of Leith in the north, Melville Street in the west and London Road in the east.

15. Lach-Szyrma was familiar with the works of Sir Walter Scott (1771–1832) which were translated into most European languages.

CHAPTER II

1. Duneidin, the 'fortress of Eydin', was the capital of the British Goddodin tribe and later a stronghold of the Angles and the Scots. By the tenth century it had become a burgh. 'Edwinenburg' is no longer believed to have been a name which was ever used.

2. Like most Continentals, Lach-Szyrma over-estimated the extent of the bloodshed during the wars of religion in Scotland. Less than a dozen people were killed during the Reformation.

3. Dioramas, invented by Daguerre and Bouton, were first exhibited in an exhibition in Paris in 1822.

4. Promised the restoration of Poland's pre-Partition frontiers by Napoleon, Polish soldiers fought with the French army in Italy, Spain and Russia.

5. George IV was the first king of Scotland to visit his kingdom since Charles II was crowned there in 1651.

6. Prince Leon Sapieha (1803–78) was one of the Poles for whom Lach-Szyrma acted as tutor on their European tour. His mother was a Czartoryska.

7. Survivors of the Bourbon royal family were given refuge at Holyrood until the fall of Napoleon in 1815.

8. Capt Alexander Macdonnell of Glengarry was the model for Scott's Fergus MacIvor in the novel *Waverley*.

9. This is the motto of the kings of Scotland.

10. Clementina Sobieska was the granddaughter of King Jan Sobieski and mother of Prince Charles Edward. In 1772 Charles Edward married Princess Louisa von Stolberg-Gedern. There were no children and they separated in 1784. Cardinal Henry was his brother.

11. Sir William Allan (1782–1850) was an historical painter who trained in London and St Petersburg. He travelled in Russia, Poland and Turkey. He became president of the Royal Scottish Academy in 1838 and Queen's Limner in Scotland in 1841.

12. Probably Feliks Janiewicz, a Pole who settled in Scotland in 1815 and anglicised the spelling of his name, replacing J with Y.

13. The Potocki family was one of a group of anglophile landowners who, in the early nineteenth century, employed Scots to introduce modern engineering and agricultural technologies on their estates.

14. Stanislaw Trembecki died in 1812

15. Count Waclaw Rzewuski (1785–1831) was a Polish poet, diarist and Orientalist.

Notes

1. The fifteenth-century Tolbooth described in *The Heart of Midlothian* had been in the High Street, at the north-east corner of St Giles.
2. Francis Jeffrey (1773–1850) was a distinguished advocate and a founder and editor of the *Edinburgh Review*. A Whig reformer, he became Lord Advocate in 1830.
3. Walter Scott was in fact deeply involved in the bankruptcies of both Constables and Ballantynes.
4. Niemcewicz and Naruszewicz were published in a series, edited by Taduez Mostowski (1766–1842), called *Wybor Pisarzow Polskich*.
5. Nicholas Copernicus (1473–1543) was born in Torun, Poland. His *De Revolutionibus* proved that the sun was the centre of the universe.
6. David Irving (1778–1860) was a literary historian and Mark Napier (1798–1897) a lawyer and editor.
7. George Buchanan (1506–82) was a humanist and a Latin poet of European renown. He was appointed classical tutor to Mary Queen of Scots and then tutor to James VI.
8. Maciej Kazimierz Sarbiewski (1595–1659) was a distinguished Latin poet whose work was translated into English by G. Hills in 1646.
9. The Royal Infirmary, which opened to patients in 1729, was the first teaching hospital in Scotland.

CHAPTER IV

1. The foundation stone of Robert Adam's Quadrangle, which was on the site of the Old College, was laid in 1789. The French Wars interrupted the building programme and William Playfair's adaptation of Adam's design was not completed till 1827.
2. Adam Smith (1723–90), author of *The Wealth of Nations*, became professor of Moral Philosophy at Glasgow University in 1755 and its Lord Rector in 1787. He spent much of his later life in Edinburgh as a Commissioner of Customs.
3. Rev Hugh Blair (1718–1800) was the minister of St.Giles and, in 1762, became the first professor of Rhetoric and Belles Lettres.
4. Alexander Monro (1733–1817) was the most distinguished holder of the chairs of Surgery and Anatomy in which he was preceded by his father and succeeded by his son.
5. James Gregory (1753–1821) followed his father in the chair of Medicine and gave his name to Gregory's Powder.
6. Rev John Playfair (1748–1819) was a mathematician and geologist who successively held the chairs of Mathematics and Natural Philosophy. He published *Illustrations of the Huttonian Theory* in 1802.
7. Dugald Stewart (1753–1828) successively held chairs in Mathematics and Moral Philosophy. He was a brilliant teacher. Like Reid, he was a critic of David Hume's philosophy.
8. Professor Thomas Brown (1778–1820) was a contributor to the *Edinburgh Review* and a colleague of Stewart's. He believed that Hume's theories could be reconciled with religious beliefs.
9. John Wilson (1785–1854) was a journalist and professor of Moral Philosophy. Under the pseudonym 'Christopher North' he wrote for *Blackwood's Magazine*, of which he and John Lockhart (1794–1854) were co-editors.
10. Sir John Leslie (1766–1832) held the chair of Mathematics in 1810 and of Natural Philosophy in 1819. Amongst his inventions were a differential thermometer, a

hygrometer and a pyroscope.
11. Thomas Charles Hope succeeded Joseph Black in the chair of Chemistry. He is reputed to have been an uninspiring teacher who did little to encourage research.
12. Rev Professor Thomas Chalmers (1780–1847) was a scientist and theologian and an outstanding orator. In 1843 he led the Disruption, the protest against the system of patronage which had been imposed on the Church of Scotland after the Union of 1707. The 470 ministers who followed him founded the Free Church.
13. Rev Archibald Allison (1757–1839) published *An Essay on the Nature and Principles of Taste* in 1790.
14. Rev John Thomson (1778–1840), Scottish landscape painter and the minister at Duddingston, then a village south of Edinburgh.
15. Antoine Laurent Lavoisier (1743–94), French chemist, a follower of Joseph Priestly and the discoverer of oxygen and of its importance.
16. Antoine-Francis de Fourcroy (1755–1809) worked with Lavoisier and Berthollet to devise the nomenclature of chemical association.
17. Claude-Louis de Berthollet (1748–1822), chemist and one of the founders of L'Ecole Normale.
18. Lecturing in the vernacular was introduced in the Netherlands in the seventeenth century and in Scotland in the eighteenth. Latin was still used for examinations in the Faculty of Medicine in Edinburgh in the early nineteenth century.
19. John Huss (1369–1415) was the founder of the Protestant movement in Bohemia and a follower of John Wycliffe. His condemnation and burning by order of the Council of Constance led to the Hussite Wars.
20. The University's collection was moved to the Royal Scottish Museum in 1865. The buildings are still linked by a bridge.
21. The Physic Garden founded by Dr Andrew Balfour and Dr Robert Sibbald was moved to Inverleith in 1822, when it became the Royal Botanic Gardens.
22. One of Lach-Szyrma's rare factual mistakes. David Gregory (1661–1708) was a distinguished astronomer and a professor of Mathematics at Edinburgh before moving to the chair of Astronomy at Oxford in 1691.

CHAPTER V

1. In 1824 Edinburgh Academy was founded by men like Scott and Cockburn, former pupils of the High School, who were conscious of its limitations.
2. Abraham Cowley (1618–67) has been described as the last of the metaphysical poets and a forerunner of the classicists. Milton placed him after Shakespeare and Spencer but Pope wrote 'Who reads Cowley now?'
3. Modelled on academies set up by Dissenters in England, the councils of market towns like Perth, Dalkeith and Jedburgh had, since the mid-eighteenth century, been setting up schools with much wider curricula. Modern languages, geography, mathematics, surveying and book-keeping were taught as well as the classics.
4. Burgh schools were supervised by the town councils but elementary schools in the country were paid for by the heritors (the landowners and major tenant farmers) and supervised by the Kirk sessions.
5. Since the late seventeenth century there had been primary schools in almost all Lowland parishes and literacy rates were high. By the 1820s the parish system began to break down in the rapidly growing industrial towns of the Central Belt, and literacy rates were beginning to fall. They remained low in the Highlands.
6. The Trustees of the Board of Manufactures had, since 1707, administered funds

for the encouragement of industry. In 1760 they set up the Trustees' Academy to train craftsmen in design. Originally housed in the University, it acquired its own premises in the early nineteenth century.

7. Francois-Pierre-Charles Dupin (1784–1873), economist and engineer, was professor of Mechanics at the Paris Conservatoire des Arts et Métiers.

8. In 1802 the Edinburgh Missionary Society established a small colony of Scots at Karass, in the foothills of the Urals. Although it survived for 30 years, it made little progress in its attempts to convert the Muslim population to Christianity. In 1813 one of the missionaries, the Rev Henry Brunton of Selkirk, published the first translation of the New Testament into Tatar-Turkish.

9. The Royal Society was founded in 1662. The Polish equivalent, the Society of the Friends of Science, functioned between 1800 and 1832 when, like the University of Warsaw, it was dissolved by the Russian government.

10. Robert James (1705–76), an English physician who published his *Medical Dictionary* in 1743.

11. The Ballantyne brothers, James (1772–1833) and John (1774–1821), founded the printing firm in which Scott became a partner.

12. Archibald Constable (1714–1827) was a bookseller and the publisher of *The Edinburgh Review*. Although a Whig, he also published Scott's novels. In 1812 he bought the copyright of the *Encyclopaedia Britannica*.

13. William Blackwood (1776–1834) was an antiquarian bookseller and publisher and one of the founders of *Blackwood's Magazine*, the Tory response to the Whig *Edinburgh Review*.

14. The Elsevier family were booksellers, publishers and printers who were active in the Netherlands between 1538 and 1712. Estienne Robert (1531–1559) was one of a family of French humanists, printers and publishers. Aldus Manutius (1449–1515) founded a printing house in Venice in 1494. The firm remained in the family for three generations.

15. *The Scotsman* was founded as a daily paper in 1817.

16. At a time when criticism of the government was considered seditious, the publication of *The Edinburgh Review,* which criticised institutions as well as literature, was of great political significance. Lach–Szyrma often uses 'scientific' as a synonym for 'critical'.

17. Sir James Mackintosh (1765–1832) was a publicist and philosopher who defended the principles of the French Revolution against Burke.

18. Henry, Baron Brougham and Vaux (1776–1868), was a British politician and reformer. A Whig Lord Chancellor from 1830–34, his major contributions were to the abolition of the slave trade, the foundation of the secular University of London and the passing of the Reform Bill of 1832.

19. John Ramsay McCulloch (1789–1864), editor of *The Scotsman*, a pupil of Ricardo and, from 1828, professor of Political Economy at University College, London. During their stay in Edinburgh he tutored the Polish students on the theories of Adam Smith.

20. William Gifford (1756–1826) was the editor of the Tory *Quarterly Review* and co-editor with John Wilson of *Blackwood's Magazine*.

21. John Gibson Lockhart (1794–1854), biographer of his father-in-law Sir Walter Scott and editor from 1825–1853 of *Blackwood's Magazine*.

22. Rev William Robertson (1721–1793), leader of the Moderates in the Church of Scotland and Principal of Edinburgh University from 1762. An historian of European renown, his other books were histories of Scotland, America and India.

Notes

1. Jan Sniadecki, philosopher and writer, published, in Polish academic journals, his interpretation of the teaching of Dugald Stewart.
2. Alexander, 10th Duke of Hamilton (1767–1852), was ambassador to the court of St Petersburg from 1806 to 1807. He made an extensive tour of Poland and Russia before returning to Scotland.
3. Anne, Baronne de Stael–Holstein (1766–1817), was the only child of the financier Jacques Neckar. An essayist and novelist, she was the greatest of French women writers of her period. Her unfinished *Considérations sur la Révolution française* was published in 1818.
4. As Prince Regent, George IV had tried to divorce his wife, the Princess Caroline. The sordid affair went on from 1808 till her death in 1821, shortly after her unsuccessful attempt to break into the coronation ceremony from which she had been banned.
5. Hugh William Williams (1773–1829). A pupil of David Allan, he travelled in Italy, Greece and the Ionian Islands. His paintings of Greece were exhibited in Edinburgh in 1822.
6. Francis Horner (1778–1817), lawyer, economist, MP and one of the founders of *The Edinburgh Review*.
7. James Hogg (1770–1835) is now better known for *The Confessions of a Justified Sinner* than for his poetry. Unlike Burns, he had had little formal education. Scott discovered him while collecting material for his *Minstrelsy of the Scottish Borders*.
8. Catherine Gordon, daughter of the Marquis of Huntly, was a Lady-in-Waiting to Queen Louise Marie of Poland. Her daughter Izabela Morsztyn married Prince Kazymierz Czartoryski in 1693.
9. Count Andrzej Zamoyski (1800–1874) and his brother Konstanty were studying at Edinburgh University in 1820. They became pioneers in the agricultural reform movement and employed Scottish farmers and engineers to introduce new technologies on their Polish estates.
10. Charles James Fox (1749–1806). Sympathetic towards both American and French revolutionaries, he led the Whig party in its opposition to the coercive measures of the Tory government. During his brief premiership in 1806 he drew up the bill which made the slave trade illegal in the British Empire.
11. David Brewster (1781–1868). Physicist and Dean of the University, he published *The Edinburgh Philosophic Journal*.
12. Benjamin Robert Haydon (1786–1846), a painter of religious and historical subjects.
13. George Watson (1767–1837), portrait painter and would-be rival of Raeburn.
14. John Galt (1779–1839), author and Canadian pioneer. His *Annals of the Parish* is the finest of a series of novels about country life in the south of Scotland.
15. David Hume (1711–1776), a philosopher of European fame as well as an historian and an economist. His scepticism prevented him from getting a university chair but his reputation as an empiricist was established by his writing. His *Treatise of Human Nature* and the posthumously published *Dialogues concerning Natural Religion* were probably the most influential of his works.
16. Founded in 1693, the scholarship was for one Polish and one Scottish Protestant student, resident in Poland, to study at Edinburgh University.
17. The Czartoryski princes boarded with Professor Pillans while studying classical literature with him.
18. Charles Maclaren (1782–1866), editor of *The Scotsman* and of the *Encyclopaedia Britannica*.
19. Thomas Morton (1781–1832), shipbuilder and inventor of the patent slip.

20. Count Ludwik Pac, a general in Napoleon's army, studied farming methods in Germany, France and Britain from 1814 to 1816. To improve his estates at Dowspuda and Raczki in north-east Poland, he recruited Scottish engineers and farmers. One of the leaders of the 1830 Rising against Russian misrule, he was exiled and his land confiscated. There is still a village called Nowa Szkocja in an area where 500 Scots settled. Many of their descendants returned to Britain in 1914; those who remained have been absorbed into the Polish nation.
21. David Ricardo (1772–1823) was a London-born stockbroker. His *Principles of Political Economy,* published in 1817, developed the ideas of Adam Smith.

CHAPTER VII

1. Hans Holbein (1497–1543), German religious painter, introduced by Erasmus to Sir Thomas More and the court of Henry VIII. His portraits of the English aristocracy of the period are of outstanding quality.
2. Federigo Zuccaro (1543–1609) painted portraits of Queen Elizabeth and Mary, Queen of Scots and founded the Academy of St Luke in Rome in 1595
3. Benjamin West (1738–1820), American painter, trained in Italy, who for 40 years enjoyed the patronage of George III. His ' Death of General Wolfe ' was one of the first pictures to depict a military hero in contemporary dress.
4. James Barry (1741–1806), Irish historical painter and professor of Painting at the Royal Academy.
5. Jean-Baptiste Du Bos (1670–1743) commented on the English lack of talent in the field of painting in his *Reflections Critiques sur la Poésie et la Peinture.*
6. Thomas Philips (1770–1845), portraitist; Sir Thomas Shee (1769–1850), portraitist; Richard Westall (1765–1836), engraver and illustrator; Sir Austin Calcott (1772–1844), landscape painter.
7. Sir David Wilkie (1785–1841). Scottish genre and portrait painter, he worked for much of his life in London and became Painter in Ordinary to the king in 1830.
8. Sir Thomas Lawrence (1769–1830), portrait painter to George III.
9. Sir Henry Raeburn (1756–1823). An outstanding portrait painter, he studied in Rome but spent his working life in Scotland. His sitters included leading figures of the Enlightenment.
10. Alexander Nasmyth (1758–1840). A pupil of Allan Ramsay, he was influenced in his landscape painting by the work of Claude Lorraine, which he had studied while in Rome.
11. Sir William Allan (1782–1850), historical painter, trained at the Royal Academy school in London and worked in St Petersburg from 1808. He travelled in Russia and Turkey before returning to Scotland in 1814.
12. David Martin (1737–97) was a portrait painter trained by Allan Ramsay but the reference is almost certainly to the English historical painter John Martin (1789–54).
13. Sir Godfrey Kneller (1646–1723), German portrait painter, trained in Amsterdam and Italy, who worked for William and Mary and George I.
14. Thomas Bruce, Earl of Elgin (1766–1843), was ambassador to Turkey from 1799 to 1803. In 1687 the Parthenon had been severely damaged when the Turks used it as a powder magazine. It was again at risk during the Greek revolt against Turkish rule in 1821.
15. John Hobhouse, Baron Broughton (1786–1869), accompanied Byron on his travels in provinces of the Turkish Empire in 1812.
16. George Gordon, Lord Byron (1788–24), was the son of the Scottish heiress Catherine Gordon of Gight and spent the first ten years of his life in Aberdeenshire. He responded to the *Edinburgh Review*'s criticism of his early poems with the satire *English Bards and Scotch Reviewers.*

Notes

1. The seat of government moved to London in 1707. Patronage was exercised in Edinburgh but was usually controlled from London. From 1746 to 1885 there was no equivalent of a Secretary of State for Scotland.
2. The new Assembly Rooms in George Street were opened in 1787, when assemblies were still very fashionable and raised considerable sums of money for charity.
3. Before the move from Old Playhouse Close to Shakespeare Square in 1769, plays had been sandwiched between concerts in order to escape the disapproval of the Church.
4. The references are to historical novels by Julian Niemciewicz, Felix Bernatowicz, Fredyryk Skarbek and Franciszek Wezykciszek.
5. August von Kotzebue (1761–1819), German dramatist, the author of about 200 dramas and comedies.
6. In 1756 the production of *The Douglas,* a play written by a minister, was considered so inappropriate that its author, the Rev Douglas Home (1722–1808), resigned his parish of Athelstaneford and moved to London.
7. Jozefa Ledochowska (1780–1849) played lead roles in tragedies performed in the Warsaw National Theatre in Krasinski Place.
8. The newly opened Waterloo Hotel was the first in Edinburgh large enough to cater for gatherings of more than 50 people.
9. Feliks Janiewicz (1762–1848), violinist, composer and conductor and a student of Haydn. He settled in Britain in 1792 and moved to Edinburgh in 1815.
10. These were popular Polish dances.
11. Michal Oginski (1765–1833), a composer and diplomat who became famous for his polonaises.
12. Niemcewicz's ballad *Duma o Zolkiewskim* was set to music by a number of composers including Kurpinski, Lessel and Szymanowski.
13. Music societies flourished in Scotland until the end of the eighteenth century. The Edinburgh Society was founded in the 1690s when membership was limited to gentleman performers. By the mid-century professionals were being employed as conductors and soloists and St Cecelia's was built as a concert hall. It was the nineteenth century before it became unfashionable for gentlemen to play musical instruments.
14. Sir Henry Bishop (1786–1865). Composer of 88 operas and director of Covent Garden, he held chairs of Music at both Edinburgh and Oxford. Of his compositions, 'Home, sweet home' is probably one of the few with which a modern audience would be familiar.
15. Wilhelm Kramer (1745–1799), violinist, and his pianist son Johann Baptiste (1771–1885), settled in London in 1772.
16. Ferdinand Reis (1784–1838), pianist and composer and a pupil of Beethoven, was in London from 1813 to 1824.
17. By the 1790s the design of the facades of New Town houses was fairly rigidly controlled by the Town Council.

CHAPTER IX

1. With one short break in 1806, the Tories had been in office since 1783. Patronage assured that the majority of those in power throughout Britain in the 1820s would be Tory supporters.
2. Anne Grant (1755–1838), poet and essayist, settled in Edinburgh in 1811 and became a friend of Scott's.
3. Joanna Baillie (1762–1851). Her dramatic poetry was acclaimed by Scott.
4. Louis Simond (1767–1831) published *Voyage d'un Français en Angleterre* in 1811.

Notes

1. In 1763 James Craig was given £30 by the Town Council to go to London and 'to remain there as long as necessary for learning everything relative to these shores (sewers)'. This was after his plan for the New Town had been accepted. Sewers in the New Town were often not laid until houses had been occupied for several years. As late as the 1820s, in lanes like Thistle Street and Rose Street intended for artisans and servants, there were neither sewers nor piped water. Farmers were fertilising their fields with the Old Town's 'night soil' till the second half of the nineteenth century. Deserted by the upper classes, the medieval city became one of the worst slums in Europe.
2. Until taxes were lowered, whisky was being distilled illegally throughout Scotland and thousands of gallons were smuggled into England.
3. Coal had been mined near Edinburgh since the twelfth century but there were few coalfields outside the Central Lowlands. Peat was widely used until improvements in transport brought down the price of coal.
4. Aeneas Silvius Piccolomini (Pope Pius II) visited Scotland in 1432 while acting as papal envoy to James I.
5. John Wilkes (1727–97) was a publicist, politician and champion of the freedom of the press. In the *North Briton* his attacks on the first Scottish Prime Minister, Lord Bute, and on Scots in general were particularly virulent.
6. Stanislaw Bzowski (c.1567–1627), a Polish church historian who studied in Rome and taught in Cracow.
7. One of the oldest cavalry regiments, the Royal Regiment of Scots Dragoons, was founded in 1674. Both their uniforms and their horses were grey and they became known as The Royal Scots Greys.
8. Prince Josef Poniatowski (1762–1813) was a nephew of King Stanislaw Augustus and a brilliant general. He fought under Kosciusko in the revolts against Russia in 1792 and 1794 and as commander-in-chief of the army of the Duchy of Warsaw in 1809. In the belief that a victorious Napoleon would restore Poland to her pre-Partition frontiers, he led the thousands of Poles who fought for France in Italy, Spain and Russia.

CHAPTER XI

1. Sanctuary rights granted to the Abbey in the twelfth century could still be claimed by debtors in the nineteenth century.
2. Duddingston House was one of the few houses built in Scotland by the Scottish architect, Sir William Chambers (1726–96).
3. Craigmillar was the main castle of the Preston family. Mary, Queen of Scots, was a guest there when the murder of her husband Darnley was being planned by some of her nobles.
4. Allan Ramsay (1685–1758), poet, bookseller and librarian of a circulating library. This was probably the first in Britain. He was the father of Allan Ramsay, the painter.
5. Maria Edgeworth (1767–1849) was a successful Irish novelist, an early advocate of the higher education of women and a friend of Sir Walter Scott. Her successful first novel *Castle Rackrent* was published in 1800.
6. Prince Adam Jerzy Czartoryski (1770–1861) was in Scotland during the 1780s and 1790s and was Lach-Szyrma's patron and employer. A wojewoda was the governor of a Polish province.
7. William Drummond of Hawthornden (1585–1649) was an inventor and historian as well as a poet. He was a friend of Ben Jonson, a descendant of the Dumfriesshire Johnstones. Jonson walked from London for a prolonged visit

during which he and Drummond were reported to have drunk the cellar dry.

8. James Thomson (1700–48) abandoned a career in the ministry and spent most of his life as a writer in London. He is best known for *The Seasons* and was a forerunner of the Romantics.

9. Robert Fergusson (1750–74), a distinguished poet who wrote in Scots and English.

10. Paper making, which had been established in the Esk valley in the early eighteenth century, was being mechanised by Alexander Cowan in the early nineteenth.

11. Archibald Primrose, 4th earl of Rosebery, moved in 1817 from the romantic Barnbougle Castle, a few yards from the sea, to the Tudor Gothic Dalmeny House which Wilkins had built on a less exposed site.

12. John McAdam (1756–1836) spent a small fortune, made in the counting house of an uncle in New York, on experiments in road making on his Ayrshire estate. In 1818 his *Essay on Scientific Repair and Preservation of Roads* advocated the use of small stones for surfacing. Macadamised roads were later bonded with tar. In 1827 he was appointed Surveyor of British Roads.

13. Lach-Szyrma was misinformed. Bukelst and Benkelsson van Bierflet were the same person, a Fleming from Vervliet in Flanders who perfected a method of curing herring in the fourteenth century.

CHAPTER XII

1. The Church of Scotland was ruled by a hierarchy of courts staffed by its ministers; the Church of England by bishops. Attempts by the Stewart kings to impose episcopalianism on the Scots after 1660 were opposed by the Covenanters.

2. Toll-bar keepers, on the excellent roads which connected England with Scotland, might be bribed to delay pursuers by letting the runaway couple through. The simple marriage ceremony, which was legal in Scotland, could be completed in a few minutes.

3. The quality of Burns' work was widely recognised. After the publication of the Kilmarnock edition of his Poems in 1786 he was feted by the Edinburgh literati and, during his tour of the Highlands and the Borders, was entertained by the gentry. When he died in 1796 he was a salaried exciseman.

4. The Vistula Legion fought in Spain from 1808–12. Many were captured by Wellington's army, which drove Joseph Bonaparte and the French out of Spain and restored Ferdinand VII to the throne.

5. Alexander Runciman (1736–1785) was a protégé of the Clerk family. He studied in Rome and became a distinguished historical painter. Ossian's Hall was destroyed by fire in 1899.

CHAPTER XIII

1. Martin. The reference is probably to St Martin of Tours (c.316–c.400).

2. Richard Cumberland (1631–1718), bishop of Peterborough and author of *De Legibus Naturae*.

3. Francis Hutcheson (1694–1746), professor of Moral Philosophy at Glasgow University, and author of *A System of Moral Philosophy*. Adam Smith attended his classes.

4. In the late second and early third centuries the Antonine Wall was the northern frontier of the Roman Empire. Built of turf, with seventeen stone forts, it ran for 37 miles between the Forth and Clyde estuaries.

5. To protect newly buried bodies, watchtowers were erected in several church-

yards near Edinburgh and iron cages – 'mort safes' – placed over the graves. To provide the distinguished anatomist Dr Knox with bodies, Burke and Hare murdered sixteen to thirty people. The scandal caused by their trial led to legislation in 1827 to legalise the use of unclaimed corpses by medical schools.

6. Lucius Cincinnatus (519–438 BC). A Roman statesman, he was twice appointed dictator but returned to his farm between periods in office.

7. Sir John Franklin (1786–1847), Arctic explorer who died on the expedition which discovered the North-West Passage in 1847. William Scoresby (1789–1857) studied at Edinburgh University . His *Arctic Regions*, published in 1820, was the first scientific description of Arctic seas and lands.

8. Serfdom did not exist in Ireland in the nineteenth century. Poverty was caused by soaring population and subdivision of peasant holdings. Serfdom died out in Scotland in the fourteenth century but could be reimposed on coal and salt miners between 1641 and 1799. Miners in England were not enserfed. In the Russian Empire serfdom was not abolished till 1866.

9. Bartolommeo Eustachio (1520–74). Italian anatomist who made important discoveries connected with the anatomy of the ear and the heart.

10. This is debatable. Lach-Szyrma may be repeating legend rather than fact.

CHAPTER XIV

1. The term 'palace' was widely used in Scotland to describe a substantial house, on an estate, which was not defensible. Hamilton Palace (James Smith, c. 1796) was undermined by coal seams and had to be demolished in the early twentieth century.

2. Chatelherault (William Adam, 1731) was built as a hunting lodge and banqueting hall and has been restored.

3. Robert Owen (1771–1858) was a Welshman. After serving an apprenticeship in a textile factory he became manager of a Manchester spinning factory and later bought the New Lanark mills from his father-in-law David Dale. In partnership with Richard Arkwright, the inventor of the spinning frame, he developed the mills and the paternalistic policies, initiated by Dale, for which the factory became famous.

4. Philipp Emanuel von Fellenberg (1771–1844), a Swiss sociologist who founded an agricultural college and an orphanage.

5. Sir Thomas More (1478–1535), humanist, statesman and Lord Chancellor of England. He was beheaded for refusing to acknowledge Henry VIII's claim to be Supreme Head of the Church of England. His *Utopia* was published in 1516.

CHAPTER XV

1. The Forth-Clyde Canal was completed in 1790 and the Union Canal, which linked it to Edinburgh, in 1822. The aqueduct carried the canal over the river Kelvin.

2. Population figures for Glasgow in 1755 were estimated by Webster to be 31,700. The 1821 Census recorded 147,000 inhabitants.

3. Lach-Szyrma uses Saxon as a synonym for Romanesque.

4. The organisation of Glasgow University seems to have been based on that of Bologna, where students were originally more powerful than the masters.

5. Joseph Hume (1777–1855), M.P. and political writer and a supporter of Poland's cause after the failure of the 1830 Rising.

6. John Napier (1550–1617), mathematician, inventor and astrologer.

7. Tobias Smollett (1721–71) served as a ship's surgeon before becoming a writer. *Roderick Random* and *Humphrey Clinker* are his best known novels.

8. James Watt (1736–1819) was the mathematical instrument maker at Glasgow

University from 1757 to 1763. Early work on the improvement of steam engines was carried out on a model of a Newcomen engine belonging to the University.

9. Robert Fulton (1765–1815) was an engineer of Irish origin who was born in Pennsylvania. His design for an improved steam engine was in general use on steamboats on the Hudson River by the 1820s.

10. Thomas Reid (1710–1796), professor of Moral Philosophy at Glasgow, whose *Inquiry into the Human Mind* challenged Hume's writing and who founded the Scottish 'Common Sense' school of philosophy.

11. William Hunter (1708–83) studied medicine at Glasgow and Edinburgh Universities and at St George's Hospital, London. He was the first great teacher of anatomy in England and a distinguished surgeon and obstetrician. He was joined in London by his brother John (1728–93). Both brothers were great collectors. William left his collection of pictures and specimens to Glasgow University and John sold his to the British government.

12. John Dolland (1706–1761) and his son Peter (1730–1820) were inventors of optical instruments and founders of the Observatory.

13. Frederick Herschel (1738–1822), English astronomer of German origin, whose telescope, with a diameter of 120 cms, was built between 1785 and 1789 with the aid of a grant from George III.

14. Anderson's Institute was founded in 1796 to provide scientific courses in physics, chemistry, mathematics, agriculture and botany. Many of the students were women. It later became the Royal Technical College and then Strathclyde University.

15. Thomas Garnett wrote in glowing terms about working conditions and educational provision at New Lanark.

16. George Birkbeck (1776–1841). A medical graduate, he gave free lectures on Natural Philosophy (Physics) to working men at Anderson's Institute. In 1824 he helped to found the Mechanics' Institute in London . This became Birkbeck College.

17. The Glasgow Asylum reflected the teaching of Dr Andrew Duncan. His belief that mentally ill patients could and should be treated was being put into practice, from 1813, at The Royal Edinburgh Asylum.

18. By the 1830s, John Dickson, a Scottish farmer who had emigrated in 1819, was producing milk and cheese of a similar quality for the Warsaw market.

CHAPTER XVI

1. Gaelic is a Celtic language closely related to Irish and Manx Gaelic; another Celtic group consists of Welsh, Breton and Cornish.

2. The tidal waves caused by the Lisbon earthquake of 1752 raised the waters of Loch Ness as well as those of Loch Lomond.

3. Rob Roy (1671–1734) was the second son of Donald MacGregor of Glengyle. After the Restoration in 1660 the penal laws against the MacGregors were repealed, only to be reimposed , because of their Jacobitism, at the Glorious Revolution of 1688–89. In the 1690s Rob Roy advanced a dubious claim to be chief of a name which remained illegal. He became an outlaw in 1716, when his lands were seized by the Duke of Montrose for non-payment of debt.

4. In 1263, after the defeat of Hakon IV at the Battle of Largs by Alexander III, the Hebrides were ceded to Scotland. The Northern Isles remained under Norse rule till 1472.

5. The Cobbler (2891 ft) is one of the lower hills on the Campbell estates but its summit is reached by a dramatic rock face.

6. This is a reference to the Campbell support for the 1665 invasion of the West of Scotland by the Earl of Argyll. He had been forced into exile by his opposition to the Catholicising policies of James VII.

Notes

1. Dunstaffnage Castle was built by the Macdougalls in the thirteenth century. For a short time after its capture by Robert the Bruce in 1309 it was a royal castle but by the fifteenth century it had become a Campbell stronghold. It is being confused with Dunadd, 25 miles south of Oban. This ancient hilltop fort was probably occupied by the Picts before it became the capital of the Scots kingdom of Dalriada, from the sixth to the eighth century.
2. The Stone of Destiny was returned to Scotland in 1996.
3. Charlemagne (742–814) was crowned in Rome in 800 as emperor of a restored western Roman Empire. This became the Holy Roman Empire.
4. The Piast dynasty ruled Poland from 960 to 1138.
5. In the 1820s whisky was being distilled throughout Scotland and thousands of gallons were being smuggled into England.
6. In the early sixteenth century Elizabeth Campbell, daughter of the 2nd earl of Argyll, was married to Lachlan MacLean of Duart. Duart was murdered by her brother, Sir John Campbell of Callander, when, some years later, he was in Edinburgh. The dukedom of Argyll was created in 1701.
7. Lach-Szyrma was deeply interested in folk music but was unfamiliar with the pentatonic scale and rhythms used in Hebridean music.
8. At the height of their power, in the fourteenth and fifteenth centuries, the Macdonalds, as Lords of the Isles, were virtually independent of their sovereigns, the kings of Scotland.

CHAPTER XVIII

1. They had walked at least 20 miles since breakfasting.
2. Johanna Schopenhauer (1766–1838) and her banker husband travelled extensively in Europe. She was the author of several novels and travel books and the mother of the German pessimist philosopher Artur.
3. Sir Joseph Banks (1744–1820), the botanist who accompanied Cook on his circumnavigation of the world in 1768–71, visited the Hebrides in 1772.
4. Barthélemy Faujas de Saint-Fond (1741–1819), French geologist, published his *Voyage en Angleterre, et Ecosse et aux Isles Hebrides* in 1789.
5. In Argyllshire, cairns usually date from the second century BC.
6. Thomas Pennant (1726–98), botanist and traveller, visited Scotland in 1769 and 1772. He published his *Tours in Scotland* in 1775.
7. Samuel Johnson (1700–84) visited Scotland with James Boswell in 1773. His *Journey to the Western Isles* was published in 1775.
8. Christianity was established in the South of Scotland by St Ninian at the end of the fourth century. St Columba's mission to the northern Picts was a century and a half later.

CHAPTER XIX

1. The route of the Caledonian Canal was surveyed by James Watt in 1773 but its construction, engineered by Thomas Telford, was delayed until the French Wars, when the creation of a safe passage between the North Sea and the Atlantic was believed to justify the expense. Opened in 1801 but not completed till 1822 at a cost of over £1,000,000, it was a financial failure.
2. English was introduced by medieval merchants, possibly as early as the twelfth century.
3. The date was 1746 and Locheil was not killed at Culloden.
4. Thomas Campbell (1777–1844), poet, critic and editor, was thrice elected Lord

Rector of Glasgow University. His best-known poems are *Lord Ullin's Daughter* and *Ye Mariners of England.*

5. Ben Nevis (4418 feet), the highest mountain in Britain, is ten miles north of Glencoe. The hills through which the River Coe runs are all under 4000 feet.
6. The Massacre of Glencoe (1692) was not a clan feud. Government troops, commanded by a Campbell of Glen Lyon, carried out orders signed by William III in London.
7. Ben Lawers is 3984 feet high.
8. The Stone was returned to Scotland over seven centuries later.
9. Agricola invaded Scotland in 80 AD and in 84 defeated the Caledonians at Mons Graupius, probably in Aberdeenshire. During the Roman occupation of South Britain the frontier fluctuated between the Tay, the Antonine Wall on the Clyde–Forth line and Hadrian's Wall between the Tyne and the Solway.
10. The Highlands and Islands are exceptionally rich in prehistoric monuments and there are several great castles and churches north of the Great Glen. Lach-Szyrma's statement again reflects the ignorance of most Lowland Scots about the culture of the Highlands.
11. There were small pockets of Roman Catholicism in the Highlands. The majority of Highlanders were Presbyterians and a significant minority in the northeast were Episcopalians. Scots and Norse were spoken in the Orkneys and Shetlands but not Gaelic.
12. Sir William Blackstone (1723–80), first professor of English Law at Oxford and author of *Commentaries on the Laws of England.*
13. Ben Lomond, unlike many Scottish mountains, is not of volcanic origin.
14. Charles-Emanuel Nodier (1780–1844) was a leading figure in the Romantic Movement whose novel *Trilby* was set in Scotland.

CHAPTER XX

1. Lord Kames (1696–1782), philosopher, lawyer and agricultural reformer.
2. George IV, the first Scottish monarch to visit his kingdom since 1652 when Charles II was crowned at Scone, did not stay at Stirling Castle.
3. Lach-Szyrma's lack of interest in the Palace of Linlithgow and the ironworks of Falkirk is surprising.

CHAPTER XXI

1. A wildly inaccurate and narrowly dynastic and racial history which must have been current in the 1820s.
2. The date now generally accepted is c. 390.
3. Privy councils and parliaments remained separate between 1603 and 1707. In 1801 Britain became the United Kingdom of Great Britain and Ireland.
4. Office in both Scotland and England was open to Protestants of either nation after 1707.
5. In most clans there was an element of selection. A brother or relative of the dead chief would be chosen rather than a son who was a minor.
6. From the fourteenth to the early seventeenth centuries, wars with England made the Middle Marches the most lawless part of Scotland. Highlanders were too far from the Borders to be directly involved in these wars. Walter Scott was largely responsible for the romanticisation of the Border Reivers.
7. Only the young heir to the chief of MacLeod had to drain the horn to prove his manhood.
8. The dynasty founded by Cormac MacAirt (c. 254–77) ruled as notional High Kings of Ireland from Tara Palace in Meath.

9. Bards were professionally trained and the office, like that of the harper and piper, was often hereditary. It was rewarded with land. The last of the bards was appointed in the early eighteenth century.
10. Robert Southey (1774–1843), poet and writer, was appointed Poet Laureate in 1813.
11. Martin Martin (d. 1719) was the factor on a Skye estate. Dr Johnson's interest in the Hebrides was roused by his *Description of the Western Isles of Scotland*, published in 1703.
12. Thomas Percy (1729–1811), antiquarian and poet, whose *Reliques of Ancient English Poetry* was published in 1765.
13. Joseph Ritson (1752–1803), an English antiquarian whose *Scottish Songs* were published in 1794.
14. John Pinkerton (1758–1826), a Scot whose *Iconographia Scotica* was strongly prejudiced against the Celts.
15. John Jamieson (1759–1838) edited Barbour's *Bruce* and Blind Harry's *Wallace* and, in 1808, published the first *Etymological Dictionary of the Scottish Language.*
16. George Finlay (1799–1875) was a classical historian.
17. David Herd (1732–1810). His *Ancient Scottish Ballads*, published in 1776, was the earliest and largest collection of European ballads.
18. Power of life and death was limited. Heritable jurisdictions were abolished in 1747–8.
19. These were all Border families.
20. Some of the powers of the chiefs, including the right to raise a private army, survived till 1747.
21. The first daily paper available in Scotland was a reprint in 1642 of the English *Diurnal Occurrences touching the daily proceedings of Parliament from the 27th December to the 3rd of January* 1642. This described the struggle between Charles I and the Long Parliament. The first Scottish weekly was the *Mercurius Scoticus* in 1651.
22. The earliest written references to dishes made of cabbages, and to shoes, made and mended by Souters (shoemakers) are from the fourteenth century.
23. Hector Boethius (1465–1536), Principal of King's College, Aberdeen and author of a Latin history of Scotland published in 1527.

CHAPTER XXII

1. Stone circles in Scotland date back to the second and third centuries BC.
2. Dr John Dee (1527–1608), English alchemist, geographer and mathematician who escaped to Hungary, and then to Poland, when accused of sorcery.
3. Wojczask Laski (1536–1605), politician and traveller, invited Dee to Poland when Dee predicted (mistakenly) that Laski would be elected king.
4. The Society in Scotland for Propagating Christian Knowledge (SSPCK) was established in 1709 to set up schools where ' religion and virtue might be taught to young and old'. The teaching was mainly in English. By 1826 there were 500 schools and 13,000 pupils but half the population was still illiterate.
5. Scots as a language has been kept alive by a literature dating from the medieval period and by continued use as part of a strong national culture.
6. Samuel Butler (1612–80). His *Hudibras* was a burlesque satire on Puritanism.
7. Lach-Szyrma is describing smallholders rather than crofters. These had no security of tenure until the late nineteenth-century Crofters' Acts gave small tenants in the Highlands special legal status.
8. Allan Ramsay (1685–1758), poet, bookseller and founder of what was probably the first circulating library in Britain. He was the father of Allan Ramsay the

painter and son of the manager of Lord Hopetoun's mines at Leadhills. As a young man he was apprenticed to a wig maker.

9. Robert Bloomfield (1766–1823) was apprenticed to a shoemaker. His poetry about rural life brought him to the notice of the Duke of Grafton who became his patron.

10. Allan Cunningham (1784–1842), a Scottish poet and the manager of Chantrey's studio. He started life as a stonemason.

11. Sir Francis Chantrey (1781–1841) was the son of small farmer and carpenter. He became one of the most successful sculptors of his generation.

12. In the *First Book of Discipline* the fathers of the Scottish Reformation tried to establish a school in every parish. It was the late seventeenth century before heritors (landowners and major tenants) were legally forced to pay for a schoolhouse and a master.

13. Literacy had been high in the eighteenth century except in the Highlands. By the 1820s it was rising in the Highlands but falling in the rapidly industrialising towns of the Central Belt.

14. Andrew Bell (1753–1832), working in Madras, developed a monitorial system in which the brightest children were taught by rote and then used to teach other pupils.

15. Joseph Lancaster (1778–1838) developed a similar system which was widely used by the nonconformist British and Foreign School Society.

16. Francis Bacon, Viscount St Albans (1561–1626), English philosopher/essayist.

17. Nova Scotia was settled by Scots in the 1620s and Pennsylvania by the English in the 1660s.

CHAPTER XXIII

1. William Symington (1763–1831) launched the first steam-powered boat in 1788. This was followed by his *Charlotte Dundas*, which towed two coal barges for 20 miles on the Forth and Clyde Canal in 1802. Robert Fulton's *Clermont*, powered by an engine built by Boulton and Watt, was in service on the Hudson River from 1807 and Henry Bell's paddle steamer the *Comet* provided a regular service on the Clyde from 1812. The first crossing of the Channel by a steamboat was in 1818. The *Savannah* crossed the Atlantic in 1819, using steam for 85 hours of the 27–day crossing. Steamboats continued to carry sail until the second part of the century.